DICTIONARY OF
DEVELOPMENT
TERMINOLOGY

Dictionary of Development Terminology

THE TECHNICAL LANGUAGE OF Builders
Lenders
Architects and planners
Investors
Real estate brokers and attorneys
Appraisers
Land taxing and zoning authorities
Government officials
Community organizers
Housing managers
Urban renewal specialists

J. ROBERT DUMOUCHEL

Housing and Community Development Consultant

McGRAW-HILL BOOK COMPANY

New York   St. Louis   San Francisco   Auckland   Düsseldorf
Johannesburg   Kuala Lumpur   London   Mexico   Montreal
New Delhi   Panama   Paris   São Paulo   Singapore
Sydney   Tokyo   Toronto

Library of Congress Cataloging in Publication Data

Dumouchel, J Robert, date.
  Dictionary of development terminology.

    1. Urban renewal—Dictionaries. 2. Housing—
Dictionaries. I. Title.
HT108.5.D84   301.5′4′03   75-9578
ISBN 0-07-018105-5

1234567890MUBP784321098765

*The editors for this book were W. Hodson Mogan and Carolyn Nagy,
the designer was Naomi Auerbach, and the production supervisor
was Teresa F. Leaden. It was set in Baskerville by
Monotype Composition Co., Inc.*

*It was printed by The Murray Printing Company
and bound by The Book Press.*

Contents

Preface

The terminology presented in this book comprises the shoptalk of builders, lenders, architects and planners, investors, real estate brokers and attorneys, appraisers, land taxing and zoning authorities, government officials, community organizers, housing managers, urban renewal specialists, and others—in short, those whose occupations combine to form the so-called development industry.

Each of the subindustries represents a highly specialized type of activity that relates specifically to all the others. The purposes of the book are, first, to facilitate communications among those in the respective subindustries and, second, to permit those on the periphery, the consumers, to understand at least the basic language spoken within the "development world."

The definitions were drawn from the author's experience of over a dozen years in the industry and from about a ton of development literature. To my knowledge, none of the sources constitute copyrighted material. For any omissions of key terminology, which I hope are few, I apologize. I do believe that it's the only reference work of its type in existence. Suggestions for improving the definitions and for including additional terms are invited. Such suggestions can be sent to the author in care of the publisher's Professional and Reference Book Division.

Hundreds of people helped me prepare this reference, some more than others. They know who they are, and they are aware of my genuine gratitude for their assistance and support over the course of years during which this material was gathered. In particular, I am grateful to those, especially clients, who were honest enough to ask for definitions of terms I used in our dealings. Their questions provided the inspiration for the book at hand.

J. Robert Dumouchel

Notes on the Definitions and Suggestions for Using the Book

The working definitions represent meanings generally accepted by their knowledgeable users; however, it must be recognized that common usage of words and terms may vary in different geographic regions.

Obsolete or defunct terminology is included for the benefit of researchers and students.

Bracketed references signify that the definition provided comes from a specific source or is peculiar to a particular program—e.g., [HUD] signifies that the definition is HUD's; [urban renewal] signifies that the definition is peculiar to the urban renewal program. Increasingly, such definitions are being adopted by the industry as a whole.

Parenthesized words indicate the customary abbreviation or acronym for the term defined—e.g., (SBA) is the abbreviation for Small Business Administration; (Fannie Mae) is the acronym for Federal National Mortgage Association.

The author has strived to avoid defining terms with technical terminology not defined elsewhere in this dictionary. The user generally will find that technical defining terms are explained elsewhere, in alphabetical order.

Abbreviations and Acronyms

AASHO American Association of State Highway Officials
AB aid to the blind
ABA American Bankers Association
ACC annual contributions contract
ACE Active Corps of Executives
ACIR Advisory Commission on Intergovernmental Relations
ACPI American City Planning Institute
ACTION American Council to Improve Our Neighborhoods
ADC aid to families with dependent children
ADP automatic data processing
ADT average daily traffic
AEC Atomic Energy Commission
AFDC aid to families with dependent children
AGC Associated General Contractors of America
AIA American Institute of Architects
AIP American Institute of Planners
AIREA American Institute of Real Estate Appraisers
ALTA American Land Title Association
AMP accelerated multifamily processing
AMPO amount to make the project operational
AO area office [HUD]
AOA Administration on Aging
AOP Apprentice Outreach Program
APHA American Public Health Association
APTD aid to the permanently and totally disabled
ARA Assistant Regional Administrator
AREUEA American Real Estate and Urban Economics Association
ARLS Area Rehabilitation Loan Specialist [HUD]
ASA American Society of Appraisers
ASA American Standards Association

ASPO American Society of Planning Officials
ASREA American Society of Real Estate Appraisers
ASTM American Society for Testing and Materials

BAB Build America Better program
BHL better housing league
BIA Bureau of Indian Affairs
BLS Bureau of Labor Statistics
BMIR below-market interest rate
BOB Bureau of the Budget
BOCA Building Officials Conference of America
BPR Bureau of Public Roads
BR or **br** bedroom
BRAB Building Research Advisory Board
BSPRA builder-sponsor's profit and risk allowance

CAA community action agency
CAC citizens advisory commission
CAE Certified Assessment Evaluator
CAI Community Associations Institute
CAP Certified Agency Program
CAP Community Action Program
CBD central business district
CCEP Concentrated Code Enforcement Program
CD community development
CDA city demonstration agency
CDC community development corporation
CDP comprehensive development plan
CEA Council of Economic Advisers
CED Committee for Economic Development
CEP Concentrated Employment Program
CFA Community Facilities Administration
CHP comprehensive health planning
CO community organization
COBOL common business oriented language
COD cash on the down payment
COG council of governments
COLC Cost of Living Council

condo   condominium
Corps   U.S. Army Corps of Engineers
CPA   Certified Public Accountant
CPC   community participation committee
CPM   Certified Property Manager
CPO   citizen participation organization
CRP   Community Renewal Program
CRS   Community Relations Service
CS   Commercial Standards
CSC   Civil Service Commission

DA or **da**   dining area
DC&E   dwelling construction and equipment
DD   degree-day
DDB   double-declining balance depreciation
DHA   direct housing allowance
DHUD   Department of Housing and Urban Development
DK or **dk**   dining-kitchen combination
DOD   Department of Defense
DOT   Department of Transportation
DR or **dr**   dining room
DU or **du**   dwelling unit

EDA   Economic Development Administration
EEOC   Equal Employment Opportunity Commission
EHPA   earned home payments account
EIOP   end of initial operating period
ELA   early land acquisition
EPA   Environmental Protection Agency

FAA   Federal Aviation Administration
FACE   federally assisted code enforcement
FAIR   fair access to insurance requirements
"Fannie Mae"   Federal National Mortgage Association
FAR   floor-area ratio
FCH   Foundation for Cooperative Housing
FDIC   Federal Deposit Insurance Corporation

Fed   Federal Reserve Board
FHA   Farmers Home Administration
FHA   Federal Housing Administration
FHA   forced hot air
FHLBB   Federal Home Loan Bank Board
FHLMC   Federal Home Loan Mortgage Corporation
FHWA   Federal Highway Administration
FIA   Federal Insurance Administration
FIC   Federal Information Center
FmHA   Farmers Home Administration
FNMA   Federal National Mortgage Association
FPHA   Federal Public Housing Administration
FRB   Federal Reserve Board
"Freddie Mac"   Federal Home Loan Mortgage Corporation
FSLIC   Federal Savings and Loan Insurance Corporation
FSPP   Federated Societies on Parks and Planning
FWA   Federal Works Agency
FY or **fy**   fiscal year

GAO   General Accounting Office
GCR   guest car ratio
"Ginnie Mae"   Government National Mortgage Association
GNMA   Government National Mortgage Association
GNRP   General Neighborhood Renewal Plan
GO bond   general obligation bond
GPO   Government Printing Office
GSA   General Services Administration

HAA   Housing Assistance Administration [HUD]
HAO   HUD area office
HAP   housing assistance payment
HAP   housing assistance plan
HBA   homebuyers association
HDC   housing development corporation
HEW   Department of Health, Education, and Welfare
HHFA   Housing and Home Finance Agency
HIP   Housing Improvement Program [Indian]
HLBB   Federal Home Loan Bank Board
HOAP   Housing Opportunity Allowance Program

HOLC   Home Owners Loan Corporation
HOME   housing ownership management entities
HOWRC   Home Owners Warranty Registration Council
HPMC   Housing Production and Mortgage Credit [HUD]
HSMHA   Health Services and Mental Health Administration
HUD   Department of Housing and Urban Development
HWP   Home Warranty Program

IAAO   International Association of Assessing Officers
ICBO   International Conference of Building Officials
ICMA   International City Managers Association
INR   impact noise area
IOP   initial operating period
IREM   Institute of Real Estate Management
IRS   Internal Revenue Service
ISPL   impact sound pressure level

JIS   Job Information Service
JOBS   Job Opportunities in the Business Sector

K or **k**   kitchen
K'ette or **k'ette**   kitchenette

LAL   limitation on artificial accounting losses
LD or **ld**   mortgagor limited distribution or limited dividend
LEAA   Law Enforcement Assistance Administration
LHA   local housing authority
LIR   land-use intensity rating
LOP   Legacy of Parks Program
LPA   local public agency
LR or **lr**   living room
LRDP   Low-Rent Demonstration Program
LU or **lu**   living unit
LUI   land-use intensity
LUMS   land utilization and marketability study

MAGIC or **Magic**   Mortgage Guaranty Insurance Corporation
MAI   Member of the American Institute of Real Estate Appraisers
MBA   Mortgage Bankers Association of America
MC   Model Cities Program
mc   moisture content
MDTA   Manpower Development Training Administration
MESBIC   Minority Enterprise Small Business Investment Company
MF or **mf**   multifamily
MFC   multifamily coordinator [HUD]
MGIC   Mortgage Guaranty Insurance Corporation
MHMA   Mobile Home Manufacturers Association
MIP   mortgage insurance premium
MIUS   modular integrated utility system
mma   maximum mortgage available
MNA   model neighborhood area
MPS   minimum property standards
MR   market rate

NA   not available
NAA   National Apartment Association
NAAO   National Association of Assessing Officers
NAB   National Alliance of Businessmen
NABM   National Association of Building Manufacturers
NAHB   National Association of Home Builders
NAHO   National Association of Housing Officials (now NAHRO)
NAHRO   National Association of Housing and Redevelopment Officials
NAIRO   National Association of Intergroup Relations Officials
NAMC   National Association of Minority Contractors
NAR   National Association of Realtors
NAREB   National Association of Real Estate Boards (now NAR)
NAREIF   National Association of Real Estate Investment Funds
NAS   National Academy of Sciences
NBS   National Bureau of Standards
NCCP   National Conference on City Planning
NCDH   National Committee against Discrimination in Housing
NCHM   National Center for Housing Management
NCHP   National Corporation for Housing Partnerships
NDP   Neighborhood Development Program
NF   Neighborhood Facilities Program

NHA   National Housing Agency
NHC   National Housing Conference, Inc.
NHP   National Housing Partnership
NIH   National Institutes of Health
NIMH   National Institutes of Mental Health
NIP   neighborhood improvement program
NIRA   National Industrial Recovery Act
NIREB   National Institute of Real Estate Brokers
NLC   National League of Cities
NLRB   National Labor Relations Board
NP   nonprofit
NPG   neighborhood planning group
NRC   noise-reduction coefficient
NRPB   National Resources Planning Board
NSF   National Science Foundation
NTO   National Tenants Organization
NYC   Neighborhood Youth Corps

OAA   old-age assistance
O&D survey   origin-destination survey
OCR   occupant car ratio
O-D survey   origin-destination survey
OEDP   Overall Economic Development Program
OEO   Office of Economic Opportunity
OEP   Office of Emergency Preparedness
OFCC   Office of Contract Compliance
OILSR   Office of Interstate Land Sales Regulation
OJT   on-the-job training
OMB   Office of Management and Budget
OMBE   Office of Minority Business Enterprise
OS   open space
OSHA   Occupational Safety and Health Administration
OSR   open space ratio

PAC   project area committee
PBS   Public Building Service [GSA]
PEP   Public Employment Program
PERT   program evaluation review technique

PFCI   Workable Program for Community Improvement
PGE   participating governmental entity
PHA   Public Housing Administration
PHS   Public Health Service
PIGS   public interest groups
PILOT   payment in lieu of taxes
PITI   principal, interest, taxes, and insurance
PLUS   Personal Living Unit System
PMI   private mortgage insurance (or insurer)
PN&R System   Project Notification and Review System
PNRS   Project Notification and Review System
POB   place (or point) of beginning
PPBS   planning-programming-budgeting system
PRA   Professional Residential Appraisal
PRS   property rehabilitation standards
PSC   Public Service Careers Program
PUD   planned unit development
PUM or **pum**   per unit per month
PWA   Public Works Administration

RA   Regional Administrator [HUD]
R&D   research and development
RAP   relocation adjustment payment
REA   Rural Electrification Administration
REAP   Rural Environmental Assistance Program
rehab   rehabilitation
REIT   real estate investment trust
RFP   request for proposals
RHA   Rural Housing Alliance
RICC   Regional Interagency Coordinating Committee
RPAA   Regional Planning Association of America
RPC   regional planning commission
RS   rent supplement program
RSVP   Retired Senior Volunteer Program
r/w   right-of-way

S&L   savings and loan association
S&P   survey and planning application

SBA   Small Business Administration
SCORE   Service Corps of Retired Executives
SCPA   Standard City Planning Enabling Act
SEC   Securities and Exchange Commission
SEOO   State Economic Opportunity Office
SESA   Social and Economic Statistics Administration
SIC   Standard Industrial Classification System
SIR   Society of Industrial Realtors
SL or **sl**   sleeping area
SMSA   Standard Metropolitan Statistical Area
SOS   Senior Opportunities and Services Program
SPA   state planning agency
specs   specifications
SPL   sound pressure level
SRA   Senior Residential Appraiser (Society of Real Estate Appraisers)
SREA   Senior Real Estate Appraiser (Society of Real Estate Appraisers)
SRO   single-room occupancy
SRS   Social and Rehabilitation Service [HEW]
SSA   Social Security Administration
STC   sound transmission class
SWAG   "scientific wild-ass guess"

TACO   tenants and certain others
TAP   Technical Assistance Program
TDC   total development cost
TL   average transmission loss
TMRP   Technology, Mobilization, and Reemployment Program
topo   topographic map, topography
TSO   time share ownership plan
TVA   Tennessee Valley Authority

UDC   urban development corporation
UL   Underwriters' Laboratories, Inc.
ULI   Urban Land Institute
ULPA   Uniform Limited Partnership Act
UMTA   Urban Mass Transportation Administration
UPA   Uniform Partnership Act
URA   Urban Renewal Administration

URA   urban renewal agency
USDA   U.S. Department of Agriculture
USES   U.S. Employment Service
USHA   U.S. Housing Act
USHA   U.S. Housing Authority

V.A.   Veterans Administration
VISTA   Volunteers in Service to America
VNA   Visiting Nurse Association

WIN   Work Incentive Program
Workable Program   Workable Program for Community Improvement
WPA   Works Projects Administration

Development Terminology

ABANDONMENT Desertion of buildings, principally residential structures, or of a neighborhood by the owner, owners, or residents, usually because they consider their real estate investment lost.

Also, relinquishment of a right-of-way or easement because it is no longer needed.

ABSENTEE LANDLORD or **OWNER** Property owner who does not occupy the property, such as one who rents it to another or leaves it vacant. Distinguished from owner-occupant.

ABSORPTION BED A pit of relatively large dimensions filled with coarse aggregate and containing a distribution pipe system into which septic tank effluent is absorbed through the bottom area.

ABSORPTION FIELD A system of trenches containing coarse aggregate and distribution pipe through which septic effluent may seep or leach into surrounding soil. Also called "disposal field."

ABSORPTION PERIOD The period of time taken by a market to adjust to fluctuations in the supply of a given product or service, such as real estate.

ABSTRACT (*See* ABSTRACT OF TITLE.)

ABSTRACT OF TITLE Legal document outlining the history of ownership of a particular property (land and/or improvement), which serves as the owner's, buyer's, or lender's assurance that the title is free or unfree of encumbrances.

ABUTTER'S RIGHTS   The right of an owner of an abutting property to see the street and be seen from it and to receive the flow of light and air from the street onto the property.

ACCELERATED DEPRECIATION   Provision of the Internal Revenue Code entitling a taxpayer to depreciation of the value of income-producing property more heavily in the early years after purchase rather than evenly over the useful life of the property; the theoretical purpose of the incentive is to foster investments in new construction or in upgrading older property. Depreciation of certain subsidized rehabilitated property can be accomplished in five years for tax purposes, according to provisions of the Tax Reform Act of 1969. (*See also* DOUBLE-DECLINING BALANCE DEPRECIATION.)

ACCELERATED MULTIFAMILY PROCESSING (AMP) [FHA]   FHA-insured-loan application processing procedures revised in 1968 to eliminate delays, reduce the number of procedural steps, and shorten the time required to obtain a mortgage insurance commitment. (*See also* SINGLE-STAGE PROCESSING.)

ACCELERATION CLAUSE   Provision in a mortgage permitting the lender to terminate the loan and demand immediate payment if terms of the mortgage are not met by the mortgagor; unless the borrower makes the immediate payment, he stands to lose his entire equity as well as the mortgaged property.

ACCELERATION LANE   In highways, a paved access road leading into the main highway traffic lanes.

ACCEPTANCE   Receiving something offered by another with the intention of retaining what is offered.

ACCESS [real estate]   The right to enter and leave a tract of land from a public way. Also called "right to enter and leave over the lands of another."

ACCESSIBILITY   Feature of a property permitting it to be easily approached by pedestrians, autos, or public transportation. Usually, the more accessible a property, the higher its value—unless accessibility impairs the property's security.

ACCESSORY BUILDING Building located on a lot and used for purpose other than that of the principal building on the same lot—e.g., a garage, storage shed.

ACCESSORY USE Use of a property for other than its principal purpose.

ACCRETION The slow buildup of lands by natural forces, such as wind, wave, or water.

ACCRUED DEPRECIATION The amount of depreciation taken on a property as of a given date.

ACCULTURATION The interchanging of the culture of individuals or of groups and the consequent exchange and/or adoption of culture traits.

ACKNOWLEDGMENT The act by which a party executing a legal document appears before an authorized officer or notary public and declares the same to be his voluntary act and deed.

ACQUISITION The purchasing of a property.

ACQUISITION AND REHABILITATION [public housing] Housing development approach through which local housing authorities purchase existing structures from private owners and rehabilitate them into public housing projects.

ACQUISITION APPRAISAL An appraisal of value placed upon a property for purposes of acquiring it, usually in conjunction with a public purpose.

ACQUISITION COST [public housing] The amount required to be expended by a local housing authority to acquire a low-rent housing or slum-clearance project.

ACQUISITION—WITHOUT REHABILITATION [public housing] Existing housing, including site, which, when acquired by a local housing authority, does not require substantial alteration, repair, or improvement or requires alteration, repair, or improvement at a cost ratio of less than 20 percent of total development cost for multifamily housing or less than 25 percent of total development cost for single-family housing (detached, duplex, or row house).

ACQUISITION—WITH REHABILITATION [public housing] Existing housing, including site, which, when acquired by a local housing authority, requires substantial alteration, repair, or improvement at a cost ratio of 20 percent or more of total development cost for multifamily housing or 25 percent or more of total development cost for single-family housing (detached, duplex, or row house). After acquisition, such work is done either by employees of the local authority, or pursuant to a contract let by the authority, or partly by force account and partly by contract.

ACRE   Unit of land measure; 43,560 square feet. As a square, an acre measures 208.71 feet on each side.

ACREAGE ZONING   Zoning intended to reduce residential density by requiring large building lots. Also called "large-lot zoning."

ACT   Usually refers to the National Housing Act of 1934 as amended by subsequent legislation.
A law passed by the U.S. Congress.

ACTIONABLE   Constituting grounds for instituting legal action.

ACTION YEAR [Model Cities]   The period of time during which HUD funds a city demonstration agency to conduct a group of Model Cities activities. A Model Cities program consists of five action years, each funded separately.
The Housing and Community Development Act of 1974 provides for the phasing out of the Model Cities Program and its supplanting by Title I-Community Development activities.

ACTION YEAR [urban renewal]   The twelve-month period during which the detailed plans of Neighborhood Development Program will be executed by a local public agency.
The Housing and Community Development Act of 1974 provides for the phasing out of the Neighborhood Development Program and its supplanting by Title I–Community Development activities.

ACTIVE INVESTOR   An investor who, in addition to investing equity capital in a project, also packages, builds, or manages a project. Distinguished from passive investor.

ACTUAL AGE   The length of time improvements have existed, as distinguished from effective age.

ACTUAL CASH VALUE   (*See* MARKET VALUE.)

ACTUAL COST [FHA]   The costs (exclusive of kickbacks, rebates, or trade discounts) to the mortgagor of the improvements involved. These costs include amounts paid for labor, materials, construction contracts, land planning, engineers' and architect's fees, surveys, taxes, interest during development, organizational and legal expenses, such allocation of general overhead expenses as are acceptable to the HUD Secretary, and other items of expense incidental to development which may be approved by the Secretary. If the Secretary determines that there is an identity of interest between the mortgagor and the contractor, an allowance for the contractor's profit in an amount deemed reasonable by the Secretary may be included.

ACTUAL DEMAND [utility]   As related to rate schedules, the actual rate of delivery of energy or fuel.

ACTUAL DIRECT LOSS OF PROPERTY [urban renewal]   Actual loss in the value of property (exclusive of goods or other inventory kept for sale) sustained by an urban renewal site occupant by reason of the disposition or abandonment of the property resulting from the site occupant's displacement. A loss resulting from damage to the property while being moved is not included.

ADDITION   (*See* SUBDIVISION.)

ADDITION [HUD]   Any construction which increases the size of a building or adds to the building, such as a porch or an attached garage or carport.

ADJUSTED ANNUAL INCOME [HUD]   The annual family income remaining after certain exclusions from gross annual income are made. The following items are excluded, in the order listed, from family gross annual income: (1) 5 percent of such gross annual income in lieu of amounts to be withheld (social security, retirement, health insurance, etc.); (2) any unusual income or temporary income, as defined by HUD; (3) the earnings of each minor in the family who is living with such family plus the sum of $300 for each such minor. (*See also* FAMILY INCOME, GROSS ANNUAL INCOME.)

ADJUSTED MARKET RENT [HUD]   Used in reference to Section 221(d)(3) BMIR projects, any rent collected on a dwelling unit in excess of the BMIR rent. It is computed by adding to the BMIR rent the lesser of (1) 20 percent of the BMIR rent or (2) of any portion of the tenant's income in excess of the applicable income admission limits.

ADJUSTED MONTHLY INCOME [HUD]   One-twelfth of adjusted annual income.

ADJUSTED MORTGAGE INSURANCE PREMIUM [FHA]   The premium paid by a mortgagee to FHA in consideration of termination of a contract of insurance by reason of prepayment in full of the insured mortgage.

ADMINISTRATION ON AGING (AOA)   (*See* OLDER AMERICANS ACT OF 1965.)

ADMINISTRATIVE COSTS [public housing]   A local housing authority's necessary expenses for management, operation, maintenance, or financing of public housing projects subsequent to their completion. Also includes the cost of financing tenant programs and services for families residing in public housing.

ADMINISTRATIVE OVERHEAD   Expenditures for salaries, wages, sundry administration costs, etc.

ADMINISTRATIVE REGULATION   A regulation promulgated by a federal agency according to its interpretation of federal statutes or policies or of an executive order issued by the President.

AD VALOREM TAX   Tax based on the real value of property rather than its income, cost, marketability, etc. The value is usually established by a public assessor. (Ad valorem means "according to value.")

ADVERSE INFORMATION REPORT [HUD]   A record of contractors and grantees whose performance has been unsatisfactory under auxiliary procedures established by the offices of the several HUD Assistant Secretaries.

ADVERSE LAND USE   Use of a tract of land that harms the value of other land in its vicinity.

ADVERSE POSSESSION   The right of an occupant to acquire title to a property after openly and peaceably occupying it continuously over a period of time (usually twenty years) without being challenged by the owner.

ADVISORY COMMISSION ON INTERGOVERNMENTAL RELATIONS (ACIR)   A permanent, bipartisan commission established by act of Congress in 1959. Its members are drawn from local and state governments and from the federal government. The commission conducts continuing studies of the problems of and relationships among the three levels of government.

ADVOCACY PLANNING   (*See* ADVOCATE PLANNING.)

ADVOCATE PLANNING   Planning on behalf or in the interest of a group to be affected by the results of a given plan.

AESTHETIC VALUE   The increase in value of a property derived from such intangible factors as its inherent attractiveness, its access to attractive views, or its general appeal to the sense of beauty of the owner or purchaser.

AFFIDAVIT   A sworn statement in writing.

AFFILIATES   [HUD]   Business concerns are affiliates of each other when, either directly or indirectly, one concern or individual controls or has the power to control another or when a third party controls or has the power to control both.

AFFIRMATIVE ACTION PROGRAM   [public housing]   Local housing authority's program to comply with court rulings that low-rent housing must be dispersed to outlying areas to effect racial and economic integration if proposed sites in such areas are otherwise desirable.

AFFIRMATIVE MARKETING PLAN   Plan required by HUD of sponsors of all HUD subsidized or unsubsidized housing to attract buyers of all minority and majority groups to the housing for initial and continued sale or rental, including provisions to the effect that the sponsor will maintain nondiscriminatory hiring policies in the operation of the housing.

AGENT   A person who acts on behalf of someone else, usually in business dealings, with authority to do so.

AGGLOMERATION   The process and/or the result of urban sprawl, particularly in relation to the unplanned overlapping of population and governmental jurisdictions.

AGGREGATE   The gravel or broken stone used in making concrete, asphalt, etc., or as backfill.

AGREEMENT OF SALE   A written agreement which serves as a contract between a purchaser and seller, setting forth the terms of the transaction.

AID TO FAMILIES WITH DEPENDENT CHILDREN   (ADC or AFDC)   Authorized by the Social Security Act of 1935 and later amendments, provides formula grants through the Social and Rehabilitation Service of HEW to states and local welfare agencies. Encourages the care of needy dependent children in their own homes or in the homes of relatives by enabling each state to furnish financial assistance or foster care for specified children.

AIR RIGHTS   Right to make use of space above property—such as highways, railroad tracts, water—for its development into a dissimilar use. Such rights can be purchased or leased from the owners of the space below.

ALCOVE   A room recessed from a larger room.

ALIENATE [real estate]   To transfer title to property to another.

ALL-CASH VALUE   Price established on a property sold for cash on delivery, as opposed to a sale accomplished with a down payment and additional payments made over a period of time.

ALLEY   A public way affording only secondary access to abutting property.

ALLEY DWELLING   Dwelling facing an alley, rather than a street or other primary access route to a building.

ALLEY INFLUENCE   The positive or negative influence on property value caused by the existence of an alley abutting on the property.

ALL-INCLUSIVE MORTGAGE   (*See* WRAPAROUND LOAN.)

ALLOTMENT   Areas set aside in residential areas for growing vegetables. A British concept.

ALTERATION   A physical change in the layout of a building or of parts of a building. (*See also* STRUCTURAL ALTERATIONS.)

AMENDATORY AGREEMENT   A supplemental project grant allocated to a locality or agency over and above the dollar amount originally allocated because of unforeseen increased costs.

AMENITY   Feature of a property that renders it more attractive, such as its accessibility, good design, and proximity to shopping or other public facilities, recreational or cultural centers, schools, and parks.

AMERICAN PUBLIC HEALTH ASSOCIATION (APHA)   Professional association of public health officials; its Committee on Hygiene of Housing in 1952 published *A Proposed Housing Ordinance,* which contains most of the health standards used in housing codes and which, in its updated form, is used as a model for numerous state and local housing codes.

AMORTIZATION The regular, periodic repayment of the principal of a loan.

AMOUNT TO MAKE THE PROJECT OPERATIONAL (AMPO) Allowance in an FHA-insured loan of an amount (ordinarily 2 percent of total replacement cost) which can be included in the mortgage insured by FHA to provide a nonprofit sponsor with working capital during the initial operating period of a project.

ANALYSIS OF LOCATION The evaluation of the qualities of a site by comparison with those of other comparable sites.

A-95 REVIEW (*See* PROJECT NOTIFICATION AND REVIEW SYSTEM.)

ANNEXATION The absorption of an area of land by a governing body into its jurisdiction.

ANNUAL ARRANGEMENTS [HUD] Processing arrangement applying to a number of categorical grant programs administered by HUD, under which HUD funds a select group of local public bodies for a number of programs rather than in separate categorical grants. The process was launched as a forerunner to special revenue sharing.

ANNUAL CONSTANT The percentage of the amount of a loan that is to be repaid annually, including principal and interest; determines the term of the loan.

ANNUAL CONTRIBUTIONS CONTRACT (ACC) [public housing] Agreement between a local housing authority and HUD, under the provisions of which the federal government guarantees permanent financing of public housing projects as well as to make up the difference between project revenues and debt service on bonded indebtedness through an annual contribution or subsidy paid to the housing authority. The authority guarantees that it will maintain the low-rent character of the project.

ANNUAL RENT [urban renewal] The amount stated in a lease agreement between an urban renewal agency and a lessee as payable by the lessee for the use of the land each year of the lease.

The amount of annual rent must not be less than fair rental value as concurred in by HUD. The minimum fair rental value is determined on the fair value of the land in fee at the time of the lease and the current annual rate of rent applicable to the locality.

The annual rent, as a minimum, must be sufficient to pay the principal and interest on any definitive loan that may be entered into to finance the payment of the capital value of the leased land.

ANNUITY   Periodic payment of a sum of money over a specified period of time.

APARTMENT   A room or group of rooms in a building rented or leased to a tenant and constituting a dwelling unit.

APARTMENT HOTEL   Hotel providing apartments, usually furnished, to long-term tenants; such hotels frequently provide their tenants with services not primarily available to the general public.

APARTMENT HOUSE   A building providing apartments for rent.

APPALACHIAN REGIONAL COMMISSION   The Commission is a joint federal-state partnership concerned with the economic, physical, and social development of the thirteen-state Appalachian region. It was created to develop plans and programs authorized under the Appalachian Regional Development Act of 1965.

The Commission consists of the governors (or their representatives) of the thirteen Appalachian states, and a permanent federal cochairman appointed by the President with the advice and consent of the Senate. The state members elect an Appalachian governor to serve as state cochairman. This position rotates every six months.

APPLICATION FEE [FHA]   Charge by FHA to a mortgagor for processing an application for mortgage insurance. The fee is $1.50 per $1,000 of the mortgage amount when a conditional commitment is requested and the same amount when a firm commitment is requested.

APPLICATION FOR MORTGAGE INSURANCE [FHA]   Request by an approved lender to FHA to insure a mortgage, submitted on an FHA-prescribed form with specific additional exhibits. (*See also* MORTGAGE INSURANCE.)

APPLICATION FOR PROGRAM RESERVATION AND PRELIMINARY LOAN [public housing]   Application submitted to HUD by a local housing authority notifying HUD that the authority intends to develop a specific number of public housing units and to conduct preliminary surveys and planning. This is the authority's first step toward the development of public housing.

APPRAISAL   An estimate of the value of a property, prepared by a professional appraiser. Appraisals are prepared on the basis of one of or a combination of any of the following: recent sales price(s) of comparable property, income value of the property, replacement cost of the building less depreciation—plus the value of the land. (*See also* ACQUISITION APPRAISAL, CAPITALIZATION APPRAISAL, COMPARABLES, COST APPROACH, DISPOSITION APPRAISAL, INCOME APPROACH TO VALUE, MARKET DATA APPROACH.)

APPRECIATION   Increase in the value of property usually attributable to a combination of inflation, higher demand, and increased accessibility or of other amenities—as opposed to increase in value attributable to improvements of the property.

APPRENTICESHIP   The process or the period during which a person is trained in a trade by working with a qualified skilled worker or journeyman.

APPRENTICESHIP OUTREACH PROGRAM (AOP)   Administered by the Manpower Administration of the U.S. Department of Labor under provisions of the Manpower Development and Training Act of 1962 and later amendments; provides project grants to seek out qualified applicants from minority groups and to assist them in entering apprenticeship programs, primarily in the construction trades. Promotes the employment of minorities but also locates, motivates, guides, and assists minorities to enter registered apprenticeship training programs.

The project funds may be used to employ a project director to maintain liaison and to develop effective working relationships with employers, unions, joint apprenticeship committees, contractor associations, youth organizations, the Department of Labor, and private organizations. Tradesmen specialists are employed by the sponsor to assist in developing material for prospective candidates and for coaching candidates. Project funds may also be used to cover certain administrative costs. Restrictions on the use of contract funds are that such funds may not be used to subsidize trainees while they are in the training programs, nor may the funds be used for any items not covered in the negotiated contract budget.

Local organizations possessing the capacity to contract and the ability and desire to carry out the objectives of the program must be able to relate to the community, unions, and contractors. Any person who wants to pursue job opportunities that are available through apprenticable occupations may participate.

APPROPRIATION   (*See* CONGRESSIONAL APPROPRIATION.)

APPROVED DISPOSITION [HUD]   The disposition (or sale) of a property by a sponsor, usually profit-motivated, to its tenants or to a cooperative or nonprofit organization with HUD approval.

APPROVED LENDER [HUD]   A financial institution approved by HUD to make loans insured by HUD. The mortgagee.

APPROVED PERCENTAGE [FHA]   Amounts to 90 percent of replacement cost in the case of an investor project, and 97 percent in the case of a management, sales, or existing construction project.

APPURTENANCE   Anything so annexed to land or used with it that it will pass with the conveyance of title to the land—e.g., a building.

APRON   A concrete ramp installed in front of a garage. Also, the trim below a window "stool."

ARCADE   A roofed passageway along both sides of which are usually located small stores, shops, or similar facilities.

ARCHITECTURAL ANALYSIS [FHA]   The analysis of the characteristics of a property to determine its quality and acceptability as physical security for mortgage insurance issued by FHA.

ARCHITECTURE   The art and science of designing buildings; the style, appearance, and character of buildings. (*See also* DESIGN ARCHITECT, SUPERVISING ARCHITECT.)

AREA OFFICE OF HUD (AO)   One of thirty-nine offices of HUD located throughout the country, established to administer HUD's assistance programs.

AREAWAY [HUD]   An open subsurface space adjacent to a building used to admit light and air or as a means of access to a basement or crawl space.

AS-BUILT DRAWINGS   Architectural drawings showing the precise method and location of construction and installation of equipment and utility lines; prepared by the architect with the cooperation of the general contractor.

"AS IS" VALUE [FHA]   Value of a property to be rehabilitated. This is determined by an appraisal based on the assumption that a prudent investor or sponsor would be justified in paying for the property, with the intention of rehabilitating it with FHA-insured mortgage financing, for occupancy by residents with incomes similar to the incomes of present occupants. The value will vary depending upon the debt service rate, type of mortgagors, rent level, etc. (Not the same as the "as is" price available in the real estate market.)

ASPHALT SHINGLE ROOFING   Roofing manufactured in single or multiple units of roofing felt saturated and coated on both sides with asphalt and surfaced on the weather side with mineral granules.

ASSEMBLAGE   The acquisition of several separate properties, usually contiguous, into a single development tract.

ASSESSED VALUE   The value of a property as established by a tax assessor, as distinguished from the market value.

ASSESSMENT   A tax levied on property by a taxing authority. A value placed on the worth of property by a taxing authority.

ASSESSMENT RATIO   The fixed relation between the market value and the assessed value of a property.

ASSESSOR   A public official who evaluates property for the purpose of taxation.

ASSET   The value of, or equity in, real property, savings, bonds, stocks, and other forms of capital investments. Does not include the value of personal property. (*See also* CONTINGENT ASSET, CURRENT ASSET, FIXED ASSET, INTANGIBLE ASSET, TANGIBLE ASSET.)

ASSET LIMITS [public housing]   The maximum amount of financial assets an applicant may possess to be eligible for occupancy in public housing or other assisted housing; such limits are established by the local housing authority.

ASSIGNEE   One to whom a transfer of interest in a property or right is made.

ASSIGNMENT   Rightful transfer of one's title, contract or option rights, lease, etc., to another.

ASSIGNMENT OF MORTGAGE   (*See* MORTGAGE ASSIGNMENT.)

ASSIGNOR   One who makes an assignment.

ASSISTANCE PAYMENT [FHA]   That portion of a Section 235 home-owner's or cooperative member's monthly mortgage payment which HUD agrees to pay under an assistance payment contract.

ASSISTANCE PAYMENT CONTRACT [FHA]   Contract between FHA and a mortgagee pursuant to Section 235(b); it provides for FHA to pay the mortgagee the difference between 20 percent of a homeowner's or co-operative member's adjusted monthly income and the required monthly payment under the mortgage for principal, interest, taxes, insurance, and mortgage insurance premium (if the mortgage bore an interest rate of 1 percent), plus a payment to the mortgagee for its expense in handling the mortgage.

ASSISTED HOUSING or PROGRAM   Housing or other program that benefits from a HUD subsidy or grant.

ASSUMPTION   (*See* LOAN ASSUMPTION.)

ATRIUM   A court surrounded on several or all sides by the walls of a house or houses. Sometimes refers to the house or houses designed around such a court.

ATTACHED HOUSE   A semidetached or row house. A house "attached" to another by reason of their sharing a party wall.

ATTACHMENT   Legal seizure of property to force payment of a debt.

ATTESTATION   The witnessing, in writing, of a legal transaction.

ATTIC [HUD]   Space immediately below a roof and above the uppermost ceiling. Inaccessible spaces are considered "structural cavities." (Not considered a full story in a building.) (*See also* HALF STORY.)

ATTIC ROOM [HUD]   Attic space which is finished as living accommodations but which is not considered a half story. Also called "finished attic."

ATTORNEY IN FACT   One who holds a power of attorney from another, allowing him to execute legal documents, such as deeds and mortgages, on behalf of the grantor of the power.

ATTRACTIVE NUISANCE The permitted use of one's property for a purpose that might entice others, especially young children, into danger.

AUTHORITY Public corporation established by a governmental entity to perform a public function. An authority's jurisdiction usually comprises a functional area (such as public housing, urban renewal, transportation) and a single area or a combination of geographic or political areas, such as a city, county, township, metropolis, state, region (or the entire nation if the authority is established by the federal government).

AUTHORIZATION (*See* CONGRESSIONAL AUTHORIZATION.)

AVERAGE ANNUAL RETURN ON EQUITY Computation of the average annual cash flow divided by the equity in a project. (Some investors also include tax savings and amortization of the loan or net proceeds of sale in their computation.)

B

BACKFILL The earth or selected material, such as aggregate, used to fill in around foundation walls after they are completed or to fill other excavated voids.

BACKING WALL Usually, a portion of a wall which reinforces the front of a wall.

BACK-TO-BACK LOTS Lots or portions of lots on opposite sides of the same portion of a rear lot line common to both.

BALANCE SHEET An accounting of assets and liabilities, usually arranged to show ratios between classes of assets and liabilities.

BALCONY [HUD] An unroofed platform enclosed by a railing or parapet and projecting from the wall of a building for the private use of tenants or for exterior access to living units located above grade. (When a balcony is roofed and enclosed with operating windows, it is considered part of the room it serves.)

BALENCY SYSTEM [construction]   A French-Italian slab system of building which combines precast wall slabs and special functional castings with poured-in-place floor slabs. Electrical wiring, radiant heat tubing, and complete plumbing trees are cast in, ready to receive fixtures, as are precast fabricated toilet compartments including fixtures.

BALLOON FRAME   A type of building framework in which the studs extend from the foundation to the eaves without interruption by horizontal members.

BALLOON MORTGAGE   A mortgage without a complete amortization schedule, leaving a substantial amount of principal to be paid upon its termination.

BALUSTER   Any of the small posts that support the upper rail of a railing, as on a staircase.

BALUSTRADE   A row of balusters supporting a top rail.

BANKRUPT   A person or entity which, through a court proceeding, is relieved from the payment of all his debts after surrender of all his assets to a court-appointed trustee.

BASE MAP   A map indicating the natural or permanent features of an area.

BASEMENT   The building level, or story or stories, located completely or partially below ground level.

BASEMENTLESS SPACE   (*See* CRAWL SPACE.)

BASE PERIOD   Point(s) in time used in analyzing data.

BASE PERIOD [relocation]   The two tax years immediately preceding displacement of a business (or, if the business concern is not in business that long, such other period as may be approved by HUD), with these provisions: that if a business concern does not qualify as a small business concern based upon the two tax years immediately preceding displacement and a renewal agency finds that its business activity during such period was not representative, the base period becomes the third and fourth tax years immediately preceding displacement.

BASE RENT The minimum amount of rent payable under the terms of a percentage lease. (*See also* BASIC RENT.)

BASIC BUILDING CODE Model building code published by the Building Officials' Conference of America; used prominently especially in the East and North Central areas of the country. (*See also* NATIONAL CODE.)

BASIC GRANT AMOUNT [community development] The amount of funds which a metropolitan area or urban county is entitled to receive by virtue of the provisions of Title I—Community Development of the Housing and Community Development Act of 1974, as determined by a formula based on factors pertaining to population, extent of poverty, and extent of housing overcrowding. (*See also* DISCRETIONARY GRANT, ENTITLEMENT AMOUNT, HOLD-HARMLESS GRANT.)

BASIC PLUMBING FACILITIES Water supply, bathing facilities, and toilet facilities (the absence of any one of which renders a home substandard according to the U.S. Bureau of the Census).

BASIC RENT [FHA] The rental rate necessary to cover vacancy and collection loss and to pay operating expenses and debt service on a hypothetical level annuity plan mortgage with interest at 1 percent. The mortgage insurance premium is not included in basic rent. (*See also* MARKET RENT.)

BASIC WATER AND SEWER FACILITIES GRANTS [HUD] Supplanted by block grants provided through Title I—Community Development of the Housing and Community Development Act of 1974. (*See also* SECTION 702 BASIC WATER AND SEWER FACILITIES GRANTS.)

BASIC YIELD The return on an investment which, theoretically, carries no risk.

BASIS POINT The equivalent in the interest rate on a loan of 1/100 of 1 percent.

BATHROOM [FHA] A room containing a tub or shower, a lavatory, and a water closet. (*See also* HALF BATH.)

BATTEN   A narrow strip of wood used as a cleat across parallel boards or to cover joints between boards.

BAUHAUS   School of design founded by German architect Walter Gropius in 1919, which emphasized the relationship between artistic form and industrial production.

BAY WINDOW   A window, supported by its own foundation, forming an opening in a wall and extending beyond the wall.

BEARING WALL [HUD]   A wall which supports any vertical load in addition to its own weight.

BEAUTIFICATION   Improving the aesthetics of man's surroundings. (*See also* URBAN BEAUTIFICATION AND IMPROVEMENT PROGRAM.)

BEDROOM COMMUNITY   (*See* DORMITORY TOWN.)

BEGINNING AMORTIZATION DATE (BEGINNING OF AMORTIZATION) [HUD]   The date one month prior to the date of the first monthly payment to principal and interest under a mortgage.

BELOW-MARKET INTEREST RATE (BMIR)   Financing device that applies to certain government-sponsored mortgage insurance programs where the mortgage carries with it an interest rate below that charged through conventional financing; it is designed to enable low- and moderate-income families to rent or buy dwelling units. The loan is made directly by the government, as distinguished from a loan from a private lender with government mortgage insurance. As the rate is below market, the mortgage is brought about by the government agreeing to buy the mortgage from a private institution. Until 1968 this was done by FNMA and now is done by GNMA, an offshoot of FNMA. (*See also* DIRECT LOAN.)

BELOW-MARKET INTEREST RATE RENT [HUD]   The rent for each dwelling unit necessary to operate a project based on the BMIR mortgage and absence of the mortgage insurance premium.

BELTWAY   A highway around an area of high traffic congestion.

BENCH MARK   A mark on a permanent object indicating elevation and serving as a reference in land surveys.

BENEFICIAL INTEREST   The derivation of profit or other benefit that results from a transaction in which the beneficiary does not own or control a principal interest in the transaction. (*See also* INTEREST [FHA].)

BENEFITED-USER CHARGE   Charge to the persons benefited for services provided by local government to finance the cost of these services, such as for water supply, sewerage, refuse collection, public parking, public transportation, and public hospital care.

BERM   A mound of earth formed to control the flow of surface water.

BETTERMENT   An improvement which adds to the cost of a property. Distinguished from a repair or replacement.

BID   Formal offer by a contractor to complete a certain amount of work for a certain price, usually within a specified period of time. "Bid" contracts are distinguished from "negotiated" contracts.

BID BOND   A bond conditioned upon the bidder on a contract entering into the contract, if he receives the award thereof, and furnishing the prescribed payment bond and performance bond. (*See also* PAYMENT BOND, PERFORMANCE BOND.)

BIDDING DOCUMENTS   Architectural drawings and specifications (including general and special conditions), bound, complete, unbroken, and applicable to all trades, together with separate copies of a bid form.

BILEVEL   A house with two levels, such as a split-level house.

BILLING DEMAND [utility costs]   The demand upon which a billing for fuel is based as specified in a rate schedule.

BINDER   Document verifying a purchaser's payment of earnest money to a property owner, usually specifying the terms of the purchase; when signed by the owner, the document often serves as a contract.

BISON SYSTEM [construction]   A slab system of building, developed in England, consisting strictly of standardized precast concrete components.

BLACK   A Negro person.

BLANKET CONDEMNATION   Condemnation of a number of properties issued simultaneously, usually immediately prior to a quick-take action. (*See also* QUICK-TAKE.)

BLANKET ENCUMBRANCE   A trust, deed, mortgage, judgment, or any other lien or encumbrance, including an option or contract to sell or a trust agreement affecting several lots or properties.

BLANKET MORTGAGE   One mortgage on a number of properties.

BLIGHT   Term used to characterize the condition of an area or building as deteriorating, usually because of lack of maintenance or because of the presence of some external factor that causes property values to decline—such as industrial traffic or pollution, construction of a major traffic artery, spot zoning, etc.

BLIGHTED AREA   Usually a neighborhood or portion of a neighborhood characterized by the existence of a degree of blight. Verging on a slum.

BLOCK   An area bounded but not transversed by streets or other physical barriers on all sides.

BLOCK BUSTING   Usually, the actions of one or more speculators to depreciate property values in an area of a city; such actions commonly consist of the spreading of rumors that "undesirable" minority groups are moving into a neighborhood, permitting the speculator to negotiate the purchase of properties at prices lower than their real market value.

BLOCK CLUB   A formal or informal association of persons living on one or both sides of a street dividing two blocks, or of persons living within a block.

BLOCK GRANT   General-purpose grant to a state or local government from the federal government. Distinguished from project grant, revenue sharing, and categorical grant program. (*See also* COMMUNITY DEVELOPMENT PROGRAM, HOUSING AND COMMUNITY DEVELOPMENT ACT OF 1974, TITLE I—COMMUNITY DEVELOPMENT.)

"BLUE-SKY" LAWS   Enforceable regulations to prevent fraud in the sale of land.

BOARD FOOT   A unit used in measuring lumber. The dimensions of one board foot are 1 inch think, 12 inches wide, and 1 foot long—or the equivalent.

BOARDING HOUSE   A residential building where, in addition to lodging, meals are provided, usually for five or more unrelated tenants but not to the general public or transients.

BOND Evidence of a debt.

A document that binds the parties to the bond to pay its face amount if certain conditions are not met. (*See also* GENERAL OBLIGATION BOND, PERFORMANCE BOND, PUBLIC BOND, REVENUE BOND, SPECIAL ASSESSMENT BOND, SURETY BOND, TAX ANTICIPATION BOND.)

BOOK COST The cost of a property as shown in the accounting records of the owner.

BOOK DEPRECIATION The accrued depreciation shown on the owner's accounts.

BOOK VALUE An owner's assessment of the value of his property, as carried in his own records or "books."

The value of a property less the total amount depreciated at the time value is established.

BORINGS Tests made to determine subsurface conditions of a building site.

BOTEL A facility providing lodging and other services for boat travelers—such as a motel provides for automobile travelers.

BOULEVARD A wide street characterized by rows of trees planted along its two sides or in its median.

BOYCOTT Organized effort to bring an organization to terms by penalizing it through refusal to deal with it commercially or socially.

BROKER A middleman who represents the interests of either buyer or seller in a transaction for a fee. An agent who does not take title to property.

BROWNSTONE A rowhouse constructed with a reddish-brown sandstone; usually refers to a structure constructed during the nineteenth century.

BUCK The frame for a door, usually metal.

BUDGET BUREAU (*See* OFFICE OF MANAGEMENT AND BUDGET.)

BUFFER ZONE   An area separating two or more types of land use from one another.

BUILDER   A person or organization that builds buildings as a principal occupation.

BUILDER COMMITMENT   [HUD]   Agreement between FHA and a builder providing for FHA to issue mortgage insurance on a specified property to be constructed; can be "conditional" when FHA agrees to insure a mortgage when construction is satisfactorily completed, in an amount and under terms preestablished, provided the eligible borrower is approved by FHA; can be "firm" when FHA agrees to insure a mortgage when property construction is satisfactorily completed and sold to an approved mortgagor, with the amount and terms stipulated upon issuance of the FHA commitment to insure.

BUILDER-SELLER MORTGAGOR or SPONSOR   [FHA]   A special type of limited distribution mortgagor which constructs or rehabilitates a multifamily project and which has entered into a written agreement with a qualified private nonprofit mortgagor to sell the project, upon final endorsement to the nonprofit corporation, at a purchase price not to exceed the certified actual cost of the project.

BUILDER-SPONSOR'S PROFIT AND RISK ALLOWANCE   (BSPRA)   [FHA]   An amount equal to 10 percent of the HUD-approved replacement cost of a project exclusive of the cost of the land.

BUILDER'S WARRANTY   A written statement by a builder warranting that a building or a construction activity was completed in conformity with a stipulated set of plans and specifications, to protect a purchaser from latent defects; usually has a one-year limit. (*See also* HOME WARRANTY PROGRAM.)

BUILDING   A structure with a roof supported by columns or walls, intended to provide shelter for persons, property, animals, or business activity. Includes roof, gutters, walls, downspouts, porches, foundations, crawl spaces, windows, floors, and doors.

BUILDING AND LOAN AGREEMENT   An instrument setting forth the rights and responsibilities of a borrower, lender, and contractor in conjunction with the making of a construction loan.

BUILDING AREA   [HUD]   The total ground area of each building and accessory building but not including uncovered entrance platforms, terraces, and steps.

BUILDING BULK   The height, depth, density, and width of a building.

BUILDING CODE   State or locally adopted ordinance or regulation enforceable by police powers under the concept of health, safety, and welfare controlling the design, construction, alteration, repair, quality of materials, use and occupancy, and related factors of any building or structure within its jurisdiction. It may include the regulation of equipment and facilities installed in the building, such as electrical, mechanical, plumbing, heating equipment, or such equipment may be regulated in separate ordinances. (*See also* PERFORMANCE CODE, SPECIFICATION CODE.)

BUILDING DEFICIENCY [urban renewal] [HUD]   Condition of buildings in an urban renewal area, including defects to a point warranting clearance; deteriorating condition because of a defect not correctable by normal maintenance; extensive minor defects which, taken collectively, are causing the building to have a deteriorating effect on the surrounding area; inadequate original construction or alterations; inadequate or unsafe plumbing, heating, or electrical facilities; other equally significant building deficiencies.

BUILDING ENCROACHMENT   (*See* ENCROACHMENT.)

BUILDING ENVELOPE   The structural frame and the basic enclosing material (e.g., brick, wood, concrete) of a building.

BUILDING HEIGHT   (*See* HEIGHT OF BUILDING.)

BUILDING INDUSTRY   (*See* CONSTRUCTION INDUSTRY.)

BUILDING LINE   Generally a line established parallel to the front street line in front of which no part of a building is allowed to project under the provisions of zoning codes.

BUILDING LOAN AGREEMENT [FHA]   Document listing HUD's requirements concerning the advancing of construction loan funds and insuring of such advances, to which the sponsor agrees, during the construction period.

BUILDING OFFICIALS CONFERENCE OF AMERICA (BOCA)   National code group which publishes and maintains a variety of model building and housing codes. (*See also* BASIC BUILDING CODE, NATIONAL CODE.)

BUILDING PERMIT   Permit issued by a municipality or other authorized entity to a builder to proceed with a given construction activity upon approval of certain plans and specifications relating to the construction activity.

BUILDING RESIDUAL TECHNIQUE   A method of assigning a value to a property in which the land is valued separately from the building; investors deduct their return on the land from their total income from the property, and the residual amount is computed to determine the value of the building.

BUILDING STANDARDS   (*See* BUILDING CODE, MINIMUM PROPERTY STANDARDS, PERFORMANCE CODE, SPECIFICATION CODE.)

BUILDING SYSTEM   The method of constructing a building—whether through industrialized techniques involving modules, through traditional techniques involving complete fabrication and/or assembly of components on site, or through a combination of both.

BUILT-IN FURNITURE [FHA]   Any article or equipment serving the purpose ordinarily performed by an item of furniture and which is designed to fulfill a function in a specific location which improves the intended function of the room. The article or equipment must be built in, that is, permanently attached as an integral and normally unremovable part of the construction. It may include such items as dressers or drawer units, wardrobe closets, kitchen cabinets and equipment, or nurses' desks. Items of furniture such as chairs, sofas, beds, and night or lamp tables are not eligible for inclusion in an FHA-insured mortgage.

BUILT-UP AREA [urban renewal]   An area in which 50 percent or more of the land is improved with buildings (not including land in excess of the needs of the buildings or their appurtenant uses or old foundations or temporary structures or temporary uses) and/or rights-of-way of improved or necessary streets and alleys.

BUILT-UP ROOFING   Roofing material consisting of membranes built up on the job from alternate layers of bituminous-saturated felt and bitumen and topped by a surfacing material.

BULK   (*See* BUILDING BULK.)

BULK REGULATIONS   Local ordinances, usually embodied in the zoning code, that control height, location, and density of building construction.

BUNGALOW   Generally, a one-story or one-and-a-half-story house with low exterior lines.

BUREAU OF INDIAN AFFAIRS (BIA)   BIA was created in the War Department in 1824 and transferred to the Department of the Interior at the time of its establishment in 1849. The Snyder Act of 1921 provided substantive law for appropriations covering the conduct of activities by BIA. The scope and character of the authorizations contained in this act were broadened by the Indian Reorganization Act of 1934.

The principal objectives of the Bureau are to actively encourage and train American Indians and Indians and Eskimos of Alaska to manage their own affairs under the trust relationship to the federal government; to facilitate, with maximum involvement of American Indians and Indians and Eskimos of Alaska, full development of their human and natural resource potentials; to mobilize all public and private aids to the advancement of American Indians and Indians and Eskimos of Alaska for use by them; and to utilize the skill and capabilities of American Indians and Indians and Eskimos of Alaska in the direction and management of programs for their benefit.

BUREAU OF LABOR STATISTICS (BLS)   The Department of Labor's Commissioner of Labor Statistics has responsibility for the Department's economic and statistical research activities. The BLS is the government's principal fact-finding agency in the field of labor economics, particularly with respect to the collection and analysis of data on manpower and labor requirements, labor force, employment, unemployment, hours of work, wages and employee compensation, prices, living conditions, labor-management relations, productivity and technological developments, occupational safety and health, structure and growth of the economy, poverty, urban conditions and related socioeconomic issues, and international aspects of these subjects.

It has no enforcement or administrative functions. Practically all the basic data it collects from workers, businessmen, and from other governmental agencies are supplied by voluntary cooperation based on their interest in and need for the analyses and summaries which result. The research and statistical projects planned grow out of the needs of these groups as well as the needs of Congress and the federal and state governments. The information collected is issued in special bulletins and in its official publication, the *Monthly Labor Review*. Publications of the Bureau include the *Consumer Price Index, Wholesale Price Index, Directory of National Labor Unions Employment and Earnings, Occupational Outlook Handbook,* and *Occupational Outlook Quarterly*. The Bureau analyzes and interprets short-run economic developments and prepares a regularly recurring report called *The Quarterly Review of Productivity, Wages, and Prices*.

BUREAU OF THE BUDGET (BOB)   (*See* OFFICE OF MANAGEMENT AND BUDGET.)

BUS LANE [transportation]   Street or highway lane intended for use primarily by buses but also used by other traffic for such purposes as making right turns. When traffic is restricted from using a bus lane, it is an exclusive bus lane or busway.

BUSWAY [transportation]   A fast link-transit mode using high-performance buses on exclusive lanes in separate rights-of-way. (*See also* BUS LANE.)

BUTT   A hinge.

BUY-BACK AGREEMENT   A provision in a sales contract to the effect that the seller will buy back a property within a specified period, usually for the selling price and in the event of the purchaser's transfer from the area.

BUYER'S MARKET   A market condition characterized by an oversupply, resulting in prices favoring the buyer. (*See also* SELLER'S MARKET.)

BUYING CLUB   An organization through which groups of residents pool their money to purchase food (usually) in large quantities at wholesale prices.

BYLAWS   Document which specifies rules, regulations, membership, and laws governing a corporation approved by some public office, usually the state.

CADASTRAL MAP   Legal map for recording of a title, indicating legal boundaries and ownership of real property.

"CALL REPORT"   A report on mortgage delinquencies. (*See also* DELINQUENCY.)

CAMPANILE A bell tower.

CAMUS SYSTEM [construction] A slab system of building, developed in France, employing a technique using factory-fabricated, precast panels. Exterior finishes, doors, windows, thermal insulation, and ventilation ducts are cast into the panels.

CANTILEVER An overhanging part of a structure supported at one end only.

CAPACITY [transportation] Number of vehicles which can reasonably be handled on a given roadway at reasonable speeds without causing congestion.

CAPE COD HOUSE A house characterized as having two stories, with the second-story cornice forming the main cornice line and the second-story rooms having dormer windows, usually built of frame construction with clapboard or shingle siding.

CAPEHART-WHERRY HOUSING Housing insured by FHA to be rented to military personnel or sold to civilians employed at military installations under provisions of Title VIII of the Housing Act of 1949, introduced by Senator Kenneth S. Wherry and amended by Senator Homer Capehart in the Housing Act of 1955. Also referred to as "Title VIII housing."

CAPITAL Money or property held by an investor in a business and available for investment purposes. (*See also* FIXED CAPITAL, FLOATING CAPITAL, WORKING CAPITAL.)

CAPITAL ACCOUNT A reporting of the investments in a business.

CAPITAL ASSET (*See* FIXED ASSET.)

CAPITAL BUDGET Budget setting forth planned, nonrecurring expenditures on capital improvements.

CAPITAL CHARGE The amount that must be paid annually to provide a return on an investment.

CAPITAL GAIN Profit made on an investment. Profit earned on an investment by an investor in an above-average tax bracket, if held for six months or longer, is taxed at a lower rate than the tax rate on ordinary income.

CAPITAL GRANT A sum of money given for a specified purpose, usually by one governmental entity to another.

CAPITAL GRANT [urban renewal] The federal cash contribution of up to two-thirds (under certain financing conditions, up to three-fourths) of the net project cost of urban renewal projects undertaken in a locality.

Title I—Community Development of the Housing and Community Development Act of 1974 substitutes a concept of block grants for capital grants.

CAPITAL GRANT PROGRESS PAYMENTS [urban renewal] (*See* PROJECT CAPITAL GRANT PROGRESS PAYMENTS.)

CAPITAL IMPROVEMENT The construction or purchase of physical facilities or equipment—such as land purchased by a public corporation or governmental entity for hospitals, parks, or other public facilities, roads, libraries, schools, city halls, water and sewer systems. Capital improvement costs do not include operating expenses.

CAPITAL IMPROVEMENT PROGRAM A governmental entity's budgeted expenditures of funds for capital improvements over a given period of time, usually based on planned needs and financial resources.

CAPITALIZATION Conversion of investments in property, stock, or other holdings into money or profit or ultimate value.

CAPITALIZATION APPRAISAL Appraisal of the value of a property on the basis of projections and analyses of anticipated future net income.

CAPITALIZATION RATE Rate used as a factor in determining the value of an asset based on the net annual earnings to be produced by the asset.

CAPITAL REQUIREMENTS The amount required for fixed capital and working capital.

CAPITAL VALUE [urban renewal] The value of land imputed from the annual rent. Determined by dividing the annual rent specified in the lease agreement by the previously concurred-in current annual rate of rent. The capital value must be not less than the fair value of the land in fee at the time of the lease. The capital value of the annual rent determined in this way provides a valid basis for comparing the proposed lease with offers to purchase.

CARPORT [HUD] A roofed space having at least one side open to the weather, primarily designed or used for parking motor vehicles.

CARRYING CHARGES The expenses incurred from owning idle property, such as the taxes on idle land or on property under construction, the cost of protective services, insurance, etc.

CASEMENT WINDOW A window using hinges on its side, permitting the window to open vertically.

CASH BALANCE [HUD] Checkbook balances of all funds in demand deposit (checking) accounts with a bank or banks at the time a financial statement or report is prepared.

CASH CREDIT The cash portion of a local share of the cost of a project which receives federal funding, as distinguished from an in-kind contribution or noncash grant-in-aid.

CASH FLOW The spendable income from an investment after paying all expenses, such as operating expenses and debt service.

CASH ON THE DOWN PAYMENT (COD) Ratio of the annual cash flow to the amount of the down payment, expressed as a percentage.

CATCH BASIN Surface drainage receptacle for collecting rainwater, from which the water is conducted by drains or conduits to a storm sewer system.

CATEGORICAL GRANT PROGRAM or CATEGORICAL PROGRAM Federal program with a single purpose resulting from its legislative enactment (such as urban renewal, basic water and sewer grant, and neighborhood facilities programs), as distinguished from a block grant system of funding. (*See also* REVENUE SHARING.)

CATWALK A partial, rough floor in an attic.

CAVEAT A notice prohibiting a party from doing a certain act, given by a party with an interest in the matter. It is intended to allow the second party to be heard before any action is taken.

CAVITY WALL [HUD] A masonry or concrete wall consisting of two wythes arranged to provide an air space within the wall in which the inner and outer wythes of the wall are tied together with metal ties.

CEBUS SYSTEM [construction]   A French building system which incorporates a flexible method of construction analysis and design applied separately to each specific project in accordance with architectural concepts and production techniques—characterized by room-sized floor-panel elements with load-bearing crosswalls of precast concrete. The system can accommodate cast-in electrical conduit, radiant heat tubing, precast plumbing venting, and waste chute technical walls or prefabricated plumbing trees.

CEILING RENT [public housing]   The highest rent that can be charged for a public housing unit by a local housing authority; it cannot exceed the rent that prevails in the locality for comparable, privately owned dwellings.

CELLAR   A building level or story located wholly or partly below ground level.

CENSUS   A counting of an area's population, demographic data, or other enumerable facts. The U.S. Bureau of the Census conducts such a count each ten years; in addition to enumerating the population, the count also includes data on minority populations, households, condition and features of housing, age groups, income levels, etc.

CENTRAL BUSINESS DISTRICT (CBD)   The principal area of a city's retail, commercial, governmental, and service functions. Often called "downtown."

CENTRAL CITY   The largest municipality in a metropolitan area. The term is used sometimes also to distinguish the center or most important part of a city from its outlying, suburban, or newer sections. Not to be confused with "core" or "slum area." (*See also* METROPOLITAN AREA.)

CENTRALIZED RELOCATION SERVICES   Relocation services provided by a central relocation agency.

CENTRAL OFFICE OF HUD   The headquarters of HUD, located in Washington, D.C.

CENTRAL RELOCATION AGENCY   A municipal agency or independent local authority or agency that provides relocation services on behalf of public agencies to displaced families, individuals, and businesses.

CERTIFICATE OF ELIGIBILITY [HUD]   Certification issued upon acceptance of a tenant's application for admission to a subsidized housing project. It confirms the tenant's eligibility to occupy the project, and states the amount of subsidy to which he is entitled. (*See also* VETERANS CERTIFICATE OF ELIGIBILITY.)

CERTIFICATE OF INCORPORATION   The instrument by which a private corporation is legally formed and in which is specified the name, location, principle, and purpose(s) of the incorporators in compliance with some designated public office, usually the state. It serves as evidence of the corporation's existence.

CERTIFICATE OF OCCUPANCY   Document issued by an official agency indicating that premises meet requirements of local codes, ordinances, or regulations. Sometimes considered a permit to occupy premises.

CERTIFICATE OF TITLE   A document stating that the title to a property is clear of defects. Such a certificate is not the same as title insurance.

CERTIFICATION [FHA Section 220]   (*See* FHA CERTIFICATION.)

CERTIFIED AGENCY PROGRAM (CAP)   An experiment by the Federal Housing Administration conducted in the late 1950s to encourage lending institutions in small cities to avail themselves of FHA's mortgage insurance programs.

CERTIFIED ASSESSMENT EVALUATOR (CAE)   A qualified member of the International Association of Assessing Officers, which establishes criteria and administers examinations prior to accepting members. (*See also* ASSESSOR.)

CERTIFIED PROPERTY MANAGER (CPM)   Person who has obtained a certificate from the Institute of Real Estate Management (an affiliate of the National Association of Real Estate Boards), verifying that certain tests have been passed and certain experience has been obtained in managing property.

CERTIORARI   A review by a higher court of proceedings conducted by inferior courts, officers, board, or tribunals to certify the record of such proceedings.

CESSPOOL [FHA]   A covered pit with open-jointed lining into which raw sewage is discharged.

CHAIN   A land measurement equal in length to 66 feet. The instrument used for measuring chain lengths of a tract of land.

CHAIN OF TITLE   A term applied to the past series of transactions and documents affecting the title to a particular parcel of land.

CHANGE ORDER   A written agreement, signed by all parties to a contract, formalizing and defining a change in the contract requirements within the scope of the original contract; establishes the consideration accruing to both parties as a result of the change. (*See also* PROCEED ORDER.)

CHANGING NEIGHBORHOOD   Usually a neighborhood experiencing significant transition of racial occupancy.

CHARTER   A document providing evidence of the incorporation of an organization.

CHASE   A space or groove left in a wall during construction to allow for passage of pipes, ducts, or conduit.

CHATTEL   Personal property, such as furniture, equipment, fixtures, automobiles, livestock—as distinguished from real estate.

CHATTEL MORTGAGE   A mortgage on chattels.

CHATTELS PERSONAL   Movable items of property, as distinguished from real estate.

CHATTELS REAL   Interests held in real estate not constituting a freehold; includes leaseholds and ownership of chattels personal attached to real estate.

CHECKMETER   Utility meter used to check consumption by individual housing units in projects where rental charges include cost of utilities. Inordinate consumption by dwelling units results in a surcharge on the tenant's rent.

CIRCULARS [HUD]   HUD statements printed and circulated to issue policies and procedures on subject matter which is inappropriate for inclusion in the applicable handbook or which is scheduled for eventual consolidation into handbooks or guides. (*See also* GUIDES, HANDBOOK, NOTICES.)

CISTERN   A man-made reservoir or tank used for storing rainwater.

CITIZEN PARTICIPATION (*See* COMMUNITY PARTICIPATION.)

CITY   The incorporated area within the legal jurisdiction of a municipal corporation chartered by a state. Also refers to the corporation itself.

CITY DEMONSTRATION AGENCY (CDA) [Model Cities]   Local agency established to administer a City Demonstration Program; responsible for planning, budgeting, and evaluating such a program. *(See also* DEMONSTRATION CITIES PROGRAM.)

CITY PLAN   (*See* GENERAL PLAN.)

CITY PLANNING   The disciplined process of establishing the social, physical, cultural, educational, transportation, public works, and other normal needs of a city over a period of time and of preparing the resources needed to provide for those needs. (*See also* PLANNING.)

CIVIC CENTER   The location within a city where most public functions are administered or occur, including governmental, cultural, and educational affairs.

CIVIL RIGHTS   The lawful rights of citizens—as distinguished from political, natural, or human rights.

CIVIL RIGHTS ACT   (*See* CIVIL RIGHTS ACT OF 1964.)

CIVIL RIGHTS ACT OF 1964   An act to enforce the constitutional right to vote, to confer jurisdiction upon the district courts of the United States to provide injunctive relief against discrimination in public accommodations, to authorize the Attorney General to institute suits to protect constitutional rights in public facilities and public education, to extend the Commission on Civil Rights, to prevent discrimination in federally assisted programs, to establish a Commission on Equal Employment Opportunity, and for other purposes. Approved July 2, 1964, and subsequently amended.

Title VI of this act applies particularly to HUD programs.

CLAPBOARD   Narrow board thicker on one edge than the other, used as siding on buildings.

CLASS OF CONSTRUCTION   The classification of buildings according to the type of material of which they are constructed; usually refers to their fire-resistant qualities—e.g., steel, concrete, masonry, frame.

CLEARANCE (*See* SLUM CLEARANCE.)

CLEARANCE PROGRAM The acquisition, demolition, and removal of structures from a defined area, and the preparation of the land for redevelopment—usually under the provisions of an approved urban renewal program. Clearance under the urban renewal program is distinguished from rehabilitation of properties. (*See also* NEIGHBORHOOD REHABILITATION, REHABILITATION.)

CLEAR TITLE A title to a property unencumbered by any claims, liens, attachments, or other defects.

CLERESTORY A windowed space which rises above lower stories to admit air and light.

CLERK OF THE WORKS Person assigned to coordinate and expedite the multiple facets of a given project.

CLOSE-OUT AMENDATORY [urban renewal] A supplemental grant intended to cover additional costs of completing an urban renewal project.

CLOSING An assembly of the parties in a transfer of property ownership, at which buyer and seller execute appropriate documents transferring title from the seller to the purchaser. (*See also* FINAL CLOSING, INITIAL CLOSING.)

CLOSING COSTS All charges paid at settlement for obtaining a mortgage loan and transferring a real estate title. Distinguished from settlement costs.

CLOUD ON TITLE An encumbrance on a title preventing the owner from holding a clear title.

CLUSTER DEVELOPMENT Development of a land tract in a clustering pattern—whether residential, commercial, industrial, institutional, etc.

CODE A systematic arrangement of a governmental entity's laws, rules, or regulations pertaining to its jurisdiction.

CODE ADMINISTRATION or CODE ENFORCEMENT The regulation by an official agency of the adherence to a governmental entity's codes by those subject to its provisions; usually refers to the administration or enforcement of minimum standards of occupancy. (*See also* FEDERALLY ASSISTED

CODE ENFORCEMENT, HOUSING AND COMMUNITY DEVELOPMENT ACT OF 1974, TITLE I—COMMUNITY DEVELOPMENT.)

CODE STANDARDS [HUD]   The requirements of local building, housing, zoning, plumbing, electrical, fire prevention, and other laws related to housing construction and to use, maintenance, and occupancy of properties.

COLD FLAT   (*See* FLAT.)

COLD-WATER FLAT   (*See* FLAT.)

COLGNET SYSTEM   A French industrialized building system fabricated in factories utilizing precision casting machinery and techniques. Consists of high-precision precast concrete floor, wall, and exterior panels.

COLLATERAL   Stocks, bonds, or property available to secure a debt. Also called "security."

COLLATERAL LOAN   A variation of conventional financing, under which a borrower is enabled to purchase a property with a smaller down payment than would be possible otherwise because the borrower's down payment is complemented by an amount of collateral obligated to the lender and available in the event of default.

COLLATERAL PLEDGE AGREEMENT   An instrument through which a seller or another contracts to deposit a sum of money in a savings account, which sum serves as collateral on behalf of a purchaser who is unable to make a down payment on the property that is satisfactory to the mortgagee.

COLLECTION LOSS   Financial loss attributable to the failure or inability to collect money amounts due, as from tenants.

COLLECTOR STREET   Street carrying traffic from minor streets to major arterial streets.

COLLEGE HOUSING [HUD]   New or existing structures suitable for dwelling use, including single-room dormitories and apartments and dwelling facilities in existing structures slated for rehabilitation, alteration, conversion, or improvement because they would otherwise be inadequate for the proposed dwelling use.

COLLEGE HOUSING PROGRAM [HUD]   Authorized by the Housing Act of 1950 and later amendments; provides grants and direct loans through the Federal Housing Administration to help colleges and hospitals finance construction or purchase of housing and related facilities. Grants may be made for periods not exceeding forty years in an amount equal to the difference in the average annual debt service required to amortize a private market loan at market interest rates and that which would be required to amortize a 3 percent loan of like term. Direct HUD 3 percent loans will be available only to institutions unable to borrow in the private market at nonexorbitant interest rates. Facilities eligible for construction or purchase include college residence halls, faculty and married-student housing, dining facilities, college unions, infirmaries and housing for student nurses, interns, and residents.

COLOR OF RIGHT   Some claim, not necessarily legal or official, indicating one's right to ownership of property.

COMBINED ROOMS [HUD]   Two or more adjacent habitable rooms which, by their relationship, planning, and openness, permit their common use. (*See also* HABITABLE ROOM.)

COMMERCIAL GARAGE [HUD]   A garage designed for the storage of five or more motor vehicles, operated for the general public. (*See also* COMMUNITY GARAGE, PRIVATE GARAGE, PUBLIC GARAGE.)

COMMERCIAL INCOME [HUD/FHA]   (*See* COMMERCIAL USE OF RESIDENTIAL PROPERTY.)

COMMERCIAL STANDARDS (CS)   Criteria of quality and methods of testing, rating, certifying, and labeling certain manufactured commodities—established by the manufacturing industry in cooperation with the Commodity Standards Division of the Office of Technical Services of the U.S. Department of Commerce.

COMMERCIAL STRIP   A generally long line of commercial establishments along one or both sides of a road.

COMMERCIAL USE OF RESIDENTIAL PROPERTY [FHA]   Any space or feature included in a property from which income is anticipated, apart from the rental of living units or which is not directly related to the housing of elderly or handicapped persons. Rental of garage space for tenant use or collection of a nominal membership fee for a recreational facility is not considered commercial income.

Commercial use is limited to that designed essentially for the use and needs of the occupants. The aggregate gross floor area devoted to commercial use should not exceed 10 percent of the gross building floor area devoted to residential use, including corridors, stairs, elevators, lobbies, etc. Laundry space, project storage space, and tenant parking space may be disregarded in the computations. Commercial uses must:

1. Be of a character and extent which is incidental to and compatible with the residential character of the property.

2. Involve a commercial use related to residential use, such as retail shops of a food, clothing, or service nature, housekeeping and personal service, and professional offices. Central dining, if included, must be considered a commercial use in profit-type projects. Inharmonious uses oriented to the general public rather than to the project are not acceptable.

3. Conform to good standards of construction and to local zoning and be acceptable to FHA.

Medical facilities may or may not be commercial uses, depending upon the extent of the services and their relationship to the mode of operation of the project.

COMMISSION A percentage of the sales price of a property paid as a fee to a broker who arranges for a sale.

A group of persons established to perform a public function.

COMMISSIONER Member of a commission. Members of an authority frequently are called "commissioners."

COMMISSIONER [FHA] (*See* FEDERAL HOUSING COMMISSIONER.)

COMMITMENT (*See* LOAN COMMITMENT.)

COMMITMENT FEE Fee paid by an applicant for a loan upon issuance of a loan commitment by a lender or upon issuance of a commitment of another type, such as a commitment to insure a mortgage by FHA.

COMMITMENT TO INSURE A report issued by a title insurance company, or its agent, showing the condition of the title and committing the title insurance company to issue a form policy as designated in the commitment upon compliance with and satisfaction of requirements set forth in the commitment.

[FHA] Documents issued in conjunction with the approval by HUD/FHA of a conditional commitment or a firm commitment.

COMMITTEE ON STATE AND LOCAL GOVERNMENT COOPERATION This

Committee was established as a presidential advisory panel pursuant to Executive Order No. 11627 of October 15, 1971, as amended, continued pursuant to Executive Order No. 11640 of January 26, 1972. It serves as an advisory panel to the Cost of Living Council, Pay Board, and Price Commission for the postfreeze Economic Stabilization Program.

The Committee in its advisory role develops, reviews, and makes recommendations on policies, mechanisms, and procedures to the Cost of Living Council, Pay Board, and Price Commission designed to stimulate voluntary cooperation by both state and local governments and individual citizens with the stabilization program. To accomplish this function, the Committee is composed of various representatives of these governments and their employee organizations.

COMMON AREAS AND FACILITIES [HUD]   Those areas of a housing project and of a property upon which it is located that are for the use and enjoyment of the owners of family units located in the project. The areas may include the land, roofs, main walls, elevators, staircases, lobbies, halls, parking space, and community and commercial facilities.

"Common space" refers usually to open areas, the use of which is shared by all tenants, as distinguished from space designated for their private use.

(*See also* RESTRICTED COMMON AREAS AND FACILITIES.)

COMMON BUSINESS ORIENTED LANGUAGE (COBOL)   Term used in the computer business to denote the terms peculiar to a project or projects undergoing computer processing.

COMMON EXPENSES [condominium] [HUD]   These include all sums lawfully assessed against the condominium unit owners by the association of such owners; expenses of administration, maintenance, and repair or replacement of the common areas and facilities; expenses agreed upon as common expenses by the association of owners; and expenses declared common expenses by provisions of FHA regulations or in the association of owners' bylaws.

COMMON PROFITS [condominium] [HUD]   The balance of all income, rents, profits, and revenues from the common areas and facilities remaining after the deduction of the common expenses.

COMMON SPACE   (*See* COMMON AREAS AND FACILITIES.)

COMMUNAL LIVING   A style of living that occurs in a communelike setting.

COMMUNE A community established as self-governing, self-supporting, and, theoretically, free from interference from others.

COMMUNITY A group of people living or working close to one another and sharing common interests.

COMMUNITY ACTION AGENCY (CAA) Agency that administers a Community Action Program.

A CAA must be designated by the state, a political subdivision of the state, a combination of such political subdivisions, or Indian tribal organizations. A state or local government (or a combination of subdivisions) may designate itself or another agency, which may be either a separate public agency or a private nonprofit organization. The director of OEO may extend financial assistance for a limited-purpose project to a public or private nonprofit agency which he finds is capable of carrying out the project in an efficient and effective manner. The director may provide financial assistance to the state agencies designated in accordance with state law to carry out functions of the appropriate State Economic Opportunity Office.

COMMUNITY ACTION PROGRAM (CAP) Program funded under provisions of the Economic Opportunity Act of 1964 and later amendments, administered by a Community Action Agency. The objectives of the CAA are to mobilize and channel the resources of private and public organizations and institutions into antipoverty action; to increase the capabilities as well as opportunities for participation of the poor in the planning, conduct, and evaluation of programs affecting their lives; to stimulate new and more effective approaches to the solution of poverty problems; to strengthen communications and mutual understanding; and to strengthen the planning and coordination of antipoverty programs in the community.

Funds may be used for administrative costs of CAAs, nonprogram staff activities, neighborhood centers in target areas, and locally developd programs which further the objectives of community action. Projects may include health, education, housing, family planning, economic development, employment, day care, community organization, and other services. Any of these programs also may be funded to meet the needs of the American Indian. Technical assistance is also available to communities in developing, conducting, and administering programs under Title II and for training for specialized or other personnel which is needed with those programs. The act provides funds for assistance to state agencies designated in accordance with state law to carry out the functions of the State Economic Opportunity Office.

COMMUNITY CENTER   A building used for recreational, social, cultural, or educational purposes to serve the members of a community.

COMMUNITY CONTROL   Authority of the members of a community to oversee the planning and/or implementation of a facility or a service.

COMMUNITY DEVELOPMENT (CD)   The process of applying the physical, social, human, financial, or other particular resources of a community toward its improvement.

A HUD term for the collective group of programs administered by the Assistant Secretary for Community Development, who has charge of urban renewal, Model Cities, water and sewer grants, neighborhood facilities, rehabilitation loans, and public facility loan programs. The term is sometimes substituted for "urban renewal," alone or in conjunction with other programs.

(*See also* HOUSING AND COMMUNITY DEVELOPMENT ACT OF 1974, TITLE I—COMMUNITY DEVELOPMENT.)

COMMUNITY DEVELOPMENT [rural]   (*See* EXTENSION PROGRAMS FOR COMMUNITY DEVELOPMENT.)

COMMUNITY DEVELOPMENT CORPORATION (CDC)   Usually, a tax-exempt corporation established through community organization to operate programs to address both immediate and long-term severe social and economic problems and eventual revitalization of a given community.

COMMUNITY DEVELOPMENT CORPORATION [HUD]   Corporation established within HUD to administer HUD's loan functions and other functions of the New Community Development Program. The Housing and Community Development Act of 1974 changed the name of the corporation to New Community Development Corporation. (*See also* TITLE VII NEW COMMUNITY LOAN GUARANTEES.)

COMMUNITY DEVELOPMENT MODEL   A representation in narrative, figures, and physical plans of the social, economic, and physical aspects of a community showing how such aspects relate to one another and how a community can develop as a whole over a period of time.

COMMUNITY DEVELOPMENT PROGRAM   Program formulated by a unit of general local government in its application to HUD for a block grant under the provisions of Title I—Community Development of the Housing and Community Development Act of 1974. Such a program states the activities to be undertaken to meet community development needs and objectives identified in the applicant's "summary community development plan," together with the estimated costs and general location of such activities. It indicates the resources, other than those provided through the block grant, which are expected to be made available toward meeting the identified needs and objectives, and it takes into account appropriate environmental factors. (*See also* HOUSING ASSISTANCE PLAN.)

COMMUNITY DEVELOPMENT REVENUE SHARING (*See* TITLE I—COMMUNITY DEVELOPMENT, URBAN COMMUNITY DEVELOPMENT SPECIAL REVENUE SHARING.)

COMMUNITY DEVELOPMENT STATEMENT [HUD] Substitute format for a community's Workable Program, identifying community development problems, annual and long-term objectives, priorities and strategies, and describing the federal programs needed in the period covered by the statement. (First used in Gary, Indiana, with HUD concurrence.)

COMMUNITY FACILITIES Public or quasi-public facilities used by a community, such as community centers, schools, parks, streets, playgrounds, and churches.

COMMUNITY FACILITIES ADMINISTRATION (CFA) Federal agency that functioned as a constituent of the Housing and Home Finance Agency until the establishment of HUD in 1965. CFA administered certain programs of federal financial assistance involving public works, college housing loans, elderly housing loans, and certain school construction programs.

COMMUNITY GARAGE A building or portion of a building providing storage for motor vehicles owned by a certain group of individuals; sometimes provides washing facilities but not other services. (*See also* COMMERCIAL GARAGE, PRIVATE GARAGE, PUBLIC GARAGE.)

COMMUNITY ORGANIZATION (CO) The organizing of a community's members towards its social, political, economic, or physical improvement.

COMMUNITY PARTICIPATION The participation by members of a community in the planning and implementation of community development programs.

COMMUNITY PARTICIPATION COMMITTEE (CPC) A voluntary group representing a segment of a community.

COMMUNITY PROPERTY Property owned jointly by a husband and wife.

COMMUNITY RELATIONS SERVICE (CRS)   The Service was created by Title X of the Civil Rights Act of 1964. It is under the general authority of the Attorney General and is headed by a director, who is appointed by the President with the advice and consent of the Senate. The Service assists communities on its own initiative, at the request of state or local officials, or upon inquiry of other interested organizations or persons.

CRS aids in resolving disputes and difficulties as they erupt and also helps communities to achieve the kind of progress which will enable them to avoid racial upheavals. Its goal is to help bring about rapid and orderly progress toward securing a life of justice, equal opportunity, and human dignity for all American citizens.

Among the activities of CRS are helping communities to identify those of their social problems that are more apparent from an objective, outside perspective; aiding communities in developing and applying their resources for rapid, orderly social and economic change in minority communities; helping to speed delivery to communities of federal programs and services designed to improve social and economic conditions; assisting minority communities to establish and strengthen constructive self-help and self-determination projects and programs; encouraging the involvement of minorities in the decision-making processes of their communities; and promoting impartial law enforcement locally and encouraging compliance with federal laws at all levels.

COMMUNITY RENEWAL PROGRAM (CRP) [HUD]   A planning program funded through the Department of Housing and Urban Development under the provisions of Section 103(d) of the Housing Act of 1949, as amended in 1959 and in later laws, to assist communities in assessing overall urban renewal needs and in developing a staged program of action to meet such needs. Since January 1971, the emphasis of the program has been on improving the capacity of cities to carry out comprehensive community development programs.

Title I—Community Development of the Housing and Community Development Act of 1974 supplanted the program with a system of block grants, the funds from which can be used to accomplish the results of CRPs.

COMMUNITY WATER OR SEWER SYSTEM   A central system which serves all living units in a given area and is not publicly owned.

COMMUTING   Traveling to and from work, usually over a fairly long distance.

COMPANY HOUSING   Housing owned by an employer and provided for employees.

COMPANY TOWN   A town or town area owned principally by the employer of the persons living in that town.

COMPARABLES   Term used by appraisers in establishing value of a property on the basis of the value of similar properties.

COMPENSABLE or COMPENSATIVE REGULATIONS   Usually, zoning regulations, newly instituted, the enforcement of which places a hardship on the property owner affected, for which he may be entitled to compensation.

COMPETITION-NEGOTIATION COMBINATION [urban renewal]   Method of offering for sale urban renewal project land in which the availability of the land is made known by public announcement; selection is made after negotiation with one or more redevelopers whose initial proposals have been determined to be most acceptable. A public hearing on the proposal is required prior to execution of the contract.

COMPETITIVE LOCATIONS [HUD]   Locations are construed to be competitive when they are improved with, or appropriate for, residential properties that are approximately similar in accommodations and are within a sales price range or rental range that proves acceptable to typical residents or prospective occupants of the same segment of the market.

COMPLETION BOND   A surety bond guaranteeing the completion of a project or building by a contractor.

COMPONENT DEPRECIATION   Depreciation, for tax purposes, of the individual components of a structure (e.g., the heating and mechanical systems, the roofing, plumbing, wiring) separately from the total structure.

COMPREHENSIVE AREAWIDE WATER AND SEWER PLANNING GRANT [rural] Authorized in the Consolidated Farmers Home Administration Act of 1961 and subsequent amendments; provides grants to rural public bodies to promote efficient and orderly development of rural communities; to provide the information necessary to avoid overlapping, duplication, underdesign, or overdesign of the community water and sewer facilities that may be constructed in the area covered by the plan.

COMPREHENSIVE COMMUNITY PLAN   (*See* COMPREHENSIVE PLAN, GENERAL PLAN.)

COMPREHENSIVE DEVELOPMENT PLAN (CDP) [Model Cities]   Initial plan prepared by cities participating in the Model Cities program; prepared during the year preceding their first action year with funds provided by HUD.

COMPREHENSIVE HEALTH PLANNING GRANTS (*See* SECTION 314(B) GRANTS.)

COMPREHENSIVE PLAN A governmental entity's official statement of its plans and policies for its long-term development. Usually related to the capital improvement program. (*See also* GENERAL PLAN.)

COMPREHENSIVE PLANNING ASSISTANCE [HUD] (*See* SECTION 701 COMPREHENSIVE PLANNING ASSISTANCE.)

CONCENTRATED CODE ENFORCEMENT PROGRAM (CCEP) [HUD] *See* FEDERALLY ASSISTED CODE ENFORCEMENT.)

CONDEMNATION Declaration by a public body having the power of eminent domain that a property will be acquired for public use, whether or not the owner is willing to sell; the owner is paid the reasonable market value of the property as established by appraisal. (*See also* BLANKET CONDEMNATION, EXCESS CONDEMNATION, INVERSE CONDEMNATION, PARTIAL TAKING.)
Declaration that a property is unfit for occupancy because it does not meet requirements of codes and that the property must be boarded up if it is not upgraded to meet code requirements.

CONDEMNATION AWARD The amount paid to the owner of property condemned as a result of a condemnation proceeding.

CONDEMNATION VALUE Value placed on a condemned property by a court of law.

CONDITION(S) [real estate] A proviso in a deed or will that, upon the happening or failure to happen of a certain event, the title of the purchaser or devisee will be limited, enlarged, changed, or terminated.

CONDITIONAL COMMITMENT [FHA] The issuance of a conditional commitment letter by FHA based on a review of the project sponsor's forms, exhibits, schematics, and brief specifications by the architect, which indicates that the project appears to have economic feasibility and that more detailed information is needed before a firm commitment can be issued. (*See also* FIRM COMMITMENT.)

CONDITIONAL CONTRACT OF SALE [public housing] Document issued by a local housing authority (with HUD approval) to a developer indicating that the authority will purchase a certain Turnkey project if certain conditions are met.

CONDITIONAL REZONING   Action through which a municipality grants rezoning but imposes specific conditions on future use of the rezoned land, either directly or by causing the owner to impose deed restrictions on his land.

CONDITIONAL USE ZONING   A land use tentatively approved by a zoning regulation, but only if each applicant satisfies stated standards. Also called "special use zoning."

CONDITIONS AND RESTRICTIONS [real estate]   The designation of the uses to which land may not be put and providing penalties for failure to comply. Commonly used by land subdividers on newly plotted areas.

CONDOMINIUM (condo)   A system of individual fee ownership of units in a multiunit structure, combined with joint ownership of common areas of the structure and land.

CONDOMINIUM MORTGAGE INSURANCE [FHA]   (*See* SECTION 221(I) CONDOMINIUM CONVERSION, SECTION 234(D) CONDOMINIUM MORTGAGE INSURANCE.)

CONDUIT   Tubing, usually metal, used to protect electric wires.

CONFESSION OF JUDGMENT   Prior consent by a tenant to any lawsuit a landlord may care to bring against him in connection with a lease and to a judgment in favor of the landlord.

CONGREGATE HOUSING   A housing project in which some or all of the dwelling units do not have kitchen facilities and connected with which there is a central dining facility to provide meals, usually for elderly persons, under terms and conditions prescribed by the sponsor (including a local housing authority) to permit a generally self-supporting operation.

CONGRESSIONAL APPROPRIATION   The amount of federal funds that can actually be spent for a given program, as established by congressional statute. Distinguished from congressional authorization.

CONGRESSIONAL AUTHORIZATION   The amount of federal funds that may be appropriated for a given program, as established by congressional statute. Distinguished from congressional appropriation.

CONSERVATION   The protection from blighting influences of good neighborhoods and structures and their preservation in a safe and sound state. Also, the prevention of further deterioration in declining areas, in which the majority of structures are not in need of major repairs, by improving or eliminating undesirable structures and through improvements in accordance with a community plan, plus effective enforcement of building, housing, zoning, and related codes.

CONSIDERATION The influencing factor in a contract, such as cash, promises, or other benefit to the seller.

CONSOLIDATED COOPERATION AGREEMENT [public housing] Document signed by a governing body of a locality and a local housing authority consolidating cooperation agreements for several public housing projects to avoid the necessity of securing separate agreements for each project undertaken by the housing authority. Also called "master cooperation agreement."

CONSOLIDATED SUPPLY CONTRACT [public housing] Contracts arranged by regional offices of HUD through which the consolidated requirements of the local housing authorities within its jurisdiction for selected common-use items (e.g., ranges, refrigerators, paint) are obtained in quantities sufficient to make purchases at advantageous prices.

CONSTANT (*See* ANNUAL CONSTANT.)

CONSTANT PAYMENT PLAN Fixed, regular, nonchanging payment schedule on a mortgage over its duration; earliest payments usually are constituted of interest charges, with later payments representing greater payments on the principal sum of the loan. Also called "level annuity plan," "level payment plan."

CONSTRUCTION COST PER SQUARE FOOT [FHA] Computed by subtracting market price of a site from FHA value of building and site and dividing the result by calculated floor area. (*See also* SQUARE-FOOT COST.)

CONSTRUCTION INDUSTRY The cumulative businesses, trades, and professionals that partake of construction and development costs.

CONSTRUCTION INDUSTRY STABILIZATION COMMITTEE The Committee was established as an agency of the United States Government by Executive Order No. 11588 of March 29, 1971, as amended by Executive Order No. 11627 of October 15, 1971. It was established as a tripartite board consisting of representatives of the public, labor, and management and was charged with the duty of stabilizing wages in the construction industry.

The Committee reviews economic adjustments embodied in collective bargaining agreements negotiated in the construction industry, as defined by the Davis-Bacon Act of March 3, 1931, as amended after March 29, 1971, to determine whether said adjustments are consistent with the goals of the Economic Stabilization Program. The Committee is further authorized to review all economic adjustments scheduled to take effect after August 14, 1971, regardless of the date on which the collective bargaining agreement was initially negotiated.

The Committee works in conjunction with seventeen craft boards which are composed of labor and management representatives of each of the construction trades. The Committee consults with the Pay Board to ensure uniform application of the criteria utilized by the Economic Stabilization Program.

CONSTRUCTION LOAN A short-term loan made to finance the cost of construction during the period of construction or rehabilitation—as distinguished from permanent financing on a building ready for occupancy. Amounts normally are distributed to the builder according to costs incurred as construction proceeds. In an FHA transaction, FHA can either "insure" payments made under such a loan or not—depending on FHA loan arrangements. FHA construction loans generally include such nonconstruction costs as architects', consultants', and attorney's fees, and land costs—all of which later can be included again in the permanent mortgage. Also called "interim loan," "short-term loan," "temporary loan."

CONSTRUCTION LOAN AGREEMENT (*See* BUILDING AND LOAN AGREEMENT.)

CONSULTANT [housing] Competent specialist retained by a housing sponsor or developer to assist in arranging the processing, financing, design, construction, equipping, operation, and management of a project. The consultant might assist in the selection and negotiation of contracts with such principals. Also called "packager."

CONSUMER COOPERATIVE [FHA] A nonprofit cooperative ownership housing corporation or trust which is the owner of an existing construction subject to an outstanding indebtedness and is approved by FHA for refinancing the indebtedness with an insured mortgage.

A nonprofit cooperative ownership housing corporation or trust organized for the purpose of purchasing an existing construction, the members and organizers of which do not have an identity of interest with the seller of the existing construction except where FHA has approved such interest as being consistent with the objectives of the cooperative.

CONSUMER CREDIT PROTECTION ACT   An act to safeguard the consumer in connection with the utilization of credit by requiring full disclosure of the terms and conditions of finance charges in credit transactions or in offers to extend credit, by restricting the garnishment of wages, and by creating the National Commission on Consumer Finance to study and make recommendations on the need for further regulation of the consumer finance industry. Approved May 29, 1968, and subsequently amended.

CONTINGENCY RESERVE [FHA]   An amount included in an FHA-insured mortgage on a proposed rehabilitation project for unanticipated costs encountered during construction. The reserve ranges from 0 to 10 percent of the estimated construction costs.

CONTINGENT ASSET   An asset that may be realized if and/or when something occurs or does not occur.

CONTOUR   Line on a topographical map connecting points of like elevation.

CONTRACT [real estate]   An agreement to sell and purchase under which title is withheld from the purchaser until such time as the required payments to the seller have been completed.

CONTRACT AUTHORITY   The total dollar limit that HUD (or other federal agencies) can commit under contracts with developers (or other constituents) for a given program as established by congressional appropriations acts.

CONTRACT AUTHORIZATION   Congressional enactment permitting federal agencies to incur obligations prior to actual appropriation by Congress of funds to cover such obligations; usually followed by an appropriation to liquidate contract authorization.

CONTRACT BUILDER   (*See* GENERAL CONTRACTOR.)

CONTRACT FOR DEED   (*See* LAND CONTRACT.)

CONTRACT FOR LOAN AND GRANT [urban renewal]   (*See* LOAN AND/OR GRANT CONTRACT.)

CONTRACTING OFFICER   The person within a contracting organization duly authorized to administer contracts for, and in the name of, the organization. The officer need not be the same person who executes the contract.

CONTRACT OF INSURANCE [FHA]   An agreement evidenced by the issuance of a mortgage insurance certificate or by the endorsement of FHA upon the credit instrument given in connection with an insured mortgage, incorporating by reference the regulations and the applicable provisions of the act.

CONTRACT OF SALE [public housing]   Contract between a Turnkey project developer and a local housing authority stipulating that upon completion of construction of the Turnkey project, in accordance with plans and specifications approved by HUD, the housing authority will purchase the project pursuant to the provisions of such contract of sale. (*See also* TURNKEY PROJECT.)

CONTRACT RENT   Rent payable by a tenant to a landlord; covers the cost of the use of a dwelling accommodation, equipment, services, and utilities supplied by a project. Does not include charges for utilities purchased by the project and sold to the tenant as a transaction separate from the rent payment, charges for excess utility consumptions, or miscellaneous charges.

CONTRACT SALE   A sale in which the seller retains title to the property sold until the buyer fulfills the terms of the contract. Distinguished from a mortgage.

CONTRACT THRIFT INSTITUTIONS   Financial institution in which the flow of funds depends upon the inflow of funds from forced savings, such as life insurance contracts and retirement fund contributions (pension funds). Distinguished from deposit thrift institutions.

CONTRACTORS AND GRANTEES [HUD]   Individuals and public or private organizations that are direct recipients of HUD funds or that receive HUD funds indirectly through nonfederal sources; all participants, or contractors with participants, in programs where HUD is the guarantor or insurer; and federally assisted construction contractors.

CONTRACTOR'S GENERAL REQUIREMENTS [FHA]   An amount that can be included in an FHA-insured mortgage to cover the general contractor's costs for construction superintendents; field engineers to provide lines and grades for locating structures and utilities on a job site; watchmen; temporary offices, sheds, and toilets; temporary heat, water, and power during construction; cleaning, rubbish removal, and building permits.

CONTRACTOR'S OVERHEAD   A general contractor's cost represented by his investment in equipment, office and administrative expenses, and such other costs as are not represented by cost of labor and material used in actual construction.

CONTROLLED ACCESS HIGHWAY   (*See* LIMITED ACCESS HIGHWAY.)

CONTROLS FOR CONSUMER AND PUBLIC INTEREST [FHA]   Conditions and provisions required by FHA in condominium and for cooperative housing projects, deemed necessary for the protection of the consumer and public interest. These controls include but are not limited to the execution of a regulatory agreement between the owners and FHA which are made applicable to a homeowners' association or cooperative corporation members or to any subsequent owner of a family unit.

CONURBATION   The locale of an agglomeration, such as a metropolitan area or a megalopolis.

CONVALESCENT   A person who is not acutely ill and does not require hospital care but who requires skilled nursing care and related medical services.

CONVENTIONAL FINANCING   Financing without the benefit of governmental mortgage insurance or subsidy.

CONVENTIONAL HOUSE   A house or housing built using standard construction methods rather than building systems techniques.

CONVENTIONAL MORTGAGE   A mortgage carrying no federal insurance from FHA or VA.

CONVENTIONAL MUTUAL HELP—NEW CONSTRUCTION [public housing]   New housing to be constructed by or for a local housing authority and utilizing in whole or in part labor of prospective occupants to be credited to them as equity toward ultimate home ownership.

CONVENTIONAL PROJECT [public housing]   Low-rent public housing project developed by a local housing authority, as distinguished from a Turnkey project.

CONVENTIONAL PROJECT [urban renewal]   Urban renewal project undertaken under provisions of Title I of the Housing Act of 1949 and later amendments, as distinguished from a Neighborhood Development Program.

CONVERSION   A building whose original use has changed; usually, single-family housing that has been divided into two or more dwellings.

CONVEY [real estate]   The act of deeding or transfering title to another.

CONVEYANCE   The transfer of title from one party to another. The document used to effect transfer of title. A deed.

COOPERATION AGREEMENT [public housing]   Contract between a local housing authority and the governing body of the municipality in which a public housing project is located, providing for the governing body to furnish municipal services and facilities to the authority—and for the authority, in turn, to make stipulated payments in lieu of taxes to the municipality.

COOPERATIVE   A legal entity permitting a group of members to mutually own (or owe) certain assets and to share mutually in the benefits derived by the group under the provisions of the entity's rules, regulations, and legal charter.

COOPERATIVE HOUSING   Housing built and owned by a cooperative.

COOPERATIVE HOUSING MORTGAGE INSURANCE [FHA]   (*See* SECTION 213 COOPERATIVE SALES, SECTION 213 INVESTOR-SPONSORED COOPERATIVE HOUSING, SECTION 221(J) CONVERSION OF MULTIFAMILY RENTAL HOUSING TO COOPERATIVE HOUSING.)

COOPERATIVE MANAGEMENT HOUSING INSURANCE FUND [FHA]   Revolving fund used by the Secretary of HUD to insure mortgages under Section 213 of the National Housing Act.

COOPERATIVE MEMBER   A member of a cooperative housing association or corporation.

CORNER INFLUENCE   The effect upon the value of a property by virtue of its location on a corner lot.

CORNER LOT   A lot abutting upon two or more streets at their intersection. (*See also* INTERIOR LOT, THROUGH LOT.)

CORNICE   The part of a roof extending horizontally beyond the wall supporting it.

CORRESPONDENT   A mortgage loan correspondent; a representative of one or several mortgage investors.

CORRIDOR [transportation]   Geographic band within which heavy traffic occurs because of large areas of traffic origin and destination; corridors may involve all modes of transportation.

COSPONSOR   Two or more groups or organizations acting corporately as one sponsor.

COST APPROACH   A method of appraisal through which the value of an improvement is established on the basis of an estimate of the cost of replacing or reproducing the improvement, minus accrued depreciation, plus the value of the land.

COST-BENEFIT ANALYSIS   A study of the probable economic or social benefits that can be expected from a given investment in a given program or investment.

COST CERTIFICATION [HUD]   The itemization of all costs of a project such that all costs can be officially verified. Usually prepared or certified by a certified public accountant.

COST OF MONEY   Interest on a loan. The rate of interest.

COST OF OCCUPANCY   The cost of occupying a property to a tenant or owner excluding operating costs—such as the fair rental value to an owner or the rent to a tenant.

COST PER SQUARE FOOT   (*See* CONSTRUCTION COST PER SQUARE FOOT, SQUARE-FOOT COST.)

COST-PLUS CONTRACT   A contract providing that the contractor's profit is fixed at a specific percentage of the actual cost of labor and materials.

COTENANT   (*See* TENANCY IN COMMON.)

COUNCIL OF ECONOMIC ADVISERS (CEA)   The Council was established in the Executive Office of the President by the Employment Act of 1946. It now functions under that statute and Reorganization Plan 9 of 1953, effective August 1, 1953. The Council consists of three members appointed by the President by and with the advice and consent of the Senate. One of the members is designated by the President as chairman.

CEA analyzes the national economy and its various segments, advises the President on economic developments, appraises the economic programs and policies of the federal government, recommends to the President policies for economic growth and stability, and assists in the preparation of the economic reports of the President to the Congress.

COUNCIL OF GOVERNMENTS (COG) Voluntary associations of officials of local governments in a metropolitan or regional area, formed to cooperate on mutual problems of their areas.

COUNTY A political subdivision of a state, empowered by the state to have jurisdiction over certain transactions and activities within its area.

COURSE [construction] A horizontal layer, as in brickwork.

COURT An open area between buildings or walls. (*See also* INNER COURT, OUTER COURT.)

COVENANT A restriction placed on a deed stipulating certain requirements the deed holder must meet or preventing him from using the property for certain purposes. (*See also* RACIAL COVENANT, RESTRICTIVE COVENANT.)

COVERAGE [HUD] The percentage of a plot area covered by buildings, including accessory buildings.

CRAWL SPACE [FHA] An unfinished accessible space below the first floor usually less than a full story in height. Also called "basementless space."

CREDIT REPORT A report on a mortgagor's financial and credit status.

CREDIT RISK [FHA] (*See* SECTION 237 MORTGAGE INSURANCE FOR SPECIAL CREDIT RISKS.)

CREDIT UNION A group of persons who agree to save their money together and make loans to one another at low interest rates; interest paid on loans is divided among the members and paid to them in the form of dividends on their savings.

CRIME INSURANCE [HUD] Authorized by Title VI of the Housing and Urban Development Act of 1970 and later amendments; provides insurance through the Federal Insurance Administration of HUD for residents of homes and apartments as well as businessmen in states where there is a critical problem of crime insurance availability at affordable rates which is not being resolved by appropriate state action.

Residents of homes and apartments and businessmen may purchase crime insurance policies through any insurance agent or broker in states which have been designated by the Federal Insurance Administrator as having a critical problem of availability or affordability.

(*See also* FEDERAL INSURANCE ADMINISTRATION.)

CRITICAL PATH METHOD   A carefully planned approach to executing a given project to streamline its execution. This approach factors into the planning as many variables and invariables as can be foreseen and provides for their surmountability as necessary.

CUL-DE-SAC   The terminus of a street or alley, usually laid out by modern engineers to provide a circular turnaround for vehicles.

CULVERT   A constructed passageway or conduit to carry drain water underground.

CURB LEVEL   The mean level of a curb in front of a lot.

CURB LINE   The dividing line between a street and the pedestrian way.

CURRENT ASSET   Asset that can be converted readily to cash, e.g., stocks, notes, inventory. Also termed "quick asset."

CURTAIN WALL   An enclosing wall which provides no structural support to the building.

CURVE OF CONSUMPTION   Chart, containing a table and curve, used by utility companies to plot changes in fuel consumption.

CUSHION   Amount included in a contractor's bid to protect himself against contingencies such as delayed approvals, bad weather, and bidding errors.

D

DAMAGES [condemnation]   The loss in value of a property resulting from the condemnation of a portion or all of the property.

DATA TRACT [HUD]   An area the approximate borders of which have been established for the purpose of indexing and classifying location, sales, and rental data. A data tract may in many instances be composed of more than one neighborhood.

DATE OF FULL AVAILABILITY   The last day of the month in which substantially all dwelling units in a project become available for occupancy.

DATE OF REEXAMINATION   Date on which the eligibility of a tenant in a federally assisted housing project for continued occupancy or for a subsidy is reexamined and any change in rent becomes effective if required.

DAVIS-BACON ACT   An act passed in 1931, and subsequently amended, requiring that all laborers and mechanics employed in certain programs of federal financial assistance involving construction activities be paid wage rates no less than those prevailing on similar construction in the locality, as determined by the Secretary of the Department of Labor.

DAY-CARE CENTER   Area set aside, often in a community center, for caring for small children while parents work or are otherwise occupied.

DEAD-END STREET   A street with an opening at one end and none at the other, usually with no cul-de-sac available at the closed end.

DEAD LOAD   The weight of all permanent construction in a building. (*See also* DESIGN LOAD, LIVE LOAD.)

DEBARMENT [HUD]   An exclusion of contractors and grantees from participation in HUD-assisted programs for a reasonable, specified period of time commensurate with the seriousness of the offense or failure or inadequacy of performance.

DEBENTURE   General term used to describe all forms of unsecured, long-term debt, whether for corporate or civil government obligations; usually applies to a certificate of debt issued by a corporation; generally secured only by the assets and the good credit of the obligor; use of the term most frequently is in connection with bonds.

DEBENTURES [FHA]   Registered, transferable securities which are valid and binding obligations issued in the name of the Mutual Mortgage Insurance Fund.

DEBT LIMIT   Legally fixed limit on the amount of money a governmental entity may borrow.

DEBT SERVICE   The required periodic payment of interest and principal on a loan; does not include the portion of mortgage payments allocated for taxes or insurance.

DECLINING AREA   An area in which physical conditions and financial values are deteriorating.

DECLINING AREA MORTGAGE INSURANCE [FHA]   (*See* SECTION 223(E) MORTGAGE INSURANCE FOR HOUSING IN DECLINING AREAS.)

DECLINING BALANCE DEPRECIATION   Form of accelerated depreciation which allows a taxpayer the same percentage of depreciation over the useful life of the property while the amount of depreciation is reduced to coincide with the declining book value.

DECLINING PAYMENT PLAN   A method of paying a loan involving periodic payments that gradually decrease as the amount of principal due is reduced over the life of the loan. Distinguished from a level payment plan.

DEDICATION [real estate]   The allocation by a landowner of a certain land area for public use or common use, such as for a street, park, or parking lot.

DEED   A legal document conveying or indicating ownership of real property.

DEED OF TRUST   A mortgage or trust deed, so-called in certain states.

DEED RESTRICTIONS   Covenants or other provisions attached to deeds specifying such restrictions as the type of structure that can be constructed on a lot, building lines, minimum construction cost, etc. (*See also* COV-ENANT, RACIAL COVENANT, RESTRICTIVE COVENANT.)

DEFAULT   Failure to meet the terms of a loan or contract. Default may lead to foreclosure.

DEFAULT [FHA]   Includes any FHA-insured mortgage transaction which is or has been in breach of a regulatory agreement or delinquent for failure to meet required mortgage payments, or which has resulted in assignment of a mortgage to FHA, foreclosure of a mortgage, or a deed in lieu of foreclosure.

DEFEASANCE CLAUSE   Legal clause, in a deed, which negates other clauses.

DEFENSE HOUSING [FHA]   Housing built under the provisions especially of the Lanham Act of 1940 to provide shelter for persons employed by defense industries. The housing ranged from permanent single-family homes to apartments, many of which were intended to last only temporarily but are still in use.

DEFERRED SALE CONTRACT   A contract under the provisions of which a purchaser pays the owner a part or all of the sale price through an obligation other than cash.

DEFICIENCY [mortgage]   The difference between what a mortgagor owes against a loan in default (including certain costs) and the proceeds from the sale of the mortgaged property.

DEFICIENCY JUDGMENT   A court ruling in a foreclosure proceeding in favor of a lender when a loan is delinquent, which permits the lender to attach all the borrower's assets to pay the difference between the amount owed by the borrower and the proceeds from the sale of the mortgaged property. (*See also* ATTACHMENT.)

DEFINITIVE LOAN [urban renewal]   A loan provided under a federal contract to enable the local public agency to finance the payment of the capital value of the leased land, or the unpaid portion thereof, into the project accounts. This loan may be obtained through private financing by the sale in the open market of bonds that are secured by the full faith and credit of the United States or through a direct loan made by HUD.

DEGREE-DAY   A unit of measure utilized as a standard for evaluating plant performance and for determining the daily requirements for fuel or heat.

DELINQUENCY [lending]   Failing to meet the original terms of an obligation, such as being late in making payments on a loan or in paying taxes.

DELIVERY [real estate]   The final and absolute transfer of a deed from seller to buyer in such a manner that it cannot be recalled by the seller. A necessary requisite to the transfer of title.

DEMISE   A transfer of a lease or a transfer of the interest in an estate.

DEMOGRAPHY   The study of the size, composition, and distribution of population and population change.

DEMOLITION   The razing of a structure, usually by a public agency as a result of an urban renewal or capital improvement program or because the structure has been condemned; demolition activities usually include clearance of the land and disconnection of utilities.

DEMOLITION GRANT PROGRAM   (*See* HOUSING AND COMMUNITY DEVELOPMENT ACT OF 1974, SECTION 116 DEMOLITION GRANT PROGRAM, TITLE I—COMMUNITY DEVELOPMENT.)

DEMONSTRATION CITIES AND METROPOLITAN DEVELOPMENT ACT OF 1966
Act that established the Demonstration Cities Program and amended certain previous housing acts. The provisions of this act are largely altered or supplanted by the Housing and Community Development Act of 1974.

DEMONSTRATION CITIES PROGRAM [Model Cities]   Most frequently called the "Model Cities program," enacted in 1966 as a federal program providing funds to localities to plan and carry out coordinated programs to solve physical and social problems of designated neighborhoods. The federal government, through HUD, pays 80 percent of the cost of developing and administering the program and may pay up to 80 percent of the local share of other federally assisted programs. Administered locally by the city demonstration agency. (*See also* MODEL CITIES SUPPLEMENTARY GRANTS.)
   The phasing out and supplanting of this program is provided for in Title I—Community Development of the Housing and Community Development Act of 1974.

DEMONSTRATION PROJECT GRANT [urban renewal]   Grant received by or through a local public agency from HUD to help finance an urban renewal activity undertaken to develop or improve methods and techniques of executing urban renewal projects. The federal share of such a grant can be up to two-thirds of the cost of the demonstration. Authorized by Section 314 of the Housing Act of 1954.

The program was eliminated by Title I—Community Development of the Housing and Community Development Act of 1974.

DENSITY   The average number of housing units, families, or persons occupying a site; usually expressed "per acre."

DENTAL GROUP   (*See* MEDICAL OR DENTAL GROUP.)

DEPARTMENT OF HOUSING AND URBAN DEVELOPMENT (DHUD) [HUD]
The Department of Housing and Urban Development was established by the Department of Housing and Urban Development Act of September 9, 1965, which became effective November 9, 1965.

The overall purpose of HUD is to assist in providing for sound development of the nation's communities and metropolitan areas.

As stated in the act, HUD was created to administer the principal programs which provide assistance for housing and for the development of the nation's communities; to assist the President in achieving maximum coordination of the various federal activities which have a major effect upon urban community, suburban, or metropolitan development; to encourage the solution of problems of housing and urban development through state, county, town, village, or other local and private action, including promotion of interstate, regional, and metropolitan cooperation; to encourage the maximum contributions that may be made by vigorous private homebuilding and mortgage lending industries to housing, urban development, and the national economy; and to provide for full and appropriate consideration, at the national level, of the needs and interests of the nation's communities and of the people who live and work in them.

(See also entries under HUD.*)*

DEPARTMENT OF TRANSPORTATION (DOT)   The Department of Transportation was established by the Department of Transportation Act of October 15, 1966, for the purpose of developing national transportation policies and programs conducive to the provision of fast, safe, efficient, and convenient transportation at the lowest cost consistent therewith. The DOT also administers uniform time matters.

DEPOSIT THRIFT INSTITUTION   Financial institution in which the flow of funds is based upon the discretion of the saver; includes savings and loan associations, mutual savings banks, and commercial banks. Distinguished from contract thrift institution.

DEPRECIATED COST   The cost of a property less accrued depreciation for tax purposes at a given point in time.

DEPRECIATION   The decline in value of a property for any reason.

The deduction from one's income taxes of a percentage of the cost of property (exclusive of the cost of land). (*See also* ACCELERATED DEPRECIATION, ACCRUED DEPRECIATION, DECLINING BALANCE DEPRECIATION, DOUBLE-DECLINING BALANCE DEPRECIATION, INCURABLE DEPRECIATION, RAPID DEPRECIATION, STRAIGHT-LINE DEPRECIATION, SUM-OF-THE-DIGITS DEPRECIATION.)

DEPRECIATION ALLOWANCE   The amount representing property value (excluding land) which can be deducted for a taxable year in accordance with a reasonably consistent plan (not necessarily at a uniform rate), so that the aggregate of the amounts set aside plus the salvage value will equal the cost or other basis of the property at the end of the estimated useful life of the depreciable property. Applies only to that part of the property which is subject to wear and tear, to decay or decline from natural causes, to exhaustion, and to obsolescence.

DEPRECIATION BASE   The amount representing the financial worth of a property which the Internal Revenue Service will recognize as depreciable. The amount never includes the value of land.

DEPRECIATION VALUE   The value of a property after depreciation.

DEPRESSED AREA   An area where a substantial proportion of the population is unemployed or underemployed.

DERELICT BUILDING   An abandoned or unoccupied substandard building that should be repaired or torn down because it constitutes a potential hazard.

DESIGN ARCHITECT   The architect who prepares the design plans and specifications for a construction project; distinguished from a supervising architect, although they are often one and the same.

DESIGN CONTEST   Competition established, usually by a public agency, to obtain a variety of architectural or planning schemes for the design of an area or a building.

DESIGN LOAD   Total load which a structure is designed to sustain safely. (*See also* DEAD LOAD, LIVE LOAD.)

DESIGN PROGRAM [public housing]   Guidelines provided by a local housing authority to architects, requiring, minimally, that plans and specifications adhere to local zoning and building requirements and HUD minimum property standards; the program usually also sets forth the type of refuse disposal, heating system, security features, materials required, and amenities desired.

DESIGN STANDARDS Standards governing the size, shape, and relationship of spaces in a building.

DETACHED HOUSE A single-family house not attached on any of its sides to any other dwelling. Distinguished from an apartment, duplex, town house, or row house.

DETAIL A fully dimensioned view of a particular portion of a project, usually prepared by an architect and constituting a component of a set of plans and specifications.

DETERIORATING HOUSING Housing unit needing more repair than would be provided in the course of regular maintenance. It has one or more defects of an intermediate nature that must be corrected if the unit is to continue to provide safe and adequate shelter. Examples of such defects are shaky or unsafe porch or steps, broken plaster, and rotted window sills or frames. Such defects are signs of neglect which lead to serious structural damage if not corrected. (*See also* DILAPIDATED HOUSING, SOUND HOUSING.)

DETERIORATING NEIGHBORHOOD Neighborhood characterized by the presence of blight.

DETERIORATION A cause of the decline in value of a property or neighborhood as a result of wear and tear, use, abuse, or lack of maintenance.

"DETROIT PLAN" [land use] Land-use plan adopted by the city of Detroit providing that the city advance a subsidy to redevelopers to offset the difference between acquisition costs in slum areas and reuse value, with the amount of the subsidy retired through the increase in tax revenues derived from the redevelopment areas.

DEVELOPER Usually an investor or group of investors who initiate a development activity.

DEVELOPMENT Any or all undertakings necessary for planning, land acquisition, demolition, construction, or equipment of a project.

DEVELOPMENT COST [public housing]   The costs incurred by a local housing authority or agency for a development and their necessary financing (including the cost of carrying charges, but not beyond the point of physical completion).

DEVELOPMENT PROGRAM [public housing]   Local housing authority's documentation to HUD of a proposed public housing project's anticipated costs of acquisition of land, construction, professional fees, salaries of involved personnel, interest expenses, appliances, and equipment needed in the project.

DEVELOPMENT RIGHTS [HUD]   An agreement to develop land only as approved by the owner of the development rights in exchange for compensation to the property owner. (*See also* LESS-THAN-FEE ACQUISITION.)

DEVISE   The disposition of land by will. A term used for land alone and never for personal property.

DILAPIDATED HOUSING [HUD]   Housing that does not provide safe and adequate shelter and in its present condition endangers the health, safety, or well-being of the occupants. Such housing has one or more critical defects or a combination of intermediate defects in sufficient number or extent to require considerable repair or rebuilding. Such defects may involve original construction, or they may result from continued neglect or lack of repair or from serious damage to the structure. (*See also* DETERIORATING HOUSING, SOUND HOUSING.)

DIRECT COSTS   The out-of-pocket expenditures made in conjunction with a project—e.g., for labor, materials, land, fees—as distinguished from overhead, administration, profit, etc.

DIRECT HOUSING ALLOWANCE (DHA)   A system of subsidizing the housing expenses of families of low and moderate income, defined by the Kaiser Commission as cash payments "made available to families according to their needs." The concept was first embodied in a rent certificate plan conceived in the late 1930s. Neither the direct housing allowance nor the rent certificate system have evolved into formal "housing programs" financed by the federal government, although demonstrations of the concept are being tested by HUD. (*See also* INCOME MAINTENANCE SUBSIDY, INCOME TRANSFER FOR HOUSING.)

DIRECT LOAN   A loan made directly by the federal government, as distinguished from loans made by private lenders and insured by the federal government.

DIRECT NEGOTIATION [urban renewal]   Method of offering urban renewal land in which, in cases where direct negotiation is permitted by law, the local renewal agency may negotiate directly with a redeveloper or redevelopers.

DIRECT REDUCTION LOAN   Loan repayable in regular and equal payments, including principal and interest, scheduled so as to retire the debt in a specific period of time; after allocation of interest from payment, the balance of the payment is applied to reduction of the principal.

DISASTER   (*See* MAJOR DISASTERS.)

DISASTER HOUSING MORTGAGE INSURANCE [FHA]   (*See* SECTION 203(H) DISASTER HOUSING MORTGAGE INSURANCE.)

DISCLAIMER   A denial or disavowal of interest of any kind in claim to a specific or general action.

DISCLOSURE OF INTEREST [HUD]   Statement by a developer naming all persons who have a financial interest in the development entity, including officers and principal members, shareholders and investors, and other parties having a substantial share or ownership interest in the developer entity.

DISCOUNTED RATE OF RETURN   A measure of financial return in which total cash flow from a project, including projections of the tax savings and the net cash proceeds of sale, is discounted back to present value tables (computations). This measure weights dollars received early in the life of a project more heavily than those received later. Also referred to as "present value rate of return."

DISCOUNT POINTS   The amount of money a borrower must pay to a lending institution to secure a mortgage loan; one point is equal to 1 percent of the amount of the loan. A device by which a lender can achieve a market yield on a loan despite the imposition of a ceiling on stated interest rates. Often called "points" or "placement fee."

DISCOUNT RATE   The amount of money not included in the interest rate of a mortgage, paid by a borrower or a seller to a lender to secure a mortgage loan.

DISCRETIONARY GRANT [community development]   A grant made to a unit of general local government participating in the provisions of Title I—Community Development of the Housing and Community Development Act of 1974, from a special fund established in the act to be used at the HUD Secretary's discretion, from a transition fund for urgent community development needs, and from the general-purpose funds for metropolitan and nonmetropolitan areas. (*See also* BASIC GRANT AMOUNT, ENTITLEMENT AMOUNT, HOLD-HARMLESS GRANT.)

DISCRIMINATION   The willful depriving of a person or of a group of the right to exercise civil or human rights.

DISCRIMINATORY PRACTICE [HUD]   Any discrimination because of race, color, creed, or national origin in lending practices or in the sale, rental, or other disposition of residential property or related facilities and group practice facilities, or in the use of occupancy thereof, if:

1. Such property is or will be constructed, rehabilitated, purchased, or financed with the proceeds of a loan or investment insured under the provisions of the National Housing Act pursuant to an application for mortgage insurance received by FHA after November 20, 1962. Or

2. Such property is offered for sale under terms which include financing under the provisions of the National Housing Act pursuant to an application for mortgage insurance received by FHA after November 20, 1962. Or

3. Such property is improved with a loan reported for insurance under Title I of the National Housing Act, the proceeds of which are disbursed after November 20, 1962. Or

4. Such property is owned by the Federal Housing Administration.

DISPLACED BY GOVERNMENTAL ACTION [HUD]   An individual or family moved or to be moved from real property occupied as a dwelling unit as a result of activities in connection with a public improvement or development program carried on by an agency of the United States or any state or local governmental body or agency.

DISPLACED FAMILY OR INDIVIDUAL   Family or individual required to move because of a public program of land acquisition or code enforcement or as a result of a major disaster as determined by the President.

DISPLACEE   A family or business or other entity displaced from a site by public action.

DISPOSAL FIELD   (*See* ABSORPTION FIELD.)

DISPOSITION APPRAISAL [urban renewal]   Appraisal prepared to establish the value of cleared land to be sold to redevelopers. Such appraisal establishes the disposition price or reuse value.

DISPOSITION PRICE [urban renewal]   Sales price of urban renewal land tracts, based upon disposition or reuse appraisal.

DISTRAINT FOR RENT (OR OTHER CHARGES)   Agreement by a tenant that his landlord is authorized to take property of the tenant and hold it as a pledge until the tenant performs the obligation which the landlord has determined the tenant has failed to perform.

DISTRESSED MORTGAGOR [VA]   An individual whose employment or service at a military base or other government installation is terminated (subsequent to November 1, 1964) as a result of the base closing, who is the owner-occupant of the dwelling on which the mortgage is in default due to his inability to make payments.

DISTRICT   A specific portion of a larger area, such as of a city.

The Housing and Community Development Act of 1974 defines as a district an area that includes all or part of the area of jurisdiction of one or more counties and one or more other units of general local government but does not include any portion of a metropolitan area.

DIVIDED INTEREST   An interest in only a part of property.

DOCTRINE OF NECESSITY   A general legal proposition stating that land cannot be condemned for public use until it is necessary to do so. (*See also* CONDEMNATION.)

DOMESTIC COUNCIL   Established in the Executive Office of the President pursuant to Reorganization Plan 2 of 1970, effective July 1, 1970, to formulate and coordinate domestic policy recommendations to the President. The Council assesses national needs and coordinates the establishment of national priorities; recommends integrated sets of policy choices; provides a rapid response to Presidential needs for policy advice on pressing domestic issues; and maintains a continuous review of ongoing programs from a policy standpoint.

The Domestic Council is composed of the President of the United States; the Vice President of the United States; the Attorney General; and the Secretaries of Agriculture, Commerce, Health, Education, and Welfare, Housing and Urban Development, the Interior, Labor, Transportation, and the Treasury; the Director of the Office of Management and Budget, the Chairman of the Council of Economic Advisers, and such other individuals as the President may designate.

DOMICILE   The locale of the legal residency of a person or corporation.

DORMER   A window whose framing protrudes from a sloping roof.

DORMITORY TOWN   A town that is predominantly residential, having few if any nonresidential services and facilities, and that serves as a residential area for an adjoining or nearby municipality or metropolitan area. Also known as "bedroom community."

DOUBLE-DECLINING BALANCE DEPRECIATION (DDB)   Depreciation for tax purposes of the value of property, depreciating it at an increased rate in the early years after purchase and at a declining rate in later years.

DOUBLE HOUSE   (*See* SEMIDETACHED HOUSE.)

DOUBLING UP   The practice of two or more families sharing a single dwelling unit, essentially to reduce the housing expenses of each family.

DOUGLAS COMMISSION   National Commission on Urban Problems, appointed by President Lyndon B. Johnson, with former Senator Paul H. Douglas as chairman.

DOWN PAYMENT   A deposit or first payment of a sum of money paid by a purchaser to a buyer in conjunction with a purchase, the full payment of which will be made over a period of time.

DOWNTOWN   (*See* CENTRAL BUSINESS DISTRICT.)

DOWN ZONING   Action by an entity authorized to adjust zoning regulations, which results in the lowering of the zoning classification of a given tract or tracts to a lesser land use.

DRAINAGE SYSTEM   A system of drain pipes, conduits, or tiles installed below earth surface to remove surface or subsurface water or sewage.

DRAW [loan]   (*See* PROGRESS PAYMENTS.)

DRIVEWAY [HUD]   A private way for the use of vehicles and pedestrians.

DROP INLET   Receptacle for collecting surface rainwater, usually built into a curb or gutter.

DROP-RATE PROVISION   Provision in a mortgage to allow a drop in the rate of interest under certain circumstances.

DRYWALL   A wall constructed with wallboard instead of plaster as its surface.

DRY WELL   A pocket dug in the earth to help drain off water which is being returned to the earth.

DRY WELL [HUD]   A covered pit with open-jointed lining, or a covered pit filled with coarse aggregate through which drainage from roofs, basement floors, foundations, drain tile, or areaways may seep or leach into the surrounding soil.

DUMMY   A person or organization (such as a corporation) which represents that it has an interest in a transaction but which really does not. Also called a "straw."

DUPLEX   A semidetached or two-family house.

DUTCH COLONIAL HOUSE   A house characterized by a gambrel roof, with exterior walls constructed of masonry or wood and with side porches.

DUTCH DOOR   A door divided horizontally in the middle to permit opening or closing of either the bottom or the top.

DWELLING   A building or portion of a building designed exclusively for residential occupancy by one family, but not including hotels or other buildings intended for use by transients.

DWELLING EQUIPMENT   Includes ranges, refrigerators, space heaters, shades, screens, work tables, etc.

DWELLING INSPECTION RECORD [urban renewal]   Record developed by an urban renewal agency used to record (1) characteristics of vacant dwelling units available in the private market to which relocated families are referred and (2) findings of inspections of accommodations located by a family on its own initiative.

DWELLING UNIT (DU or du)   A building or portion of a building, such as an apartment, designed for occupancy by only one family.

E

EARLY ACQUISITION [urban renewal]   (*See* EARLY LAND ACQUISITION.)

EARLY LAND ACQUISITION (ELA) [urban renewal]   Provision of federal urban renewal regulations permitting local public agencies to acquire land immediately upon approval of a survey and planning application by HUD—provided state urban renewal enabling legislation also contains such provisions.

EARNED HOME PAYMENTS ACCOUNT (EHPA) [public housing]   A sum placed in a prospective homebuyer's account, by a local housing authority, representing the equity a tenant has earned in return for performing certain maintenance functions, usually under provisions of the Turnkey III program.

EARNEST MONEY   Advance payment of part of the purchase price to bind a contract for property.

EASEMENT   Permanent or limited right of use obtained by a public agency or public utility from a landowner. (*See also* FACADE EASEMENT, RIGHT-OF-WAY.)

EAVE   The lower portion of a roof that projects beyond the wall.

ECOLOGY   The broad study of the interrelationships of organisms (human and animal) and their physical environment.

ECONOMIC BASE   The sum of all economic activities that produce income for a city population or other large entity.

ECONOMIC DEVELOPMENT ACT   (*See* ECONOMIC DEVELOPMENT ADMINISTRATION, PUBLIC WORKS AND ECONOMIC DEVELOPMENT ACT OF 1965.)

ECONOMIC DEVELOPMENT ADMINISTRATION (EDA)   EDA was established September 1, 1965, by the Secretary of Commerce to carry out most of the provisions of the Public Works and Economic Development Act of 1965 as amended. The primary function of EDA is the long-range economic development of areas with severe unemployment and low family income problems. It aids in the development of public facilities and private enterprise to help create new, permanent jobs.

The EDA program includes public works grants and loans; business loans for industrial and commercial facilities; guarantees for private working capital loans; and technical planning and research assistance for areas designated as "Redevelopment Areas" by the Assistant Secretary.

Areas designated under Title I are eligible only for public works grants.

Redevelopment Areas in designated multicounty Economic Development Districts are eligible for bonus grants for public works projects. Cities designated as "Growth Centers" for such districts are eligible for EDA assistance for projects which provide employment opportunities and services for residents of Redevelopment Areas.

EDA technical assistance is available to help alleviate or prevent excessive unemployment, underemployment, or outmigration in any area confronted by any of these problems.

ECONOMIC DEVELOPMENT GRANTS AND LOANS Authorized by the Public Works and Economic Development Act of 1965 and later amendments; provides direct loans and project grants through the Economic Development Administration to states, political subdivisions, or nonprofit organizations to assist the construction of public facilities needed to initiate and encourage long-term economic growth in designated geographic areas where economic growth is lagging behind the rest of the nation.

ECONOMIC INTEGRATION The integration of families or persons of various income levels in a residential project or community.

ECONOMIC LIFE The period during which a building produces a profit to its owner.

ECONOMIC OPPORTUNITY ACT OF 1964 An act to mobilize the human and financial resources of the nation to combat poverty in the United States. Approved August 20, 1964, and subsequently amended. Established the "war on poverty." (*See also* OFFICE OF ECONOMIC OPPORTUNITY.)

ECONOMIC RENT The amount of rent required to pay all operating costs of a building, including debt service and profit. Sometimes viewed as the rent level set by the forces of supply and demand in a given market. Economic rent may differ from contract rent.

EDUCATIONAL USES [urban renewal] [HUD] Those uses related to the functions of teaching or research or to the housing, feeding, and care of students and faculty; or otherwise intended for the primary benefit of students and faculty.

EFFECTIVE AGE   The age of improvements measured in comparison with similar improvements, as distinguished from actual age.

EFFECTIVE GROSS INCOME   The total possible income generated by a project less an allowance for vacancies and bad debts.

EFFECTIVE INCOME [FHA]   (*See* NET EFFECTIVE INCOME.)

EFFICIENCY APARTMENT OR UNIT   A small apartment comprising only one room (plus a separate bathroom) which serves as the occupant's living room, bedroom, and kitchen.

EFFLUENT   Liquid discharged from a sewage treatment plant or from a lake or reservoir.

EGRESS [real estate]   The right to leave a tract of land. This term is used interchangeably with "access."

EKISTICS   The science of human settlements.

ELDERLY HOUSING [HUD]   Housing with design features and facilities intended for use by persons aged sixty-two or over. (*See also* SECTION 202 ELDERLY HOUSING.)

ELDERLY PERSON   Any person, married or single, who is sixty-two years of age or over. (*See also* FAMILY.)

ELDERLY UNIT   Usually, a housing unit designed for occupancy by elderly persons, as distinguished from a family unit.

ELECTRIC BRANCH SERVICE   That part of an electric distribution system from the service equipment to the development receptacle.

ELEVATION DRAWING   Drawing of a building or other development as seen from a horizontal view without perspective.

ELEVATOR STRUCTURE [HUD]   A structure for which an elevator is required by the HUD minimum property standards for multifamily housing and/or by local building codes.

ELIGIBLE APPLICANT A person or entity that meets the criteria for applying for a particular form of federal financial assistance.

ELIGIBLE DISPLACEE Family, individual, or household entitled to receive relocation assistance or relocation payments.

EMERGENCY LOANS [rural] Direct loans provided through the Farmers Home Administration to assist farmers and ranchers in continuing their normal farming and ranching operations following several losses caused by natural disasters; for operating and living expenses and to (1) replace equipment and livestock damaged or destroyed by natural disasters and (2) make real estate repairs made necessary by natural disasters.

These loans are not made to finance major adjustments and expansions in farming and ranching operations and are generally not made to refinance secured debts. Exceptions are made when (1) a loan is being made to repair or replace an essential farm home or essential farm service buildings damaged or destroyed by a major disaster declared by the President and (2) it is necessary to refinance secured debts in order for the applicant to retain the property or carry the secured debts in an orderly manner. The total amount of the loan for all purposes must be within the applicant's repayment ability and he must meet security requirements.

These loans are made in counties designated as emergency loan areas by the Secretary of Agriculture and in any other county, without a designation, where only a small number of loans will be made. In either event, there must have been severe damage by a major disaster declared by the President or a natural disaster determined by the Secretary of Agriculture.

EMINENT DOMAIN The legal right of a government or other entity to acquire private property for public use upon payment of just compensation to the owner. (*See also* CONDEMNATION.)

EMPTY NESTERS Usually refers to suburban couples whose children have grown and found their own housing.

ENABLING DECLARATION The basic document used in creating a condominium when a master deed is not readily adaptable, in which case the enabling declaration functions as a master deed.

ENABLING LEGISLATION Legislation authorizing governmental or other entities to carry out an activity, as under the provisions of a federal program.

ENCROACHMENT An unauthorized extension of a structure or part of it upon land owned by someone other than the owner of said structure.

ENCUMBER   To burden the title to a parcel of land with a lien or charge such as a mortgage.

ENCUMBRANCE   A lien, liability, or charge upon a title. (*See also* LIEN, TITLE DEFECT.)

END OF INITIAL OPERATING PERIOD (EIOP) [public housing]   (*See* INITIAL OPERATING PERIOD.)

ENERGY CONSERVING EQUIPMENT   As defined in the Housing and Community Development Act of 1974, any addition, alteration, or improvement to an existing or new structure designed to reduce total energy requirements of that structure, and which is in conformity with such criteria and standards as are prescribed by the Secretary of HUD in consultation with the National Bureau of Standards.

ENTAIL   A provision in a will restricting inheritance of property to a certain line of descendants.

ENTITLEMENT AMOUNT [community development]   Amount of block grant funds to be received by a unit of general local government, under the provisions of Title I—Community Development of the Housing and Community Development Act of 1974, consisting of its basic grant amount and/or its hold-harmless grant. (*See also* BASIC GRANT AMOUNT, DISCRETIONARY GRANT, HOLD-HARMLESS GRANT.)

ENTREPRENEUR   A person who organizes a business venture at his own risk.

ENVIRONMENT   The sum total of that which surrounds us. The environment is constituted of natural and man-made factors.

ENVIRONMENTAL DEFICIENCIES [urban renewal]   Characteristics of an area including overcrowding or improper location of structures on the land; excessive dwelling unit density; conversions to incompatible types of uses, such as rooming houses among family dwellings; obsolete building types, such as large residences or other buildings which through lack of use or maintenance have a blighting influence; detrimental land uses or conditions, such as incompatible uses, structures in mixed use, or adverse influences from noise, smoke, or fumes; unsafe, congested, poorly designed, or otherwise deficient streets; inadequate public utilities or community facilities contributing to unsatisfactory living conditions or economic decline; and other equally significant environmental deficiencies.

ENVIRONMENTAL EDUCATION ACT   An act to authorize the United States Commissioner of Education to establish education programs to encourage understanding of policies and support of activities designed to enhance environmental quality and maintain ecological balance. Approved October 30, 1970, and subsequently amended.

ENVIRONMENTAL PLANNING   That part of the planning process which is concerned primarily with the physical environment and its effect upon planning considerations.

ENVIRONMENTAL PROTECTION AGENCY (EPA)   EPA was established in the executive branch as an independent agency pursuant to Reorganization Plan 3 of 1970, effective December 2, 1970. It was created to permit coordinated and effective governmental action to assure protection of the environment by the systematic abatement and control of pollution through proper integration of a variety of research, monitoring, standard setting, and enforcement activities.

As a complement to its other activities, EPA coordinates and supports research and antipollution activities by state and local governments, private and public groups, individuals, and educational institutions. EPA also reinforces efforts among other federal agencies with respect to the impact of their operations on the environment, and it is specifically charged with making public its written comments on environmental impact statements and with publishing its determinations when those hold that a proposal is unsatisfactory from the standpoint of public health or welfare or environmental quality. In all, EPA is designed to serve as the public's advocate for a livable environment.

EQUAL EMPLOYMENT OPPORTUNITY COMMISSION (EEOC)   Created by Title VII of the Civil Rights Act of 1964 and became operational July 2, 1965. Title VII was amended by the Equal Employment Opportunity Act of 1972. The Commission has two purposes: (1) to end discrimination based on race, color, religion, sex, or national origin in hiring, promotion, firing, wages, testing, training, apprenticeship, and all other conditions of employment and (2) to promote voluntary action programs by employers, unions, and community organizations to put equal employment opportunity into actual operation.

EQUAL HOUSING OPPORTUNITY   Principle enforced by law holding that all citizens of the United States have the same right to inherit, purchase, lease, sell, hold, and convey property.

EQUIPMENT IN VALUE [FHA]   Those household items and appliances which are acceptable by local law, custom, and applicable FHA standards. Excluded are items which, by established custom, are supplied by occupants and removed when he vacates premises as well as chattels prohibited by law from becoming realty.

EQUITY   The owned interest in a property, over and above mortgages, liens, etc. The amount of cash invested in a project.

EQUITY INSURANCE   Insurance protecting a homeowner's estate against foreclosure in the event of his death, disability, illness, etc.

EQUITY OF REDEMPTION   Mortgagor's right, after paying the debt and other costs, to redeem a mortgaged property if mortgage terms are not met.

EQUITY SKIMMING   The practice, with intent to defraud, of (1) purchasing dwellings subject to a loan in default at the time of purchase or in default within one year subsequent to the purchase and the loan is secured by HUD or VA insurance, or if the loan is made by VA; (2) failing to make payments under a mortgage or deed of trust as the payments become due; and (3) applying or authorizing the application of rents from such dwellings for personal use.

EQUIVALENT ELIMINATION [public housing]   Elimination from a locality's substandard housing stock of a number of substandard housing units equal to the number of standard housing units constructed or rehabilitated by a local housing authority.

ESCALATOR CLAUSE   Provision in an agreement permitting the adjustment of price based on a change in other conditions or terms.

ESCHEAT   A reversion of title to a property to the state in those cases where an individual dies without heirs or devisees and without a will.

ESCROW   A procedure whereby a disinterested third party handles legal documents and/or funds on behalf of a seller and/or buyer.

ESTABLISHED INVESTMENT   The amount of costs incurred by an investor in, and necessary for, carrying out all works and undertakings for the development of a project. It includes the premium charge for the first operating year and the cost of all necessary surveys, plans, and specifications; architectural, engineering, or other special services; land acquisition; site preparation, construction, and equipment; a reasonable return on the funds paid out by the investor for development, up to and including the initial occupancy date; and expenses in conjunction with initial occupancy. (*See also* TOTAL DEVELOPMENT COST.)

ESTATE   A person's possessions. The degree of interest one has in real property. (The greatest interest in real estate is fee simple estate.)

ESTIMATED INVESTMENT   The estimated cost of development of a project.

ETHNIC GROUP   Group of persons of the same race with a common heritage of customs, language, religion, culture.

EVICTION   Legal ousting of a tenant from a property.

EVIDENCE OF SITE CONTROL   An option or a purchase agreement, or a title to verify the authority of one to plan improvements on a given site.

EXAMINATION FEE [FHA]   A charge made to a mortgagor by FHA for processing applications for conditional and firm commitments—the standard total charge for which is 0.3 percent of the mortgage amount.

EXAMINATION OF TITLE   The interpretation of the record title to real property based on the title search or abstract.

EXCEPTION [real estate]   In legal descriptions, that portion of lands to be deleted or excluded. Also, an objection to title or encumbrance on title.

EXCEPTION INCOME LIMITS [FHA]   Provision of the Section 235 and 236 programs that up to 20 percent of the periodic assistance payments authorized to be contracted can be used on behalf of families whose incomes exceed 135 percent of the public housing income limits for a given community; generally, the exception income limits are 90 percent of the income limits for the Section 221(d)(3) BMIR program.

EXCESS CONDEMNATION   The condemnation of more land than is actually needed to meet the public purpose of the condemnation.

EXCESS EARNINGS   The net income derived from a project in excess of the minimum annual amortization charge and the minimum annual return (if any) and income taxes (if any).

EXCESS INCOME [FHA]   Applies usually to the Section 236 and Section 221(d)(3) BMIR programs. It is (1) the amount by which a tenant's income exceeds the applicable maximum income admission limits or (2) project income shown on an annual financial statement for a project as being in excess of financial requirements and allowed distributions for the year. Such funds must be deposited to the residual receipts account.

EXCESS-INVESTMENT INTEREST   The interest paid on a loan against investment property minus the net income from the investment in the property.

EXCESS RENTAL INCOME [FHA]   Used in reference to Section 236 projects, it is any rent collected in excess of the basic rent for an individual dwelling unit. (Such funds must be remitted to HUD monthly.)

EXCLUSIVE AGENCY LISTING   (*See* EXCLUSIVE LISTING.)

EXCLUSIVE LISTING   A listing with a single real estate broker, precluding listings with other brokers.
    Under an "exclusive agency listing," the seller agrees that the broker will be the only agent with whom the property will be listed for a specified period of time, but the agreement does not rule out the seller's producing a buyer himself, in which event the agent is not entitled to a commission.
    Under an "exclusive-right-to-sell listing," the agent is entitled to a commission on the sale of a property, regardless of whether the seller found the purchaser.

EXCLUSIVE-RIGHT-TO-SELL LISTING   (*See* EXCLUSIVE LISTING.)

EXCULPATORY CLAUSE [lease]   Agreement by tenant not to hold the landlord or landlord's agents liable for any acts or omissions, whether intentional or negligent on the part of the landlord or the landlord's authorized representatives or agents.

EXECUTION   The pursuance or carrying forth of the provisions of a plan or contract.

EXECUTION SALE   Sale of a property to permit payment of a judgment.

EXECUTIVE OFFICE OF THE PRESIDENT   Under authority of the Reorganization Act of 1939, various federal agencies were transferred to the Executive Office of the President by the President's Reorganization Plans I and II, effective July 1, 1939. Executive Order No. 8248 of September 8, 1939, established the various divisions of the Executive Office and defined their functions with the exception of those agencies established in or transferred to the Executive Office by subsequent legislation.

EXECUTIVE ORDER A federal regulation promulgated by the President of the United States, as distinguished from an administrative regulation or statutory regulation.

EXECUTOR OR EXECUTRIX A person appointed by a probate court to carry out the terms of a will.

EXECUTOR'S DEED Deed wherein the executor of an estate is the grantor.

EXISTING CONSTRUCTION OR STRUCTURE [HUD] A project or building constructed prior to the filing of an application for mortgage insurance, frequently in conjunction with a rehabilitation project.

EXPENSE RATIO Total project expense expressed as a percentage of its effective gross income.

EXPERIMENTAL HOUSING MORTGAGE INSURANCE [FHA] (*See* SECTION 233 MORTGAGE INSURANCE FOR EXPERIMENTAL HOUSING.)

EXPRESS SERVICE [transportation] Transit operation over long distances with minimum number of stops.

EXPRESSWAY Highway with full or partially controlled access, some signalized grade intersections, and grade separations at major crossings.

EXPROPRIATION The voluntary surrendering of something one owns or claims to own. Sometimes used synonymously with "condemnation."

EXTENDED FAMILY The nuclear family plus grandparents and other close relatives. (*See also* NUCLEAR FAMILY.)

EXTENSION PROGRAMS FOR COMMUNITY DEVELOPMENT [rural] Authorized by the Smith-Lever Act and later amendments; provides formula grants and advisory services and counseling through the U.S. Department of Agriculture Extension Service and through land-grant colleges to help communities become more involved in assisting people to improve their knowledge and skills in working together in decision making and upgrading skill groups; in development and expanding business and industry to increase income and employment opportunities; in developing facilities and services to meet standards of health, education, recreation, and other needs of society; and in conserving and using natural resources for the fullest benefit of all citizens.

EXTENT OF HOUSING OVERCROWDING   The number of housing units in a given area with 1.01 or more persons per room, based on data compiled by the U.S. Bureau of the Census and referable to the same point in time.

EXTENT OF POVERTY   The number of persons in a given area whose incomes are below the poverty level, based on data referable to the same point in time. Determined by the Secretary of HUD according to criteria provided by the Office of Management and Budget, reflecting regional or area variations in income and cost of living.

EXTRAORDINARY MAINTENANCE   Work that is not recurrent, is substantial in scope, and is performed in connection with specific work programs. Whether performed by the owner or regularly employed staff, specific labor force, or under contract, the expenditure involved would otherwise materially distort the level trend of ordinary maintenance expense. (*See also* ORDINARY MAINTENANCE, PREVENTIVE MAINTENANCE.)

EXURBANITE   A person living beyond the suburbs, in exurbia, but who earns his living in or near the central city area of a metropolitan area.

EXURBIA   The area surrounding a metropolitan area beyond the suburbs, occupied essentially by families usually of relatively high income.

F

FACADE EASEMENT [HUD]   In historic preservation programs, agreement by an owner to retain intact the exterior of a structure and such outbuildings and amenities as are relevant to the history or design of the structure.

FACED WALL [HUD]   A wall in which the masonry facing and the backing are so bonded as to exert a common reaction under load.

FACTORY AND SHOP LUMBER Lumber used for manufacturing windows, doors, millwork, and similar items. (*See also* STRUCTURAL LUMBER, YARD LUMBER.)

FACTORY BUILDER (*See* HOME MANUFACTURER.)

FAIR ACCESS TO INSURANCE REQUIREMENTS (FAIR) (*See* FEDERAL INSURANCE ADMINISTRATION, URBAN PROPERTY PROTECTION AND REINSURANCE.)

FAIR CASH VALUE (*See* MARKET VALUE.)

FAIR HOUSING LAWS Federal, state, or local laws prohibiting discrimination in the sale, rental, or financing of housing, for any reason. (*See also* FAIR HOUSING PROGRAM.)

FAIR HOUSING PROGRAM Authorized by the Civil Rights Act of 1968, Title VIII, and administered by the Civil Rights Division, Department of Justice, to provide freedom from discrimination on the basis of race, color, religion, or national origin in connection with the sale, rental, and financing of housing.

Specialized services are provided to anyone. The services are aimed at assuring freedom from discrimination in the sale, rental, and financing of housing units. A private suit alleging discrimination may be filed in the appropriate federal or state court. The Attorney General is authorized to bring civil actions in federal courts when he has reasonable cause to believe that any person or group of persons is engaged in a pattern or practice of discrimination or when he has reasonable cause to believe any group has been denied such rights in a case of general public importance.

FAIR LABOR STANDARDS ACT OF 1938 Act as amended, to provide for establishment of fair labor standards in employment in and affecting interstate commerce and for other purposes. Also known as the Wage and Hour law.

FAIR MARKET RENT [Section 23] The housing assistance payment plus the rent collected from the tenant for a Section 23 housing unit, as approved by HUD.

FAIR PLAN (*See* URBAN PROPERTY PROTECTION AND REINSURANCE.)

"FAIR-SHARE HOUSING" The planned allocation of subsidized housing units to every community within a metropolitan area.

FAMILY [HUD] Two or more persons related by blood, marriage, or operation of law who occupy the same dwelling or units; a handicapped person who has a physical impairment which is expected to be of long-continued and indefinite duration, substantially impedes his or her ability to live independently, and is of such a nature that this ability to live independently could be improved by more suitable housing conditions; or a single person sixty-two years of age or older.

The Housing and Community Development Act of 1974 adjusts the definition of elderly or handicapped family to include two or more elderly, disabled, or handicapped individuals living together or one or more such individuals living with another person who is found to be a person essential to their well-being.

(*See also* EXTENDED FAMILY, NUCLEAR FAMILY.)

FAMILY INCOME [HUD]   Gross income from employment, pensions, or other sources of all members of a family. (*See also* ADJUSTED ANNUAL INCOME, GROSS ANNUAL INCOME.)

FAMILY OF VEHICLES [transportation]   Variety of transit vehicles designed for different service levels, e.g., minibus in congested areas and over-the-road bus for express service.

FAMILY UNIT [HUD]   A one-family housing unit including the undivided interest in the common areas and facilities and such restricted common areas and facilities as may be designated.

Sometimes, a housing unit designed for occupancy by a family as distinguished from elderly persons. In the latter case, the proper term is "elderly unit."

FAMILY UNIT PRICE [FHA]   The price, including closing costs, for which a family unit (usually in a condominium housing project) is sold to the mortgagor.

"FANNIE MAE"   (*See* FEDERAL NATIONAL MORTGAGE ASSOCIATION.)

FARMERS HOME ASSOCIATION (FmHA, FHA, FmHA) along with other Department of Agriculture agencies, operating through state, area, and county Rural Development Committees, assists other federal, state, and local agencies to make their services known and effective in local rural areas. The agency operates under three principal statutes: the Consolidated Farmers Home Administration Act of 1961; Title V of the Housing Act of 1949; and Part A, Title III of the Economic Opportunity Act of 1964. Applications for loans are made at the agency's 1,754 local county offices, generally located in county-seat towns. (*See also* RURAL HOUSING LOANS.)

FARM LABOR HOUSING LOANS AND GRANTS [rural]   Authorized by the Housing Act of 1949 and later amendments; loans and grants available through the Farmers Home Administration for construction, repair, or purchase of housing; acquiring the necessary land and making improvements on the land for the housing; and developing related facilities including recreation areas, central cooking and dining facilities, small infirmaries, laundry facilities, fallout shelters, and other essential equipment and facilities to serve domestic farm laborers.

FASCIA   The finishing member used to conceal the ends of the rafters of a building.

FAST LINE [transportation]   High-speed transit line.

FEASIBILITY ANALYSIS OR STUDY [FHA]   A study to determine whether a proposed project is economically feasible in terms of site acceptability, number and size of housing units, rents, expenses, net income, land value, project budget, cash requirements, and mortgage amount.

FEASIBILITY LETTER [FHA]   (*See* INITIAL COMMITMENT.)

FEASIBILITY SURVEY [urban renewal]   A survey of an area deemed blighted, using federal funds to determine if it is feasible to undertake an urban renewal project or projects within that area. Seeks to resolve special problems that might arise before survey and planning applications are submitted or afterward while HUD is reviewing them. Examples are questions of legal powers, local financial capacity, relocation resources, or, in special circumstances, eligibility of project areas.

FEDERAL AGENCY   Any department, independent establishment, government corporation, or other agency of the executive branch of the federal government except the American National Red Cross.

FEDERAL CAPITAL GRANT   (*See* CAPITAL GRANT.)

FEDERAL CRIME INSURANCE   (*See* CRIME INSURANCE, FEDERAL INSURANCE ADMINISTRATION.)

FEDERAL DEPOSIT INSURANCE CORPORATION (FDIC)   The Corporation was organized under authority of Section 12B of the Federal Reserve Act, approved June 16, 1933. By legislation approved September 21, 1950, Section 12B of the Federal Reserve Act as amended was withdrawn as part of the Federal Reserve Act and made a separate law known as the

Federal Deposit Insurance Act. The act also made numerous amendments to the former deposit insurance statutes.

FDIC was established to promote and preserve public confidence in banks and to protect the money supply through provision of insurance coverage for bank deposits. It does not operate on funds appropriated by Congress. Its income is derived from assessments on deposits held by insured banks and from interest on the required investment of its surplus funds in government securities.

FEDERAL FINANCIAL ASSISTANCE   Assistance through grant or contractual arrangements; assistance in the form of loans, loan guarantees, or insurance; and, in addition, award of procurement contracts notwithstanding any quid pro quo given.

FEDERAL GRANT-IN-AID PROGRAM   A program of federal financial assistance other than loans and other than the assistance provided by community development block grants under provisions of Title I—Community Development of the Housing and Community Development Act of 1974. (*See also* BLOCK GRANT, CATEGORICAL GRANT PROGRAM, REVENUE SHARING.)

FEDERAL HIGHWAY ADMINISTRATION (FHWA)   FHWA became a component of the Department of Transportation pursuant to the Department of Transportation Act (80 Stat. 932). It carries out the highway transportation programs of the Department of Transportation under pertinent legislation or provisions of law cited in Section 6(a) of the act.

FHWA encompasses highway transportation in its broadest scope, seeking to coordinate highways with other modes of transportation to achieve the most effective balance of transportation systems and facilities under cohesive federal transportation policies as contemplated by the act.

FHWA is concerned with the total operation and environment of the highway systems, with particular emphasis on improvement of highway-oriented aspects of highway safety.

FEDERAL HOME LOAN BANK BOARD (FHLBB)   The Board was made an independent agency in the executive branch under Section 109(a)(3) of the housing act amendments of 1955. The purpose of FHLBB is to encourage thrift and economical home ownership through supervision of the Federal Home Loan Bank System, the Federal Savings and Loan System, and the Federal Savings and Loan Insurance Corporation.

The Board consists of three members, appointed by the President by and with the advice and consent of the Senate. Not more than two members may be members of the same political party. Members are appointed for a term of four years each.

Expenses of the Board are paid by assessments against the regional Federal Home Loan Banks and the Federal Savings and Loan Insurance Corporation, and charges against institutions examined by its Office of Examinations and Supervision. All these activities are self-supporting and do not require the appropriation of United States Treasury funds.

FEDERAL HOME LOAN BANK SYSTEM (*See* FEDERAL HOME LOAN BANK BOARD.)

FEDERAL HOME LOAN MORTGAGE CORPORATION (FHLMC) (Popularly known as "Freddie Mac.") Federal corporation established under provisions of the Emergency Home Finance Act of 1970 "to increase the availability of mortgage credit for the financing of urgently needed housing, and for other purposes." FHLMC is under the direction of the Federal Home Loan Bank Board; its principal function is to purchase mortgages from savings and loan institutions in the secondary mortgage market.

FEDERAL HOUSING ADMINISTRATION (FHA) An agency of HUD which administers the housing insurance program; the agency through which interest subsidies and rent supplements are obtained. (*See also entries under* FHA.)

FEDERAL HOUSING AUTHORITY Federal agency established in 1934 which was replaced by the Federal Housing Administration.

FEDERAL HOUSING COMMISSIONER The Commissioner of the Federal Housing Administration. The FHA Commissioner is also the HUD Assistant Secretary for Housing Production and Mortgage Credit.

FEDERAL INSURANCE ADMINISTRATION (FIA) [HUD] The Administrator of the FIA is the principal adviser to the HUD Secretary on insurance matters, particularly on those administered by the FIA. In all insurance programs, the Administration utilizes the cooperation of other federal agencies, state and local governments, and the private insurance industry. The FIA conducts studies and makes recommendations of alternative programs of insurance and financial assistance in meeting natural and other disasters and similar occurrences. FIA administers the flood insurance program, riot insurance program, and crime insurance program.

FEDERAL LOAN AGENCY Federal agency established by Reorganization Plan No. 1 on July 1, 1939 (approved by Congress on June 7, 1939) to coordinate the work of numerous other federal agencies in operation at the time, including several with housing functions. The same plan established the Federal Works Agency. Its function was supplanted by the National Housing Agency, which was established by Executive Order No. 9070, of February 24, 1942.

FEDERALLY ASSISTED CODE ENFORCEMENT (FACE)   Code administration or enforcement activity undertaken under provisions of Section 117 of the Housing Act of 1965, which authorized HUD to make grants to cities and counties to assist them in carrying out programs of intensive code compliance, including street and similar improvements, to "arrest the decline of deteriorating areas." Eligible property owners in FACE areas are entitled to obtain Section 115 housing rehabilitation grants and/or Section 312 housing rehabilitation loans. Such activities, with the exception of the Section 312 loans, are to be phased out and supplanted under provisions of Title I—Community Development of the Housing and Community Development Act of 1974.

FEDERALLY ASSISTED PROJECT [urban renewal]   An urban renewal project for which federal financial assistance is made available to local public bodies under provisions of the Housing Act of 1949. Includes advances for survey and planning work, loans for project operations, and grants to defray the larger part of the deficit, if any, remaining after land disposition proceeds have been applied against the total cost of the project. The Housing and Community Development Act of 1974 provides for the phasing out of such projects in favor of the institution of Title I—Community Development activities. (*See also* NEIGHBORHOOD DEVELOPMENT PROGRAM, TITLE I—URBAN RENEWAL.)

FEDERALLY ASSISTED URBAN RENEWAL PROJECT   (*See* NEIGHBORHOOD DEVELOPMENT PROGRAM, TITLE I—COMMUNITY DEVELOPMENT, TITLE I—URBAN RENEWAL.)

FEDERAL NATIONAL MORTGAGE ASSOCIATION (FNMA) (Popularly known as "Fannie Mae.")   From 1938 until 1968, a federal agency providing a stimulus for the expansion of mortgage capital in the secondary mortgage market, principally in connection with mortgages insured or financed under certain HUD or VA programs. The Housing and Urban Development Act of 1968 transferred certain FNMA functions to GNMA and established FNMA as a private corporation operating with federal sponsorship. In its new format, FNMA continues to operate in the secondary mortgage market, buying mortgages at par and selling certain of them to GNMA. (*See also* GOVERNMENT NATIONAL MORTGAGE ASSOCIATION, TANDEM PLAN.)

FEDERAL PROJECT   Any project owned or administered by the U.S. Housing Authority.

FEDERAL PUBLIC HOUSING ADMINISTRATION (FPHA)   *(See* PUBLIC HOUSING ADMINISTRATION.)

FEDERAL RESERVE BOARD (Fed or FRB)   The Federal Reserve System was established pursuant to authority contained in the act of December 23, 1913, known as the Federal Reserve Act. As stated in the preamble, the purposes of the act are "to provide for the establishment of Federal Reserve Banks, to furnish an elastic currency, to afford means of rediscounting commercial paper, to establish a more effective supervision of banking in the United States, and for other purposes."

The System comprises the Board of Governors; the Federal Open Market Committee; the twelve Federal Reserve Banks and their twenty-four branches situated in different sections of the United States; the Federal Advisory Council; and the member banks, which include all national banks in the fifty states of the United States and such state banks and trust companies as have voluntarily applied to the Board of Governors for membership and have been admitted to the System.

FEDERAL SAVINGS AND LOAN ASSOCIATIONS   These associations are provided for by Section 5 of the Home Owners Loan Act of 1933 as amended. They are chartered and supervised by the Federal Home Loan Bank Board and may be either new institutions or converted from state-chartered institutions upon application. *(See also* HOME OWNERS LOAN CORPORATION.)

FEDERAL SAVINGS AND LOAN INSURANCE CORPORATION (FSLIC)   The Corporation was created by Title IV of the National Housing Act, approved June 27, 1934, to insure the safety of savings in thrift and home-financing institutions. The operations of FSLIC came under the supervision of the Federal Home Loan Bank Board. The Corporation insures the safety of savings up to $20,000 for each qualified investor's account in an insured institution. All federal savings and loan associations and those state-chartered building and loan, savings and loan, homestead associations, and cooperative banks which apply and are approved are insured.

To prevent the default of an insured institution or restore it to normal operation, the Corporation may make loans to, purchase assets of, or make a financial contribution to such an institution. In the event of a default by any insured institution, payment of each insured account is made by the Corporation as soon as possible.

FEDERAL SHARE   The amount of money that a federal agency will contribute to a program of federal financial assistance. (*See also* PROJECT GRANT.)

FEDERAL SHARE [urban renewal]   A grant representing two-thirds of the net project cost of an urban renewal project in cities over 50,000 population; three-fourths in cities under 50,000 population, and in "economically depressed" areas, and in cities that pay their own urban renewal survey, planning, administrative, legal, and certain other expenses.

FEDERAL WORKS AGENCY (FWA)   Federal agency established by Reorganization Plan No. 1 on July 1, 1939 (approved by Congress on June 7, 1939) to coordinate the work of numerous other agencies in operation at the time, including several with housing functions. The same plan established the Federal Loan Agency. Its housing functions were absorbed by the National Housing Agency, which was established by Executive Order No. 9070, of February 24, 1942.

FEE   A charge.
[real estate]   The property owned completely by the holder.

FEEDER SYSTEMS [transportation]   Part of the family of vehicles used to bring passengers to or from fast link stations in low- or medium-density areas.

FEE SIMPLE   Direct ownership of real property.

FEE SIMPLE ESTATE   The greatest interest in a parcel of land that it is possible to own. Sometimes designated simply as "fee."

FEE SIMPLE TITLE PURCHASE MORTGAGE INSURANCE   (See SECTION 240 MORTGAGE INSURANCE FOR PURCHASERS OF LEASED HOUSING.)

FENESTRATION   The arrangement and proportion of windows in solid wall areas.

FHA APPRAISAL   Appraisal by FHA to establish the insurable value of a property on which mortgage insurance has been or will be requested.

FHA CERTIFICATION [Section 220]   Certification by FHA that housing units developed in an urban renewal area will be insurable under the provisions of Section 220 of the National Housing Act.

FHA COMMISSIONER   (*See* FEDERAL HOUSING COMMISSIONER.)

FHA COMMITMENT   A commitment by FHA to provide mortgage insurance under the terms of a conditional commitment or firm commitment.

FHA CONDITIONAL COMMITMENT   (*See* CONDITIONAL COMMITMENT.)

FHA-INSURED LOAN   (*See* INSURED MORTGAGE.)

FHA-INSURED MORTGAGE   (*See* INSURED MORTGAGE.)

FHA-INSURED PROJECT   (*See* INSURED MORTGAGE.)

FHA INSURING OFFICE   (*See* INSURING OFFICE OF HUD-FHA.)

FHA NO. 300   Publication *FHA No. 300* containing HUD's established minimum property standards for single-family and duplex housing units.

FHA NO. 2600   Publication *FHA No. 2600* containing HUD's established minimum property standards for multifamily housing construction.

FHA VALUE   The estimated price that typical buyers would be warranted in paying for a property (including the structure, all other physical improvements, and land) for long-term use or investment, assuming the buyer to be well-informed and acting intelligently, voluntarily, and without necessity.

FIDUCIARY   A person responsible for acting on behalf of another; the relationship between the person so charged and the person for whose benefit he acts.

FILTERING DOWN PROCESS   The process by which housing units originally or once occupied by middle- and upper-income families decline in relative quality and become available to occupants of lesser income.

FINAL CAPITAL GRANT PAYMENT   [urban renewal]   The final payment from HUD to a local public agency at the time of financial settlement at completion of the project. This payment covers the remainder of the federal capital grant payable.

FINAL CLOSING   Closing transaction at which permanent financing is provided on a given project.

FINANCING COST   The fee(s) paid to obtain financing, usually to the lender.

FINANCING FEE [FHA]   The amount a mortgagor pays to a construction loan lender. Usually, FHA allows this fee to be no more than 2 percent of the amount of the mortgage.

FINANCING STATEMENT [real estate]   A document prepared for filing with the Registrar of Deeds or Secretary of State indicating the encumbrances on personal property or fixtures with a debt.

FINDER'S FEE   A fee paid to one who secures business for another.

"FINDERS-KEEPERS" POLICY [public housing]   Policy under which, when a local housing authority follows a plan of operation in which standard dwellings occupied by low-income families are placed under lease (in a Section 23), the authority also advises all eligible applicants on its waiting lists that if any applicant finds a suitable standard dwelling that will be made available for the leasing program by the owner, the dwelling will be leased and assigned to the applicant, providing normal leasing terms can be arranged with the owner.

FINDING OF FEASIBILITY [FHA]   (*See* INITIAL COMMITMENT.)

FINISHED ATTIC   (*See* ATTIC ROOM, HALF STORY.)

FINISH GRADE   The top surface elevation of lawns, walks, drives, or other improved surfaces after completion of construction or grading operations.

FIRE AREA [HUD]   The floor area of a story of a building within exterior walls, party walls, fire walls, or any combination thereof.

FIRE DOOR [HUD]   A door including its frame, so constructed and assembled in place to prevent or retard passage of flame or hot gases.

FIRE SAFETY EQUIPMENT   As defined the Housing and Community Development Act of 1974, any device or facility designed to reduce the risk of personal injury or property damage resulting from fire and which is in conformity with such criteria as are prescribed by the Secretary of HUD.

FIRE STOP   Cross members between the joists of a building intended to retard the spread of fire.

FIREWALL [HUD]   A wall with qualities of fire resistance and structural stability which subdivides a building into fire areas and which resists the spread of fire.

FIRM COMMITMENT [FHA]   A firm commitment from FHA to a lender to insure a mortgage on a project based upon FHA's approval of complete working drawings, specifications, and construction contract cost estimates.

FIRM OBLIGATION [FHA]   A firm commitment by FHA to insure a Section 235 or 236 mortgage and to make assistance payments to the purchaser or renter of the housing unit.

FIRNKAS SYSTEM [construction]   An American building system that uses precast concrete bearing wall slabs and precast prestressed floor plant with a concrete topping.

FIRST MORTGAGE   A mortgage, the holder of which has first claim on the property (if foreclosure occurs).

FIRST-MORTGAGE BOND   A bond secured by a first mortgage on real estate.

FIRST-ROUND PLANNING GRANT [Model Cities]   Grants from HUD to the first seventy-five cities selected to participate in the Model Cities program.

FIRST STORY [FHA]   The lowermost story of a building which has at least half its total floor area designed for and finished as living accommodations. Utility, storage, and heating space finished in same manner as improved floor area is included. Location of first story is based upon use of space rather than location of door or finished grade.

FIRST USER   The first occupant of a housing unit that has been newly constructed or rehabilitated.

FISCAL YEAR (FY or fy)   The accounting year of a particular entity. It may or may not coincide with a calendar year. The federal government's fiscal year is July 1 to June 30.

FISCAL ZONING   The establishment of zoning regulations in such a way as to attract land uses which add more in property taxes or local sales taxes than they require in public services.

501(C)(3) AND 501(C)(4) CORPORATIONS   Tax-exempt organizations recognized by the Internal Revenue Service as organized and operated exclusively for religious, charitable, educational, and other specified tax-exempt purposes. What distinguishes a 501(c)(3) from a 501(c)(4) corporation is that contributions to the former are tax deductible.

5M SYSTEM   A low-rise building system utilizing factory-made components, developed as a package and site assembled; includes steel columns and joists, wood infill panels, and a variety of claddings.

FIXED ASSET   An asset that cannot be converted readily into cash, such as real estate, land, machinery and equipment, furniture, and fixtures.

FIXED CAPITAL   The amount invested in fixed assets.

FIXED GUIDEWAY TRANSIT [transportation]   Fast line transit mode using exclusive rights-of-way and capable of fully automated operation.

FIXED-PRICE COMPETITION [urban renewal]   Method of offering urban renewal project land in which the price is announced in advance. Competition is based on factors other than price, such as design, qualifications and organization of the redeveloper, benefits to the community, rents or sales prices, or value of the improvements to be provided by the redeveloper.

FIXTURE [real estate]   Any item of personal property so attached to real property that it becomes a part of the real property.

FLASHING [HUD]   Sheet metal or other impervious material used in roof and wall construction to protect a building from seepage of water.

FLAT   An apartment or other type of dwelling located entirely on one floor, as distinguished from one in which living areas are located on separate floors and are connected by a stairway. Cold-water flats are rented without running hot water; cold flats are rented without a built-in heating system.

   "Flat," actually, is a British term for "apartment."

FLAT COST   In a construction project, the cost of labor and materials only.

FLAT RENT [public housing]   Rent charged for a public housing unit, established on the basis of unit size, as distinguished from graded rent or income rent.

FLEXIBLE FORMULA [public housing]   Method of establishing the amount of federal annual contributions for housing leased under Section 23 or Section 10(c), based upon the development cost of comparable new projects.

FLOATING CAPITAL   An amount of money invested in current assets, such as inventory and accounts receivable.

FLOATING ZONE   A land area described in the text of zoning regulations but not placed on the zoning map until a developer applies for rezoning.

FLOOD INSURANCE [HUD]   Authorized by the Housing and Urban Development Act of 1968 and later amendments; makes provision in states or areas to enable persons to purchase insurance against losses from physical damage to or loss of real property caused by floods or mud slides in the United States. (*See also* FEDERAL INSURANCE ADMINISTRATION.)

FLOOD PLAIN   An area susceptible to flooding by the overflow of a water body, no matter how seldom.

FLOOR AREA [architectural] [HUD]   The total floor area of one story within exterior enclosing walls of a building or between exterior walls and firewalls of a building.

FLOOR AREA [site planning] [HUD]   The total floor area of all stories devoted to residential use, including halls, stairways, elevator shafts, and other related nonresidenttial use, measured to outside faces of exterior walls.

FLOOR-AREA RATIO (FAR)   The square-foot amount of total floor area (all stories) for each square foot of land area of a property.

FLOOR PLAN   A drawing of a horizontal floor of a structure showing partitions, doors, windows, etc.

FLOW-THROUGH   (*See* PASS-THROUGH.)

FOOTING   The lower part of a foundation, which rests on the ground.

FORBEARANCE AGREEMENT   Any agreement under which a creditor agrees to await payment of a debt that has become due.

FORCED-SALE VALUE   (*See* LIQUIDATION VALUE.)

FORECLOSURE   The termination of the rights of a mortgagor to a mortgaged property.

FORFEITURE   The loss of one's rights because of failure to abide by the terms of an agreement.

FORMULA GRANT   Grant approved on the basis of measurable factors, such as population, highway mileage, income. Distinguished from project grant.

FORWARD FUNDING [public housing]   Procedure authorized in the Housing Act of 1970, providing that HUD pay a local housing authority the amount of subsidy obligated in the HUD-approved operating budget of the authority at intervals through the authority's fiscal year.

FOUNDATION WALL [HUD]   A wall, below or partly below grade, providing support for the exterior or other structural parts of a building.

FOURPLEX   A row house containing four dwellings.

"FREDDIE MAC"   (*See* FEDERAL HOME LOAN MORTGAGE CORPORATION.)

FREEDOM OF INFORMATION ACT   On July 4, 1967, certain amendments to the public information section of the Administrative Procedure Act took effect. These amendments have become popularly known as the "Freedom of Information Act."

The Freedom of Information Act provided for making information held by federal agencies available to the public unless it comes within one of the specific categories of matters exempt from public disclosure. The legislative history of the act makes it clear that the primary purpose was to make information maintained by the executive branch of the federal government more available to the public. At the same time, the act recognized that records which cannot be disclosed without impairing rights of privacy or important government operations must be protected from disclosure.

Virtually all agencies of the executive branch of the federal government have issued regulations to implement the Freedom of Information Act. These regulations inform the public where certain types of information may be readily obtained, how other information may be obtained on request, and what internal agency appeals are available if a member of the public is refused requested information.

Agency decisions to withhold identifiable records requested under the act are subject to judicial review.

Persons interested in information on various aspects of the federal government, including programs and services, may visit or phone the Federal Information Centers maintained throughout the country by the General Services Administration.

FREEHOLD   A right of title to property.

FREEWAY   Highway with full control of access, all crossroads grade-separated, and interchanges with major crossroads. Accommodates heavy traffic at high speeds.

FRONTAGE   The length of a lot line along the principal side of a property.

FRONTAGE ROAD   (*See* SERVICE ROAD.)

FRONT MONEY   Money needed before a project becomes a reality, as before interim or permanent financing is obtained.

FRONT MONEY LOANS [HUD]   (*See* SECTION 106 AND 106(B) NONPROFIT SPONSOR "SEED MONEY" AND PLANNING LOANS.)

FROST LINE   The depth below finish grade where frost action on footings or foundations is improbable.

FULL COVENANT AND WARRANTY DEED   A deed wherein the seller guarantees (1) lawful possession; (2) quiet enjoyment, free of molestation, disturbance, or claims; (3) unencumbrance of the title; (4) further assurance that he will execute any additional assurance of title to the property; (5) a warranty of the title forever.

FURNITURE   (*See* BUILT-IN FURNITURE, STREET FURNITURE.)

G

GABLE The triangular portion of the end wall of a building, formed by a sloping roof.

GABLE ROOF A roof that slopes up from only two walls of a building.

GAMBREL ROOF A roof characterized by ridges having two slopes, the lower of which is the steeper.

GAP COMMITMENT (*See* STANDBY COMMITMENT.)

GARAGE [HUD] A building or enclosure primarily designed or used for storage of motor vehicles. (*See also* COMMERCIAL GARAGE, COMMUNITY GARAGE, PRIVATE GARAGE, PUBLIC GARAGE.)

GARDEN APARTMENTS Apartments characterized by their location (usually in a suburb or away from the city center) and their construction in two- or three-story buildings unserviced by elevators.

GARDEN CITY A town planned for industry and healthful living, large enough to permit a full measure of social life, surrounded by a permanent belt of open or rural land (greenbelt).

GAZEBO Ornamental garden structure from which a view may be enjoyed; often constructed of light metal or wood.

GENERAL ACCOUNTING OFFICE (GAO) An independent agency in the legislative branch, GAO was created to assist the Congress in providing legislative control over the receipt, disbursement, and application of public funds.

GAO audits the receipt, expenditure, and application of public funds by the departments and agencies of the federal government. The primary purpose of these audits is to make for the Congress independent examinations of the way in which government agencies are discharging their financial responsibilities. This includes looking into the efficiency of operations and program management and determining whether government programs are achieving the purposes intended by Congress and whether alternative approaches have been examined which might accomplish these objectives more effectively and more economically.

The scope of the work of GAO extends not only to the programs and activities which the federal government itself conducts but also to the activities of state and local governments, quasi-governmental bodies, and private organizations in their capacity as recipients under, or administrators for, federal aid programs financed by loans, advances, grants, and contributions. The interest of GAO also extends to certain activities of those having negotiated contracts with the government.

GENERAL CONTRACTOR A builder who builds on land owned by others, usually according to the owner's plans. Also called "contract builder."

GENERAL NEIGHBORHOOD RENEWAL PLAN (GNRP) [HUD] A preliminary plan (conforming, in the determination of the local governing body, to the general plan of the locality as a whole and its Workable Program for Community Improvement), outlining the urban renewal activities proposed for the area involved; provides a framework for the preparation of urban renewal plans; and indicates generally, to the extent feasible in preliminary planning, the land uses, population density, building coverage, prospective requirements for rehabilitation and improvement of property, and any portions of the area contemplated for clearance and redevelopment. Funding for such activities was authorized by the Congress in 1956.

Title I—Community Development of the Housing and Community Development Act of 1974 substituted a system of block grants for the federal GNRP system.

GENERAL OBLIGATION BOND (GO bond) Bond issued to finance a city's or state's general financial obligations, which will be repaid from general revenue sources such as taxes. Distinguished from a revenue bond.

GENERAL PARTNERSHIP An association of two or more persons or entities to carry on as coowners a business for profit. Distinguished from limited partnership.

GENERAL PLAN A comprehensive, long-range plan officially recognized as a guide for the physical growth and development of a community, together with the basic regulatory and administrative controls needed to attain the physical objectives. Basic components of the plan for physical development are a land-use plan, thoroughfare plan, community facilities plan, and public improvements program. Essential regulatory and administrative controls in a general plan are a zoning ordinance and sub-division regulations. Also called "city plan," "comprehensive community plan," and "master plan." (*See also* COMPREHENSIVE PLAN.)

GENERAL REQUIREMENTS [FHA]   (*See* CONTRACTOR'S GENERAL REQUIRE-MENTS.)

GENERAL REVENUE SHARING   Revenue sharing concept enacted through the State and Local Financial Assistance Act of 1972, providing formula grants to states and units of local government to fund a wide variety of activities largely at the discretion of the governing body of the recipients.

GENERAL SERVICES ADMINISTRATION (GSA)   GSA was established by section 101 of the Federal Property and Administrative Services Act of 1949, effective July 1, 1949. The act consolidated and transferred to the agency a variety of real and personal property and related functions formerly assigned to various agencies. Subsequent laws assigned other related functions and programs.

GSA provides for the government an economical and efficient system for the management of its property and records, including construction and operation of buildings; procurement and distribution of supplies; utilization and disposal of property; transportation, traffic, and communications management; stockpiling of strategic materials; and the management of the governmentwide automatic data processing resources program.

GEODESIC DOME   Developed by R. Buckminster Fuller, a building system consisting of triangular space frames that create self-reinforcing roof and siding units based on mathematically precise divisions of a sphere. Factory assembled, preinsulated, triangular space frames are bolted together to form the finished building.

GHETTO   The area of a city in which minority groups are restricted—overtly or by virtue of their economic condition, race, nationality, or religion—to living.

"GINNIE MAE"   (*See* GOVERNMENT NATIONAL MORTGAGE ASSOCIATION.)

GIRDER   A wood or steel horizontal member designed to carry a load between two supports.

GOING FEDERAL RATE   The annual rate of interest paid on public housing, urban renewal, or other bonds or loans, determined according to the statutes or regulations governing the pertinent program.

GOVERNMENTAL ACTION   Direct construction by all instrumentalities of government, e.g., public buildings, military installations, highways, schools, playgrounds, low-rent projects by local housing authorities, power projects.

Slum clearance, urban redevelopment, and urban renewal activities of all instrumentalities of government, e.g., land acquisition, site clearance, rehabilitation work financed both publicly and privately (pursuant to publicly sponsored enforcement of voluntary programs), privately financed new construction on a publicly sponsored clearance site, publicly financed projects on-site.

Enforcement of housing standards and the demolition, closing, and improvement of dwelling units through actions of public bodies or courts, e.g., code enforcement, including health and safety ordinances, occupancy ordinances.

Privately financed construction of public buildings under lease-purchase agreements with government instrumentalities, e.g., federal buildings built under such agreements with the General Services Administration and the Post Office Department.

Slum clearance and urban development activities and construction on the clearance site by private groups and organizations having the power of eminent domain, e.g., public utilities, limited-dividend housing corporations.

Construction by quasi-public bodies such as state universities.

Removal and demolition of publicly owned buildings by all instrumentalities of government, e.g., publicly owned defense housing, Veterans' Reuse housing, dwellings on grounds of public institutions.

Removal and demolition of privately owned buildings by a public body in the interest of public health, welfare, and safety (not necessarily connected with the code enforcement activities mentioned above), e.g., flood-control operations, fire-fighting operation.

Eviction of overincome tenants in low-rent projects operated by a public body, e.g., projects financed with federal aid, state-aided projects.

Displacement resulting from tenants' inability to pay increased rents as a result of publicly sponsored rehabilitation or of improvements made in connection with the enforcement of housing standards.

GOVERNMENT NATIONAL MORTGAGE ASSOCIATION (GNMA) (Popularly known as "Ginnie Mae.")   A federal agency within HUD established by the Housing and Urban Development Act of 1968 to buy and sell mortgages on properties insured under certain HUD programs in the secondary mortgage market from or to private lenders, including the Federal National Mortgage Association, as a means of expanding the supply of mortgage investment capital. (*See also* FEDERAL NATIONAL MORTGAGE ASSOCIATION, TANDEM PLAN.)

GRADE (*See* FINISH GRADE, GRADIENT, NATURAL GRADE, SUBGRADE.)

GRADED TAX SYSTEM Real estate tax system under which land is taxed at a higher rate than improvements, on the theory that such land will be developed to its highest and best use.

GRADIENT [HUD] The slope, or rate of increase or decrease in elevation, of a surface, road, or pipe, usually expressed in percent or in inches of rise or fall per horizontal linear foot.

GRANT A payment of cash, as distinguished from a loan.

GRANT-IN-AID Cash payments, land donations, or in-kind contributions of improvements, services, or use of facilities made as a share of the cost of a project.

GRANT RESERVATION [urban renewal] Reservation of federal funds for a capital grant to be made in connection with a specific urban renewal project. Made in connection with approval of the initiation of surveys and planning for a project, to assure that grant funds will be available under existing statutory authorizations when needed during the actual undertaking of the project.

GRANTEE [real estate] A person who acquires an interest in land by deed, grant, or other written instrument.

GRANTEES [HUD] (*See* CONTRACTORS AND GRANTEES.)

GRANTOR [real estate] A person who, by written instrument, transfers to another an interest in land.

GRANTSMANSHIP The ability to obtain grants or subsidies or other financial assistance.

GRAY AREA A deteriorating neighborhood.

GREENBELT (*See* GARDEN CITY.)

GRESHAM'S LAW OF NEIGHBORHOODS The theory that minority groups, including the poor, will cause the deterioration of neighborhoods into which they move and cause a consequent decline in property values.

GREY AREA (*See* GRAY AREA.)

GRID In surveying, two superimposed sets of equidistant parallel lines intersecting at right angles.

GRIDIRON PLAN A street plan under which streets are installed at right angles to another, forming a gridiron pattern on a map. Distinguished from a radial street system.

GROSS ANNUAL INCOME [HUD] The total income, before taxes and other deductions, received by all members of the tenant's household. Included in this total are income from all wages, social security payments, retirement benefits, military and veteran's disability payments, unemployment benefits, welfare benefits, interest and dividend payments, and such other income items as the Secretary of HUD considers appropriate. (*See also* ADJUSTED ANNUAL INCOME, FAMILY INCOME.)

GROSS FLOOR AREA [HUD] The sum of all floor areas of headroom height within the exterior walls, measured from the exterior faces of exterior walls or from the center line of walls separating buildings. Built-in garages and commercial, basement, and other areas within the exterior walls are included. Excluded are recessed, extended, or continuous balconies, carports, accessory buildings, patios, porches, or terraces and all other areas outside of the exterior walls.

GROSS LEASE Lease agreement generally providing for the lessor to pay real estate taxes, insurance, and all maintenance in addition to rent and utilities.

GROSS POSSIBLE INCOME The total rent or income obtainable from a property if all units and space are occupied and all rents paid.

GROSS PROJECT COST [urban renewal] The amount of cash expenditures for all undertakings necessary in planning and carrying out an urban renewal project plus the amount of such local grants-in-aid as are furnished in forms other than cash. May include outlays for planning, land purchase, clearance, site improvements, relocation, and carrying charges incurred up to the time of the project's completion. May also include the value of local contributions such as donations of land, demolition work, streets and utilities, parks, public buildings, and other public facilities. (*See also* NET PROJECT COST.)

GROSS PROJECT INCOME The total rents and revenues from other income derived from, or in connection with, a project during an operating year.

GROSS RENT Contract rent plus an estimate of the value or cost to a tenant for reasonable amounts of utilities purchased by tenants and not included in contract rent.

GROUND RENT The rent paid for the use of land which is rented or leased rather than purchased.

GROUNDS Lawns, roads, walks, and other paved areas, trees and plants, fences, play areas, drainage facilities, etc.

GROUP HOUSING PROJECT A housing project consisting usually of five or more buildings located on at least a three-acre tract in one ownership which is not subdivided into customary streets and lots or when the existing or contemplated street pattern make it impractical for zoning authorities to apply normal zoning regulations.

GROUP PRACTICE FACILITY [FHA] A facility which is primarily for the provision of preventive, diagnostic, and treatment services by a medical, dental, optometric, osteopathic, or podiatric group to ambulatory patients, in which patient care is under the professional supervision of persons licensed to practice medicine, dentistry, optometry, osteopathy, or podiatry.

GROUP PRACTICE MEDICAL FACILITIES MORTGAGE INSURANCE (*See* TITLE XI MORTGAGE INSURANCE FOR GROUP PRACTICE MEDICAL FACILITIES.)

GROUP PRACTICE UNIT [FHA] A private nonprofit organization of one of the following types:

1. An organization which undertakes to provide (directly or through arrangements with a medical or dental group) complete dental, medical, optometric, osteopathic, or podiatric care or any combination thereof. It may also provide health insurance to members or subscribers on a group practice prepayment basis.

2. An organization established for the purpose of providing dental, medical, osteopathic, podiatric, or optometric care or for performing functions related to such care through arrangements for the use of the group practice facility by a medical or dental group.

GROWTH CENTER [EDA] (*See* ECONOMIC DEVELOPMENT ADMINISTRATION.)

GUIDELINE A statement suggesting how a given policy or regulation might be implemented.

GUIDES [HUD] HUD statements used to provide pertinent program participants with material of an advisory nature; generally, guides supplement or augment handbook issuances. (*See also* CIRCULARS, HANDBOOK, NOTICES.)

GWINN AMENDMENTS [public housing] Provisions in public housing statutes that prohibit occupancy by a member of a subversive organization designated as such by the Attorney General.

H

HABITABLE ROOM [HUD] A space used for living, sleeping, eating, cooking, or combinations thereof; not including bathrooms, toilet compartments, closets, halls, storage rooms, laundry and utility rooms, basement recreation rooms, and similar spaces. (*See also* COMBINED ROOMS.)

HABITAT-UNIMENT SYSTEM [construction] A Canadian-U.S. building system characterized by the use of factory-molded concrete shell configurations in combination with various factory-produced and installed interior subsystems.

HALF BATH [FHA] A room containing a lavatory and a water closet. Also called "toilet room." (*See also* BATHROOM.)

HALF STORY [FHA] An area finished as living accommodations located wholly or partly within the roof frame and having a floor area at least half as large as the story below. (Space without 5 feet of clear head room is not considered as floor area. (*See also* STORY.)

HALFWAY HOUSE A residential building sponsored by an agency that seeks to help persons who have been imprisoned or otherwise institutionalized (as in a mental institution) readjust to society.

HALFWAY HOUSING Partially completed housing construction, the condition of which is attributable to the lack of financing for its completion.

HAND A lineal measure consisting of 4 inches.

HANDBOOK [HUD] Statements issued by HUD concerning specific categorical programs and promulgating permanent policies, procedures, and instructions that must be followed by administering agencies. (*See also* CIRCULARS, GUIDES, NOTICES.)

HANDICAPPED PERSON A person found to have a physical impairment which is expected to be of long, continued, and indefinite duration, substantially impeding his or her ability to live independently, and is of such a nature that this ability could be improved by more suitable housing conditions. (*See also* FAMILY.)

HARBOR LINE An arbitrary line set by authorities on navigable rivers, beyond which wharves and other structures may not be built. Also called "line of navigation."

HARD-CORE RENTER A renter who can be considered a fairly permanent resident.

HATCHWAY An access door to an attic or a cellar.

HEADER A horizontal cross member used to construct a frame across openings.

HEADWALL Retaining wall at the end of a culvert or drainage conduit.

HEALTH CENTER A building or area in a building providing health care services and/or facilities to a community.

HEAVY INDUSTRY Businesses requiring large tracts of land to accommodate their nature and function—such as mills, foundries, refineries, packing plants—generally characterized as producing noise, vibration, heavy truck traffic, and fumes.

HEIGHT OF BUILDING Usually, the vertical distance measured from the highest of one of three places—the street curb level, the established or mean street grade, or the average finished ground level adjoining the building if it sets back from the street line—to the highest point of the roof.

HEIGHT ZONING Zoning regulations that limit the height of buildings in certain areas.

HELIPORT   An area of land or of a building specifically designated as the regular place of landing and takeoff for helicopters.

HELLER-PECHMAN PLAN   Proposal that Congress contemplate a different approach to funding or assisting states and local communities in participating in categorical programs, involving distribution of funds on a less conditional and narrowly targeted basis through revenue sharing. Proposed to the Joint Economic Committee of Congress in 1967 by a group that included Professor Walter W. Heller of the University of Minnesota and Joseph A. Pechman of the Brookings Institution.

HEREDITAMENT   Anything that can be inherited.

HIATUS [real estate]   A gap or space unintentionally left between when attempting to describe adjacent parcels of land.

HIGHEST AND BEST USE   The use that will provide the greatest net income to the land which, when capitalized, will result in the greatest land value (taking into consideration applicable zoning codes).

HIGH-RISE   A building with enough stories to require that it be served with an elevator; usually, four or five stories or more. Generally, buildings that stand out on a skyline as taller than others are classified as high-rise.

HIGH-RISE APARTMENTS   Apartments located in multistory buildings (usually five or more) served by elevators.

HILL-BURTON PROGRAM [health]   Authorized by the Public Health Service Act; provides formula grants, direct loans, or insured loans to state and local governments, hospital districts or authorities, and nonprofit organizations through the Health Services and Mental Health Administration of HEW. The purpose is to assist the states in planning for and providing hospitals, public health centers, state health laboratories, outpatient facilities, emergency rooms, neighborhood health centers, long-term care facilities (nursing homes, chronic disease hospitals, and long-term units of hospitals), rehabilitation facilities, and other related health facilities.

HIP ROOF   A roof sloping upward from four walls of a building.

HISTORICAL COST   The total cost of a property in the life of an ownership, including original acquisition, betterments, and capital improvements.

HISTORIC AREA [HUD] A geographically delimited unit possessing a significant concentration of historic sites, buildings, and structures unified by events or aesthetically by plan or physical developments stemming from one or several periods.

HISTORIC PRESERVATION PROGRAM Authorized by the National Historic Preservation Act of 1966; provides project grants through the National Park Service to prepare comprehensive statewide historic surveys and plans for the preservation, for the public benefit, of districts, sites, buildings, structures, and objects significant in American history, architecture, archaeology, and culture.

Funds can be used to help finance state surveys and plans for historic preservation, staff salaries, equipment and materials, and travel necessary to accomplish the purpose of the program. Funds can also be used to acquire historic property and to finance development costs such as research, preparation of plans and specifications, project costs, and certain donated services. Not eligible are administrative costs following the restoration of the site phase, such as interpretive expenses, the cost of installing and maintaining exhibit devices, and certain other expenses.

Only eligible applicants are the National Trust of Historic Preservation and states operating under programs administered by a state liaison officer appointed by the governors.

Public and private owners of historic property listed on the National Register of Historic Places may benefit.

HISTORIC SITE [HUD] The location of a historic event, building, or structure.

HISTORIC STRUCTURE [HUD] Works constructed by man and connected to the earth, which are judged to have historical significance, such as houses, monuments, bridges, commercial buildings, and industrial facilities.

HOISTWAY [HUD] An enclosed shaft in which one or more elevators is designed to travel.

HOLD-HARMLESS [community development] Principle, advanced in conjunction with Title I—Community Development of the Housing and Community Development Act of 1974, under which units of general local government are entitled to receive funds with which to phase out certain categorical grant programs consolidated by the legislation and to phase in to the funding of such programs with block grants provided through the 1974 act.

HOLD-HARMLESS AGREEMENT A legally valid agreement between two parties providing that one party assumes the liability of the other.

HOLD-HARMLESS AMOUNT [community development] The amount of funds representing the average past level of funds received by a unit of general local government under provisions of certain categorical grant programs consolidated by Title I—Community Development of the Housing and Community Development Act of 1974, used to determine the amount of a hold-harmless grant to such units of general local government. (*See also* BASIC GRANT AMOUNT, ENTITLEMENT AMOUNT, HOLD-HARMLESS GRANT.)

HOLD-HARMLESS GRANT [community development] The amount of funds which a unit of general local government is entitled to receive in excess of its basic grant amount under provisions of Title I—Community Development of the Housing and Community Development Act of 1974. (*See also* BASIC GRANT AMOUNT, ENTITLEMENT AMOUNT, HOLD-HARMLESS AMOUNT.)

HOLDOVER TENANT A tenant who continues to occupy a rented dwelling unit after his lease term has expired.

HOLLOW-NEWEL STAIR A circular staircase built around a well hole.

HOME-BASED TRIP [transportation] A trip that begins or ends at the residence of the traveler.

HOMEBUYERS ASSOCIATION (HBA) [HUD] An incorporated organization of all families who have agreed to buy a home, usually under provisions of the Turnkey III program.

HOME IMPROVEMENT LOAN [FHA] A loan, advance of credit, or purchase of an obligation representing a loan or advance of credit, made to finance the improvement of an existing structure used primarily for residential purposes. (*See also* TITLE I PROPERTY IMPROVEMENT LOAN INSURANCE.)

HOME LOAN BANK BOARD (HLBB) (*See* FEDERAL HOME LOAN BANK BOARD.)

HOME MANUFACTURER A builder who uses assembly line techniques to produce sectionalized units or packages of materials for rapid assembly on site. Also called "factory builder."

HOME OCCUPATION　An occupation conducted in a home, usually of a service nature. Zoning codes often restrict the use of a dwelling unit for home occupations to certain types of services. A home occupation constitutes an accessory use of a property.

HOMEOWNERS ASSOCIATION　An association of homeowners having responsibilities with respect to common property of a project or specific area or subdivision, including condominium associations.

HOME OWNERS LOAN CORPORATION (HOLC)　Federal agency established under provisions of the Home Owners Loan Act of 1933 to refinance the mortgages of distressed home owners. Loans in the amount of $3.1 billion refinanced over a million homes in HOLC's first three years. The agency was liquidated in 1951.

HOME OWNERS WARRANTY REGISTRATION COUNCIL (HOWRC)　*(See* HOME WARRANTY PROGRAM.)

HOME RULE　The right of self-government of political jurisdictions within a state.

HOMESTEAD　The dwelling place of a family, including house, accessory buildings, and land.

HOMESTEAD EXEMPTION　The legal exemption of one's homestead from attachment in a bankruptcy proceeding.

HOME WARRANTY PROGRAM (HWP)　Insurance against faulty workmanship and materials for certain components of houses for certain periods of time, instituted by the National Association of Home Builders and administered by its Home Owners Warranty Registration Council. *(See also* BUILDER'S WARRANTY.)

HOSPITAL [FHA]　A facility which provides community service for inpatient medical care of the sick or injured (including obstetrical care); where not more than 50 percent of the total patient days during any year are customarily assignable to the categories of chronic convalescent and rest, drug and alcoholic, epileptic, mentally deficient, mental, nervous and mental, and tuberculosis; and which is a proprietary facility or facility of a private nonprofit corporation or association, licensed or regulated by the state (or, if there is no state law providing for such licensing or regulation, by the municipality or other political subdivision in which the facility is located).

HOSPITAL MORTGAGE INSURANCE [FHA] (*See* SECTION 242 MORTGAGE INSURANCE FOR HOSPITALS.)

HOSPITAL USES [urban renewal]   Those uses related to the functions of a hospital in providing care and treatment of the ill or injured, including the housing, feeding, and care of resident interns, physicians, and nurses.

HOTEL   A residential building occupied or used principally as a temporary place of lodging; hotels may or may not provide meals and there are usually no cooking facilities in guest rooms. (*See also* APARTMENT HOTEL.)

HOUSE   A building designed for residential occupancy. The term generally applies to a detached house.

HOUSEHOLD   A family or individual living alone.

HOUSING   Defined by the Douglas Commission as "both a product and a process." The process is obvious. The product "includes all of the immediate physical environment, both within and outside of buildings, in which families and households live, grow, and decline. It is largely manmade. Its primary functions are three: to provide (1) comfortable shelter; (2) a proper setting, both within the structure and in its neighborhood, for the day-to-day activities of families and households, of small informal groups of children and adults, and of the individuals who make them up; and (3) the locus or location of families and other groups within the larger physical pattern of the family."

HOUSING ACT OF 1937   (*See* U.S. HOUSING ACT.)

HOUSING ACT OF 1949   Federal law establishing among other provisions, as national policy, "the goal of a decent home and a suitable living environment for every American family"; the federal financing of slum clearance activities by localities (now known as the "urban renewal program"); and public responsibility for relocating families displaced by clearance activities.

The Housing and Community Development Act of 1974 provides for the phasing out of the urban renewal program and ancillary programs and activities and for their supplanting by block grant funding under Title I—Community Development.

HOUSING ACT OF 1954   Federal legislation broadening the provisions of the Housing Act of 1949, including the introduction of the concept of housing rehabilitation as an inherent feature or possibility under the urban renewal program; the establishment of the requirement that localities adopt an official Workable Program for Community Improvement to be eligible to participate in certain programs of federal financial assistance; the broadening of relocation assistance to families and businesses; and the provision of incentives to localities to develop new community facilities, new schools, and other institutions—the cost of which could be credited against the local share of urban renewal program costs. It was with the 1954 housing act that the term "urban renewal" replaced the term "slum clearance" in the language of the field.

The Housing and Community Development Act of 1974 provides for the phasing out of many of the provisions of the 1954 act and their supplanting through a system of block grant financing under Title I—Community Development.

HOUSING ACT OF 1959   A further broadening of the provisions of the 1937 and 1949 housing acts, including the vesting in local housing authorities of "the maximum amount of responsibility in the administration of the low-rent housing program" and the establishment of the Community Renewal Program.

The CRP has been supplanted by Title I—Community Development of the Housing and Community Development Act of 1974.

HOUSING ALLOWANCE   (*See* DIRECT HOUSING ALLOWANCE.)

HOUSING AND COMMUNITY DEVELOPMENT ACT OF 1974   Omnibus act providing for

1. The phasing out of Title I—Urban Renewal activities (including the Community Renewal Program, the Neighborhood Development Program, Section 115 housing rehabilitation grants, the Section 116 demolition grant program, the Section 117 federally assisted code enforcement program, and most other related and ancillary grants and programs), the Demonstration Cities Program ("Model Cities Program"), Section 702 basic water and sewer facilities grants, and Section 703 neighborhood facilities grants. This act provides for supplanting of the aforementioned categorical grant programs through a system of block grant financing available to units of general local government under the provisions of Title I—Community Development.

2. Significant technical reforms in the public housing program established in the National Housing Act of 1937 (including the renaming of the Section 23 leased housing program to the Section 8 housing assistance program), Section 202 elderly housing, the Sections 235 and 236 interest subsidy programs, and rural housing programs.

3. Major revisions in the Section 701 comprehensive planning program.

4. The establishment of new mobile home construction standards.

5. Numerous other technical amendments to previous housing acts.

HOUSING AND HOME FINANCE AGENCY (HHFA)   Until 1965, when HUD supplanted HHFA, HHFA was the federal agency responsible for the principal federal activities concerned with housing and community development. Established on a permanent peacetime basis on July 27, 1947, under government Reorganization Plan No. 3, the HHFA was an independent agency, with its major program operations carried out by five constituents under the general coordination of the Office of the Administrator of the HHFA. The five major program constituents were the Federal Housing Administration, the Public Housing Administration, the Federal National Mortgage Association, and the Community Facilities Administration.

HOUSING AND URBAN DEVELOPMENT [HUD]   *(See* DEPARTMENT OF HOUSING AND URBAN DEVELOPMENT.)

HOUSING AND URBAN DEVELOPMENT ACT OF 1968   Act establishing a broad range of programs of federal financial assistance, including the Section 235 and Section 236 programs, Neighborhood Development Program, the FAIR plan—and reorganizing FNMA and GNMA operations.

Title I—Community Development of the Housing and Community Development Act of 1974 phases out and supplants the Neighborhood Development Program.

HOUSING ASSISTANCE PAYMENT (HAP) [public housing]   Subsidy payments made to the owner of Section 23 leased housing units by local housing authorities on behalf of tenants. The HAP plus the rent collected from the tenant equals the total fair market rent for the unit. The Housing and Community Development Act of 1974 renamed the Section 23 program Section 8, under provisions of Title II—Assisted Housing. *(See also* SECTION 8 HOUSING ASSISTANCE PAYMENT PROGRAM, SECTION 23 LEASED HOUSING.)

HOUSING ASSISTANCE PLAN (HAP)   Basic document in a unit of general local government's application for participation in the provisions of Title I—Community Development of the Housing and Community Development Act of 1974. The HAP includes such features as a survey of housing conditions in the applicant's community, an estimate of the needs for housing assistance of lower-income persons, a statement of goals for the development of new or rehabilitation of existing dwelling units, an indication of the general location of proposed housing development and/or rehabilitation activities, and a map showing where minority groups are concentrated in the community. (*See also* COMMUNITY DEVELOPMENT PROGRAM.)

HOUSING ASSOCIATION   An organization of persons seeking to effect changes in housing conditions, policies, programs, or regulations.

HOUSING AUTHORITY   (*See* LOCAL HOUSING AUTHORITY.)

HOUSING CODE   Official regulations establishing minimum standards of occupancy which housing units must meet to be occupied legally. Such codes usually govern spatial, ventilation, wiring, plumbing, structural, and heating requirements. Housing codes normally apply to existing housing, as distinguished from housing to be constructed. Also called "housing ordinance," "minimum housing code," "minimum housing standard."

HOUSING CONSULTANT   (*See* CONSULTANT.)

HOUSING DEVELOPMENT CORPORATION (HDC)   A multipurpose, private housing corporation established to serve a given geographic area—such as a neighborhood, city, state, or region—by providing technical assistance, lending seed money, and directly sponsoring housing developments. The board of directors generally is represented equally by community people, the business community, and local governmental officials.

HOUSING EXPENSES   (*See* MONTHLY HOUSING EXPENSE.)

HOUSING FOR THE ELDERLY [HUD-FHA]   Eight or more new or rehabilitated living units which are specially designed for use and occupancy by elderly persons. (*See also* SECTION 202 ELDERLY HOUSING.)

HOUSING IMPROVEMENT PROGRAM (HIP)   (*See* INDIAN-HOUSING IMPROVEMENT PROGRAM.)

HOUSING INVENTORY   (*See* HOUSING STOCK.)

HOUSING OPPORTUNITY ALLOWANCE PROGRAM (HOAP)   Authorized by the Emergency Home Finance Act of 1970; provides subsidies through the Federal Home Loan Bank Board to provide payments to upwardly mobile moderate-income families whose annual incomes are too high to allow them to participate in HUD's subsidized housing programs but too low to allow them to obtain conventional mortgage loans.

The assistance, which is in the form of a $20 allowance for a period of not more than sixty months, can be applied only to the contractually required monthly payment of a twenty-five- to thirty-year first mortgage for the purchase of a single family home or condominium unit. Eligible families may not have incomes in excess of the HOAP regular family income limits. The assistance can be obtained through loans originated by any participating member of the Federal Home Loan Bank Systems. Borrowers may not use HOAP to refinance their present homes. Rental properties are not eligible.

Any family consisting either of two married persons living together or a head of household with at least one dependent person may apply for a HOAP allowance. The applicant applies for HOAP at any participating member of the Federal Home Loan Banks System. The participating member will determine the applicant's eligibility; income should not exceed specified HOAP regular family income limit and must be insufficient to warrant making of the requested loan but for availability of HOAP allowance. Also, security property must meet program requirements: i.e., single-family home or condominium unit.

HOUSING ORDINANCE (*See* HOUSING CODE.)

HOUSING OWNERSHIP MANAGEMENT ENTITIES (HOME) Ownership system for subsidized housing projects proposed by the National Center for Housing Management, Inc., through which consortia of local financial institutions and housing management corporations would own and manage FHA-subsidized multifamily projects.

HOUSING PRODUCTION AND MORTGAGE CREDIT (HPMC) [HUD] The office of the HUD Assistant Secretary for HPMC, who is also the Federal Housing Commissioner, administers the HUD programs and functions which assist in the production and financing of housing and in the conservation and rehabilitation of the housing stock.

These programs include the insurance, under the National Housing Act, of mortgages and loans made by private lending institutions for the purchase, construction, rehabilitation, repair, and improvement of single-family and multifamily housing, the low-rent public housing program, and the homeownership assistance, interest-reduction, rent supplement, and college housing programs. The functions assigned to the Assistant Secretary/HPMC are those required from preapplication through construction completion and the execution and closing of a contract or mortgage or other credit financing instrument as well as actions which are a direct extension of the construction and production phase, which may occur after final endorsement.

(*See also* FEDERAL HOUSING ADMINISTRATION.)

HOUSING PROJECT A project of a private or public investor designed and used primarily for the purpose of providing dwellings occupied by tenants under a rental (lease) or purchase agreement—including all property (real and personal), contracts, rights, and choses in action acquired, owned, or otherwise held by the investor. (*See also* LOW-INCOME HOUSING PROJECT.)

HOUSING REHABILITATION GRANT (*See* SECTION 115 HOUSING REHABILITATION GRANTS.)

HOUSING REHABILITATION LOAN (*See* SECTION 312 HOUSING REHABILITATION LOANS.)

HOUSING STARTS Housing units placed under construction.

HOUSING STOCK The quantity of housing units in a geographic area. Also called "housing inventory."

HOUSING TYPE The architectural or building style of housing, such as garden or high-rise apartments, row houses, attached or detached.

HOUSING UNIT A dwelling unit.

HUD AREA OFFICE (HAO) (*See* AREA OFFICE OF HUD.)

HUD AUDIT An audit of the books, records, or performances of contractors or grantees and others doing business with HUD.

HUD CENTRAL OFFICE (See CENTRAL OFFICE OF HUD.)

HUD–FHA The Department of Housing and Urban Development–Federal Housing Administration. The term is used in lieu of FHA wherever it occurs except in the case of the assistant regional administrator for FHA, which will read the assistant regional administrator for HPMC.

HUD PG-46 HUD's established minimum property standards for the construction of housing for the elderly ("with special consideration for the handicapped").

HUD REGIONAL ADMINISTRATOR (RA) The top official in a regional office of HUD.

HUD REGIONAL OFFICE (*See* REGIONAL OFFICE OF HUD.)

HUNDRED PERCENT LOCATION   The location, usually within a central business district, with the highest land value.

I

IDEAL COMMUNITIES   Theoretical projections of utopian concepts (not in actual existence).

IDENTITY OF INTEREST   Direct financial relationship between the principals of a project. Various forms of identity of interest are recognized by HUD. (*See also* INTEREST [FHA].)

IMPACT AID   (*See* SCHOOL ASSISTANCE IN FEDERALLY AFFECTED AREAS.)

IMPROVED AREA OR IMPROVED LAND   A land area that has been prepared for construction upon it, as by the installation of utility connections or services, streets, sidewalks, etc.

IMPROVED VALUE   The market value of a property, including its value after appreciation over its actual cost.

IMPROVEMENT [building] [HUD]   Conservation, repair, restoration, rehabilitation, conversion, alteration, enlargement, or remodeling of a building.

IMPROVEMENT ON LAND   Structures built on a tract of land.

IMPROVEMENTS [land development] [FHA]   Water lines and water-supply installations; sewer lines and sewage disposal installations; steam, gas, and electric lines and installations; roads; streets; curbs; gutters; sidewalks; storm drainage facilities; and other installations or work, whether on or off the site of the mortgaged property, which FHA deems necessary or desirable to prepare land primarily for residential and related uses or to provide facilities for public or common use. Related uses may include industrial uses, with sites for such uses to be in proper proportion to the size and scope of the developments. The public or common facilities include only such buildings as are needed in connection with water-supply or sewage disposal installations or steam, gas, or electric lines or installations and such buildings other than schools, as the FHA considers appropriate, which are to be owned and maintained jointly by the property owners.

IMPROVEMENTS TO LAND   Curbs, sidewalks, drains, sewers, fills, etc., installed to make land usable for development.

IMPUTED NET RENT   The gross rental value of a property minus all necessary expenses of ownership, including depreciation and insurance.

INCHOATE CURTESY [real estate]   The imperfected interest which the law gives a husband in the lands of his wife; the interest which, upon the death of the wife, may ripen into possession and use.

INCHOATE DOWER [real estate]   The imperfected interest which the law gives a wife in the lands of her husband; the interest which, upon the death of the husband, may ripen into possession and use.

INCINERATION   The burning of waste material.

INCOME ADMISSION LIMITS   (*See* INCOME LIMITS.)

INCOME APPROACH TO VALUE   A method of appraisal through which the value of a property is determined through analysis of the income produced by the property.

INCOME CEILING   (*See* INCOME LIMITS.)

INCOME LIMITS [HUD]   The family income limits that are established by HUD for admission into HUD-assisted projects for low- and moderate-income families and which may not be exceeded if the families are to be eligible to rent or buy and remain eligible for a subsidy. The income limits are based on family size, type of dwelling unit, and cost of living in the area. Each HUD program has its own income limits.

INCOME MAINTENANCE SUBSIDY   An unrestricted cash subsidy to a person or family of limited financial means intended to augment the recipient's income; such funds can be used to purchase food, obtain better housing, pay medical bills, or whatever. (*See also* DIRECT HOUSING ALLOW-ANCE.)

INCOME MIX Generally, the same as economic integration.

INCOME-PRICE RATIO Ratio established by dividing the net income from a property by the selling price.

INCOME PROPERTY Property that is expected to produce an income to its owner from rents or leases.

INCOME RECERTIFICATION [HUD] (*See* RECERTIFICATION OF INCOME.)

INCOME TRANSFER FOR HOUSING A cash subsidy paid to a person or family of limited financial means, restricted to use for obtaining good or better housing; usually paid in the form of a direct housing allowance or rent certificate. (*See also* INCOME MAINTENANCE SUBSIDY.)

INCREMENT TAX A tax on the increased value of a property, levied or assessed on the basis of the appreciation of its value.

INCURABLE DEPRECIATION Depreciation in value of a property caused by deteriorating conditions and/or functional obsolescence which cannot be corrected—at least, not with any degree of economic feasibility.

INDEMNIFY To make payment for a loss.

INDENTURE A deed involving two or more principals which stipulates that each has certain rights, responsibilities, and obligations to the other.

INDIAN HOUSING DEVELOPMENT PROGRAM Authorized by the Snyder Act of 1921 and subsequent legislation applicable to programs administered by HUD and HEW; provides training, advisory services and counseling, dissemination of technical information.

The program's purpose is to eliminate substandard housing among American Indians in the 1970s in accordance with the joint plans of the Departments of Health, Education, and Welfare, Housing and Urban Development, and Interior, in conjunction with the Indian-housing improvement program.

Assistance is provided to Indian tribes in establishing local housing authorities to obtain benefits of HUD housing programs, in carrying out construction of the projects, and in managing them. Assistance is restricted to Indian tribes that are able to establish local housing authorities and carry out programs under the U.S. Housing Act of 1937, as amended, the U.S. Housing Act of 1949 as amended, and the rules and regulations of the Department of Housing and Urban Development.

Indians and other persons who meet the income criteria and other rules and regulations of the legally established local Indian housing authorities are eligible to participate.

INDIAN HOUSING IMPROVEMENT PROGRAM (HIP)   Authorized by the Snyder Act of 1921 and subsequent legislation applicable to programs administered by HUD and HEW; provides Bureau of Indian Affairs project grants of up to $3,500 for repairs, $5,000 for transitional housing, $3,500 for down payment to obtain housing loans, and $16,000 for a new house.

The program is mainly devoted to housing improvement. The Bureau does, however, build an entire house in special situations where no other program will meet the need, i.e., extremely isolated areas or reservations where only a very small number of homes are needed.

Indians in need of financial assistance to help repair or renovate existing homes or who need new houses and cannot be helped by any other federal program may participate. Indians who have the financial ability to provide their own housing are not eligible to participate.

Formula and matching requirements are not required; however, HIP money is used in conjunction with other federal or privately financed programs that are appropriate to repair or build housing. This also includes the recipients' self-help efforts where possible and practical.

INDIGENOUS   Native, or belonging to a region or an area.

INDIGENT   Poor, destitute.

INDIRECT COSTS   The costs of a development not reflected in the price of land or building(s), such as legal and organizational expenses, financing, taxes and insurance during construction, and architectural and engineering fees.

INDIVIDUAL [urban renewal]   A person who is not a member of a family. An elderly individual is one who is sixty-two years of age or over at the time of displacement. A handicapped individual is one who has a physical impairment which is expected to be of long-continued and indefinite duration and which substantially impedes his ability to live independently.

INDIVIDUAL MORTGAGE [FHA]   A mortgage covering an individual single-family dwelling which has been released from a multifamily sales project mortgage.

INDUSTRIAL DEVELOPMENT BOND   A bond, usually tax exempt, issued by a public authority or corporation to finance the construction of facilities to house industry.

INDUSTRIALIZED HOUSING   Housing units or portions of housing units (such as walls, rooms, plumbing components) produced in factories using mass production techniques. (*See also* HOME MANUFACTURER.)

INDUSTRIAL PARK   An area specially zoned for use by industry, frequently served by a management operation through which special services or facilities are made available to the occupants of the area.

IN-FILL HOUSING   Housing units built on vacant lots in built-up areas of a city. (*See also* SCATTERED-SITE HOUSING.)

INFILTRATION   The replacement, over a period of time, of one social group by another.

INFORMATION   (*See* FREEDOM OF INFORMATION ACT.)

INFORMATION SYSTEM   Schematic approach to the organization and dissemination of information.

INGRESS [real estate]   The right to enter a tract of land. Often used interchangeably with "access."

INITIAL CLOSING [FHA]   Closing conference held following the issuance of a firm commitment by HUD-FHA. At this conference HUD places its initial endorsement, assuring mortgage insurance, on the credit instrument or mortgage, permitting the lender to make progress payments toward the project. Distinguished from final closing. Also called "initial endorsement."

INITIAL COMMITMENT [FHA]   A letter issued by FHA to a sponsor or prospective lender, establishing that a proposed project appears feasible and, usually, inviting the sponsor to proceed with the preparation of an application for conditional or firm commitment. Also termed "feasibility letter" or "finding of feasibility."

INITIAL ENDORSEMENT [FHA]   (*See* INITIAL CLOSING.)

INITIAL OCCUPANCY   The date on which a tenant first assumes possession of or occupies an individual dwelling unit.

INITIAL OCCUPANCY DATE   The last day of the calendar month in which 90 percent of the dwellings in a project are occupied.

INITIAL OPERATING DEFICIT   The deficit incurred by a project before it becomes self-supporting.

INITIAL OPERATING PERIOD (IOP) [public housing]   First quarter in which occupancy of a project, recently constructed or rehabilitated, achieves 95 percent occupancy.

INITIAL RENT-UP PERIOD [FHA]   (*See* RENT-UP PERIOD.)

INITIATION DATE [public housing]   (*See* PROJECT INITIATION DATE.)

IN-KIND CONTRIBUTION   A service—such as contributed manpower or time of workers or use of a facility or equipment contributed to a project —which serves to help constitute a grant-in-aid toward the financing of a project. Distinguished from a cash credit and noncash grant-in-aid.

INNER CITY   An urban area which does not necessarily have political, geographic, racial, or economic outlines or boundaries but which, in general, was recognized popularly as a central shopping and residential part of a city prior to World War II.

INNER COURT [HUD]   An open, outdoor space enclosed on all sides by exterior walls of a building or by exterior walls and property lines on which walls are allowed to be constructed. (*See also* COURT, OUTER COURT.)

IN-SERVICE LOAN   (*See* SECTION 222 MORTGAGE INSURANCE FOR SERVICEMEN'S HOUSING.)

INSPECTION FEE [FHA]   A charge by FHA to a mortgagor for the costs of its construction inspections. The standard charge is 0.5 percent of the mortgage amount.

INSTALLMENT CONTRACT   Contract for property purchase providing for the payment of the purchase price in periodic installments.

INSTITUTIONAL USE   The use, usually of land, by a governmental entity, a nonprofit organization, or some other body having a public character— e.g., hospitals, schools, city halls, libraries.

INSTRUMENT   A legal document, such as a contract, will, lease, deed, or mortgage note.

INSURANCE   A contract of indemnity against specific perils.

INSURANCE CONTRACT [FHA]   (*See* CONTRACT OF INSURANCE.)

INSURANCE OF ADVANCES [HUD/FHA]   Arrangement between HUD/FHA and a construction loan lender providing for HUD/FHA to insure the construction loan against a project—distinguished from insurance upon completion.

INSURANCE OF TITLE   Insurance as to who owns a specified interest in designated real estate and showing as exceptions to the insured interest the defects, liens, and encumbrances which exist as against that insured interest. Also called "title insurance."

INSURANCE UPON COMPLETION [HUD/FHA]   Arrangement between HUD/FHA and a construction loan lender providing for HUD/FHA to insure the permanent loan against a project but not the construction loan—distinguished from insurance of advances.

INSURED ADVANCES   (*See* INSURANCE OF ADVANCES.)

INSURED MORTGAGE [FHA]   A mortgage which has been insured by the issuance of a Mortgage Insurance Certificate or by the endorsement of the credit instrument by FHA.

INSURING OFFICE OF HUD-FHA   HUD office established to process FHA mortgage insurance programs. Currently, there are thirty-eight insuring offices located throughout the country. (*See also* AREA OFFICE OF HUD.)

INTANGIBLE ASSET   An asset that has no negotiable substance—e.g., goodwill, copyrights, trademarks.

INTENSITY PATTERN   The quality of interaction and activity of a population or population group.

INTEREST [FHA]   The term "interest" is not limited to a financial interest in the sense of profits, dividends, fees, and legal guarantees but also includes nonfinancial interests such as a pledge of support, not constituting a legal or financial obligation, given by a parent organization to its member groups or a pledge of other nonfinancial support designed to convince HUD that a proposal will be feasible. (*See also* BENEFICIAL INTEREST.)

INTEREST [money]   The price one pays for the use of another's money, usually expressed as a percentage.

INTEREST REDUCTION PROGRAM [FHA]   FHA programs that subsidize the market interest rate of mortgage loans for low- and moderate-income housing to lower the cost of rent or monthly payments to the renter or purchaser of the housing. [*See also* SECTION 235(I) INTEREST SUBSIDY, SECTION 236 INTEREST REDUCTION (OR SUBSIDY) PROGRAM.]

INTEREST SUBSIDY   Federal subsidy, paid to a lender on behalf of a home renter or purchaser, in some amount between the market rate of interest and an established lower rate. [*See also* INTEREST REDUCTION PROGRAM. SECTION 235(I) INTEREST SUBSIDY, SECTION 236 INTEREST REDUCTION OR SUBSIDY PROGRAM.]

INTERFACE [transportation]   Transfer between transit lines or modes and stops or stations to accomplish such transfer.

INTERGOVERNMENTAL PERSONNEL ACT OF 1970   An act to reinforce the federal system by strengthening the personnel resources of state and local governments, to improve intergovernmental cooperation in the administration of grant-in-aid programs, to provide grants for improvement of state and local personnel administration, to authorize federal assistance in training state and local employees, to provide grants to state and local governments for training of their employees, to authorize interstate compacts for personnel and training activities, to facilitate the temporary assignment of personnel between the federal government and state and local governments, and for other purposes. Approved January 5, 1971.

INTERGOVERNMENTAL RELATIONS   The relationships between and within governmental units.

INTERIM ASSISTANCE AREA [HUD]   An area which HUD has approved for a grant designated to assist the locality in carrying out programs to alleviate harmful conditions in slums or blighted areas, as provided for in Section 118 of Title I of the Housing Act of 1949 as subsequently amended.

Title I—Community Development of the Housing and Community Development Act of 1974 supplants this program with a system of block grants.

INTERIM ASSISTANCE PROGRAM   (*See* SECTION 118 INTERIM ASSISTANCE PROGRAM.)

INTERIM FINANCING [FHA]   A loan, usually temporary, which covers the land cost, construction cost, current real estate taxes, and other incidental expenses attributable to the construction period. (*See also* CONSTRUCTION LOAN.)

INTERIM LOAN [construction]   (*See* CONSTRUCTION LOAN.)

INTERIM MANAGEMENT [HUD]   The management of property which is vacant at the time of acquisition by a public agency or which becomes vacant afterwards. Such property cannot be rented to off-site tenants but may be used for temporary relocation of site occupants.

INTERIOR LOT   A lot whose side lines do not abut upon a street. (*See also* CORNER LOT, THROUGH LOT.)

INTERMEDIATE CARE FACILITY [HUD]   A facility operated by a proprietary or nonprofit organization licensed or regulated by a state or other governmental entity for the accommodation of persons who, because of incapacitating infirmities, require minimum but continuous care but are not in need of continuous medical or nursing services. (*See also* SECTION 232 MORTGAGE INSURANCE FOR NURSING HOMES.)

INTERNATIONAL CONFERENCE OF BUILDING OFFICIALS (ICBO)   National code group which publishes and maintains a variety of model building and housing codes; publisher of the *Uniform Building Code*. (*See also* NATIONAL CODE.)

INTERSTATE LAND SALES ADMINISTRATOR [HUD]   The HUD Interstate Land Sales Administrator exercises HUD's responsibilities under the Interstate Land Sales Full Disclosure Act. The administrator heads the Office of Interstate Land Sales Registration, which administers and enforces registration and disclosure requirements which apply to developers who sell land through the use of any means of interstate commerce or the mails. Pursuant to the provisions of the act and HUD regulations, developers of all nonexempt subdivisions containing fifty or more lots must file a Statement of Record with the Office of Interstate Land Sales Registration and furnish each purchaser with a printed Property Report in advance of the time that they sign the sales contract. Developers who do not comply with the statutory and regulatory requirements may be subject to administrative proceedings, civil proceedings to enjoin the acts or practices, and criminal prosecution.

INTESTATE   Designates the estate or condition of failing to leave a will at death. (*See also* TESTATE.)

INVERSE CONDEMNATION   Legal process through which a property owner claims damages for loss of property value arising out of the failure of a condemning body to complete a proposed condemnation action.

INVESTOR   A person, group of persons, or partnership; or a corporation, company, association, trust, or other legal entity; or a combination of two or more corporations, companies, associations, trusts, or other legal entities —any of which receives the economic benefits and is liable for the taxes resulting from an ownership position in a project. (*See also* ACTIVE INVESTOR, PASSIVE INVESTOR.)

INVESTOR PROJECT [FHA]   A project owned by a mortgagor that intends to sell the project to the mortgagor of a management project.

INVESTOR-SPONSOR   Private, profit-making organization that undertakes the development of housing projects for sale at a profit to a nonprofit cooperative corporation. The allowable profit is limited and the mortgage amount available to the sponsor is a lower percentage of project cost than is the case for nonprofit cooperative mortgagors. (*See also* LIMITED DISTRIBUTION OR LIMITED DIVIDEND MORTGAGOR.)

INVITATION FOR PROPOSALS [public housing]   Local housing authority's legal solicitation of Turnkey proposals from developers, usually published in the form of letters of invitation to developers, legal notices in newspapers, news stories, etc.

ISOMETRIC   A three-dimensional drawing using parallel isometric lines and no perspective of the subject.

J

JAMB   The vertical sides of a door or window frame.

JERRY-BUILT   Built poorly, of cheap materials.

JOB CORPS   Federal program authorized by the Economic Opportunity

Act of 1964; provides residential centers for young men and women, aged sixteen through twenty-one, in a coordinated program of basic education, skill, training, and constructive work experience. Normally entails a two-year period of service for enrollees.

JOB OVERHEAD [FHA]   (*See* CONTRACTOR'S GENERAL REQUIREMENTS.)

JOINER   A carpenter whose principal task is to finish interior woodwork.

JOINT TASK FORCE OF HUD AND HEW   Task force established to coordinate the social services aspects of HUD's and HEW's various aid programs to localities. Originally established in 1961 between the Housing and Home Finance Agency and HEW.

JOINT TENANCY   Where two or more persons hold real estate jointly for life, the survivors to take the interest of the one who dies.

JOURNEYMAN   A worker who has finished learning his trade.

JUDGMENT [real estate]   A decree of a court; the lien or charge upon the lands of a debtor resulting from the court's award of money to a creditor.

JUDGMENT LIEN [real estate]   The charge upon the lands of a debtor resulting from the decree of a court properly entered in the judgment docket.

JUNIOR LIEN   A lien recorded on a property subsequent to the recording of a prior lien.

JURISDICTION   The area in which a governmental or other entity has authority.

JUST COMPENSATION   The fair compensation of one whose property has been acquired, usually through condemnation.

JUVENILE DELINQUENCY PREVENTION AND CONTROL ACT OF 1968   An act to assist the courts, correctional systems, community agencies, and primary and secondary public school systems to prevent, treat, and control juvenile delinquency; to support research and training efforts in the prevention, treatment, and control of juvenile delinquency; and for other purposes. Approved July 31, 1968, and subsequently amended.

K

KAISER COMMITTEE President's Committee on Urban Housing, appointed by President Lyndon B. Johnson, with Edgar F. Kaiser as chairman.

KERNER COMMISSION National Advisory Commission on Civil Disorders, appointed by President Lyndon B. Johnson, with Governor Otto Kerner of Illinois as chairman.

KEY TENANT A prestigious tenant in a commercial shopping center or building whose presence is expected to help attract other tenants to lease space in the same area.

KITCHEN (K or k) [HUD] Space, 60 square feet or more in area, used for cooking and preparation of food.

KITCHENETTE (K'ette or k'ette) [HUD] Space, less than 60 square feet in area, used for cooking and preparation of food.

L

LABOR HOUSING (*See* FARM LABOR HOUSING LOANS AND GRANTS.)

LAND ASSEMBLY (*See* ASSEMBLAGE.)

LAND BANKING Acquiring land for future use, usually by a public body or agency; intended to control urban or suburban development or sprawl.

LAND CLEARANCE Generally implies slum clearance.

LAND CONTRACT   A contract for the purchase of land on an installment basis. Upon payment of last installment, the deed is delivered. Also called "contract for deed."

LAND DEVELOPMENT   The process of making, installing, or constructing improvements on vacant land.

LAND GRANT   Government land granted to an educational institution, railroad, etc.

LANDLORD   The owner of property that is leased to another.

LANDMARK   Any conspicuous object that helps establish land boundaries or the location of a property.

LAND USE [urban renewal]   The type of use of a lot or parcel of property; for example, a lot occupied by a factory is an industrial land use. The general categories of land uses include: residential, commercial, industrial, public, semipublic, and institutional. Existing land uses within an urban renewal area and the proposed land uses in the urban renewal plan must be considered in determining the urban renewal area's eligibility for federal loan and grant assistance.

LAND-USE INTENSITY (LUI)   The overall relationships of structural mass and open space of a developed property or a development plan. A land-use intensity rating (LIR) establishes minimum amounts of space for open space, nonvehicular livability space, and recreation space for each square foot of floor area of a property. (*See also* OPEN SPACE RATIO.)

LAND-USE REGULATIONS   Zoning, official maps, and subdivision regulations to guide or control land development.

LANHAM ACT [housing]   Federal law passed in 1940 authorizing the construction of defense housing by the Public Works Administration, much of which housing was managed by local housing authorities. Since the war, Lanham Act housing has been sold by the federal government to private interests, to local housing authorities, and to returning veterans.

LARGE FAMILIES [HUD]   Families which include four or more minors.

LARGE-LOT ZONING   (*See* ACREAGE ZONING.)

LATENT DEFECTS   Hidden defects arising from faulty construction, presumably unknown to an owner or contractor.

LAW ENFORCEMENT ASSISTANCE ADMINISTRATION (LEAA) This was established June 19, 1968, by the Omnibus Crime Control and Safe Streets Act of 1968 as amended. LEAA is under the general authority of the Attorney General and is headed by an administrator. The administrator and the two associate administrators are appointed by the President, with the advice and consent of the Senate. The act, as amended in 1970, provides that except for present incumbents, one of the two associate administrators must be of a different political party from the President.

The purpose of LEAA is to assist state and local governments to reduce crime. "Law enforcement" as defined in the act encompasses all activities pertaining to crime prevention or reduction and the enforcement of the criminal law. The block grant concept embodied in the legislation implies that more authority and power should be shifted to state and local levels of government to decentralize operations of the federal government.

The Agency's operations are managed by the Office of Criminal Justice Assistance, which is responsible for actual grant operations, providing technical assistance to the states through the ten regional offices and coordinating policy recommendations; the National Institute of Law Enforcement and Criminal Justice, which has the responsibility for LEAA research and development programs; and the Office of Operations Support, which provides supportive services including management evaluation, administrative management, systems analysis, and program support.

Block planning funds are granted to each state to finance development of an annual comprehensive law enforcement plan. The plan is prepared by the State Planning Agency (SPA) and reflects the needs of city and county as well as state governments. LEAA planning grants provide agencies throughout the state with the resources to create program concepts and set up detailed plans for carrying out these programs.

LEAD-BASED PAINT POISONING PREVENTION ACT An act to provide federal financial assistance to help cities and communities to develop and carry out intensive local programs to eliminate the causes of lead-based paint poisoning and local programs to detect and treat incidents of such poisoning, to establish a federal demonstration and research program to study the extent of the lead-based paint poisoning problem and the methods available for lead-based removal, and to prohibit future use of lead-based paint in federal or federally assisted construction or rehabilitation. Approved January 13, 1971.

LEAPFROGGING Process in which development "jumps over" expensive vacant land at the immediate urban fringe or within developed areas in favor of cheaper land farther out.

LEASE   A grant of the use of lands or property for a term of years in consideration of the payment of a monthly or annual rental. (*See also* SUBLEASE.)

LEASE-BACK   A transaction in which an owner sells a property and then leases it back from the buyer.

LEASED HOUSING [public housing]   Housing leased by local housing authorities from private owners for low-income families, who receive a subsidized rent through the authority. (*See also* SECTION 8 HOUSING ASSISTANCE PAYMENT PROGRAM, SECTION 23 LEASED HOUSING.)

LEASED HOUSING—NEW CONSTRUCTION [public housing]   New housing which is constructed pursuant to an agreement between a local housing authority and a builder and which upon completion will be leased by the local authority from the owner under a contract which permits the local authority to sublease these units to low-income families in accordance with an established rent schedule. (*See also* SECTION 8 HOUSING ASSISTANCE PAYMENT PROGRAM, SECTION 23 LEASED HOUSING.)

LEASED HOUSING—WITHOUT REHABILITATION [public housing]   Existing housing which does not involve new construction or substantial rehabilitation and which is leased by a local housing authority from an owner under a contract which permits the local authority to sublease these units to low-income families in accordance with an established rent schedule. (*See also* SECTION 8 HOUSING ASSISTANCE PAYMENT PROGRAM, SECTION 23 LEASED HOUSING.)

LEASED HOUSING—WITH REHABILITATION [public housing]   Existing housing, including site, which requires substantial alteration, repair, or improvement at a cost ratio of 20 percent or more of total development cost for multifamily housing or 25 percent or more of total development cost for single-family housing (detached, duplex, or row house). Such work is done pursuant to an agreement between a local housing authority and an owner. Upon completion, it is leased by the local authority from the owner under a contract which permits the local authority to sublease these units to low-income families in accordance with an established rent schedule.

The total development cost for leased housing with rehabilitation should represent the estimated value of the units after rehabilitation. (*See also* SECTION 8 HOUSING ASSISTANCE PAYMENT PROGRAM, SECTION 23 LEASED HOUSING.)

LEASEHOLD MORTGAGE   Mortgage on a leased property.

LEGACY OF PARKS PROGRAM (LOP)   A HUD-sponsored program which, as of July 1971, consolidated HUD's open space, historic preservation, and urban beautification and improvement programs. The name was changed in January 1972 to Open Space Land Program. (*See also* TITLE IV OPEN SPACE LAND PROGRAM.)

LEGAL AND ORGANIZATIONAL EXPENSES [FHA]   Mortgagor costs allowable by FHA in insured mortgages; ordinarily limited to expenses incurred in organizing the mortgagor corporation, developing the proposal for submission to FHA and other necessary governmental agencies, and for necessary services during closings and construction.

Organization expenses include necessary expenses customarily incurred by prudent, knowledgeable sponsors for reasonable reimbursement for time devoted to the proposal, travel and communications, and consultations in keeping with the complexity of a project.

Legal expenses are limited to those incurred for initial and final closings; tax advice during organization of mortgagor corporations only; and preparation of documents and representation for and during organization of the mortgagor entity.

LEGAL EXPENSES [FHA]   (*See* LEGAL AND ORGANIZATIONAL EXPENSES.)

LESSEE   One who takes land or property, upon a lease. Also known as the "tenant."

LESSOR   One who grants land or property under a lease. Also known as the "landlord."

LESS-THAN-FEE ACQUISITION [HUD]   The acquisition of only certain rights to a property, such as a facade easement, a simple easement, or development rights. Form or method of acquisition in a historic preservation program.

LETTER OF CONSENT [urban renewal]   A letter of consent to undertake limited urban renewal execution activities during the project planning stage constitutes a determination that expenditures by the local public agencies for such activities will not be excluded from gross project cost solely because such activities are performed prior to the effective date of a contract for loan and grant. If such activities are permitted under state and local law, HUD may issue a letter of consent to an LPA.

LETTER OF CREDIT A letter indicating that the bearer is entitled to use a sum of money in the amount stipulated in the letter; certified by the issuer.

LETTER OF INTENT [public housing] Letter of intent to enter into contract of sale of Low-Rent Housing Project to local housing authority. Obligates the parties to a proposed Turnkey project to enter into a contract to sell the finished project when completed in accordance with plans prepared by the developer and approved by the local authority (and HUD).

LEVEL ANNUITY PLAN [FHA] A plan for paying off an FHA-insured mortgage which provides for payment of principal, interest, and mortgage insurance premiums at a constant level throughout the mortgage term.

LEVEL PAYMENT PLAN (*See* CONSTANT PAYMENT PLAN, LEVEL ANNUITY PLAN.)

LEVERAGE The borrowing of a portion of the money required for the purchase of an investment at an interest rate less than the rate of return generated by the investment; the result is to raise the rate of return on the equity capital invested.

LIEN A hold, claim, or a charge allowed a creditor upon the lands of a debtor. (*See also* ENCUMBRANCE, TITLE DEFECT.)

LIEN WAIVER Affidavit signed by a contractor or subcontractor certifying that invoices for all labor and materials have been properly submitted and that all lien rights have been waived on payment of such invoices.

LIFE ESTATE A grant or reservation of the right of use, occupancy, and ownership for the life of an individual.

LIFE SUPPORT SYSTEMS All the opportunities, services, and public and private programs required by people in the day-to-day pursuit of their lives.

LIFE TENANT A tenant of a property who may occupy it until his death.

LIGHT INDUSTRY Businesses whose operation requires less land than heavy industry and whose operation normally is not objectionable because of noise, heavy truck traffic, fumes, etc.

"LIKE KIND" [IRS] The nature or character of goods or property, as distinguished from grade or quality.

LIMITATION ON ARTIFICIAL ACCOUNTING LOSSES (LAL) Proposal by George P. Shultz, Secretary of the Department of the Treasury, that would ban the practice of applying deductible losses on certain investments to offset taxes on other unrelated income.

LIMITED ACCESS HIGHWAY A highway, usually provided in a built-up area, designed to permit through traffic to avoid interference from traffic to and from properties built beyond its right-of-way. Also called "controlled access highway."

LIMITED DISTRIBUTION OR LIMITED DIVIDEND MORTGAGOR (LD or ld) [HUD] A mortgagor corporation restricted as to distributions of income by the laws of the state of its incorporation (or by FHA); or a trust, partnership, association, individual, or other entity restricted by law or by FHA as to distributions of income and regulated as to rents, charges, rate of return, and methods of operation in such form and manner as is satisfactory to the FHA to effectuate the purposes of the legislation.

LIMITED PARTNERSHIP A partnership in which the liability of one or more (but not all) of the partners is limited to the amount of capital contributed (or agreed to be contributed) to the partnership. Distinguished from general partnership.

LINE [transportation] Route followed by a scheduled transit system vehicle.

LINE OF NAVIGATION (*See* HARBOR LINE.)

LINK A term of land measurement, equal to 1/100 chain or 66/100 foot.

LIQUIDATION VALUE The price a property would bring if the owner were forced to liquidate it into cash, as distinguished from selling it willingly. Also called the "forced-sale value."

LIQUIDITY The ability to or ease of transforming an investment to cash.

LIS PENDENS A notice recorded in the official records of a county to indicate that a suit is pending affecting the lands where the notice is recorded.

LISTING An agreement, not necessarily in writing, under the terms of which a real estate broker agrees to sell a property for a seller, who agrees to allow the broker to do so, for which the broker will be paid a fee. (*See also* EXCLUSIVE LISTING, MULTIPLE LISTING, OPEN LISTING.)

LISTING CONTRACT   Contract documenting the terms of a listing.

LIVE LOAD   The weight of all moving and variable loads that may be placed on or in a building, such as snow, wind, occupancy, etc. (*See also* DEAD LOAD, DESIGN LOAN.)

LIVING UNIT (LU or lu) (*See* DWELLING UNIT.)

LOAD   (*See* DEAD LOAD, DESIGN LOAD, LIVE LOAD.)

LOAD FACTOR [utilities]   The ratio of the average electrical load over a designated period of time to the peak load in that period.

LOAN   An advance of funds or credit, evidenced by a note secured by a security instrument.

LOAN AGREEMENT   (*See* BUILDING AND LOAN AGREEMENT.)

LOAN AND/OR GRANT CONTRACT [urban renewal]   Contract between HUD and a local public agency for the undertaking of an urban renewal project. Under the contract, the federal government agrees to make a loan and/or a capital grant to the local renewal agency to carry out the project under the terms and conditions stated therein.

This system was rendered obsolete by Title I—Community Development of the Housing and Community Development Act of 1974, which institutes a system of block grants to finance urban renewal-type activities.

LOAN ASSUMPTION   Transaction under which the buyer of a property assumes responsibility for an existing loan or mortgage on the property. The terms of such a transaction establish whether the buyer or the seller becomes or remains personally liable for the original debt.

LOAN COMMITMENT   Decision by a lending institution, after reviewing a loan application and the borrower's qualifications, to issue a loan.

LOAN CONSTANT   (*See* ANNUAL CONSTANT.)

LOAN MATURATION OR MATURITY   The end of the term of a loan.

LOAN ORIGINATION FEE [FHA]   A charge by a mortgagee to a mortgagor to compensate the mortgagee for obtaining FHA approval of the mortgage.

LOAN PACKAGE   Interim (or construction), standby, and permanent financing arrangements.

LOAN RATIO   The ratio of the amount of a mortgage loan to the value of property mortgaged.

LOAN SERVICING   The collection of payments on a loan and the handling of tasks related to such collection activity by or on behalf of a mortgagee or other lender.

LOAN SURVEY   A survey of land prepared by a registered surveyor for a lender prior to the disbursement of loan funds covering the tract or improvements thereon. (*See also* PLAT OF SURVEY, SPOTTED SURVEY.)

LOAN-VALUE RATIO   The amount of a loan in relation to the value of the security for the loan.

LOCAL APPROVAL   Approval by the appropriate unit of local government—usually of the provisions of a project involving federal financial assistance.

LOCAL AUTHORITY   (*See* LOCAL HOUSING AUTHORITY.)

LOCAL GOVERNMENT   Any county, city, village, town, district, or other political subdivision of any state.

LOCAL GRANT-IN-AID [urban renewal]   A contribution made by a state, local, or other entity to assist in the financing of an urban renewal project. Must amount to at least one-third of the net project cost in cities over 50,000 populaion or at least one-fourth in cities under 50,000 population unless the locality bears the full planning, administrative, and legal expenses of the project, in which case the local grant-in-aid is required to cover at least one-fourth the net project cost (in cities over 50,000 population). May be made in the form of cash, land, site clearance, project improvements, supporting facilities, etc.

Under the provisions of Title I—Community Development of the Housing and Community Development Act of 1974, no local grant-in-aid is required to obtain block grant financing.

LOCAL HOUSING AUTHORITY (LHA)   Any state, county, municipality, or other governmental entity or public body which is authorized under state enabling legislation to engage in the development or administration of low-rent public housing or slum clearance.

LOCAL ISSUING AGENCY   Term used to denote either the local public agency or the local housing authority in documents used in both the urban renewal and the low-rent housing programs.

LOCAL PUBLIC AGENCY (LPA)   Synonymous with "local urban renewal agency." Official body empowered to contract with the federal government for assistance in carrying out urban renewal projects. May be a state, county, municipality, or other governmental entity or public body, or two or more such entities, authorized to undertake the project for which federal financial assistance is sought. In most cases it is a separate body, such as a redevelopment authority or a local housing authority, with an unpaid governing policy board or commission, usually appointed by the principal executive officer of a city and served by a professional staff.

Under the provisions of the Housing and Community Development Act of 1974, LPAs may be designated by units of general local government to conduct Title I—Community Development activities.

LOCAL PUBLIC BODY   A county, city, or other political subdivision within which a land development project or part of such project is established and any other political subdivision, public agency, or instrumentality of one or more states, counties, or political subdivisions empowered under law to take or withhold any action required in connection with the establishment of such project.

LOCAL RENEWAL AGENCY   (*See* LOCAL PUBLIC AGENCY.)

LOCAL SERVICE [transportation]   Transit service providing frequent stops at low speeds for pickup and delivery as close to origin and destination as possible.

LOCAL SHARE   A contractor or grantee's share of the cost of a program financed with a federal project grant.

LOCAL SHARE [urban renewal]   The difference between the urban renewal net project cost and the federal share—either one-third or one-fourth. Local share can be paid either in cash or through local grants-in-aid.

There is no "local share" of the cost of Title I—Community Development activities, which are financed by block grants under the provisions of the Housing and Community Development Act of 1974.

LOCAL URBAN RENEWAL AGENCY (*See* LOCAL PUBLIC AGENCY.)

LOCATION ANALYSIS (*See* ANALYSIS OF LOCATION.)

LOCK-IN Characteristic of a mortgage without a prepayment privilege.

LONG-TERM LEASE [urban renewal] [HUD] A lease for a period of time usually more than forty years but in no event less than twenty-five years.

LOS ANGELES AMENDMENT (*See* PHILLIPS AMENDMENT, ROANOKE AMENDMENT.)

LOT A plot, parcel, or tract of land with fixed boundaries, occupied or designated for occupancy by one building and its accessory building(s) or uses. (*See also* CORNER LOT, INTERIOR LOT, THROUGH LOT.)

LOT DEPTH The mean horizontal distance of a lot from the front street line to its rear line.

LOT LINE [HUD] A legally defined line dividing one parcel of property from another.

LOT-LINE WALL [HUD] A wall adjoining and parallel to the lot line used primarily by the party upon whose lot the wall is located. (Lot-line walls may share common foundations.)

LOT WIDTH The mean horizontal distance between the side lines of the lot measured at right angles to the depth.

"LOUISVILLE CASE" 1935 federal court case in which the decision prevented, in effect, the federal Public Works Administration, from acquiring property locally through eminent domain to build housing and returned to the states and their jurisdictions the public control over individual property rights.

LOUVER A screened slotted opening usually at the gable ends of a house installed to provide ventilation. An opening covered by ventilating slats to keep out rain.

LOW- AND MODERATE-INCOME SPONSOR FUND Revolving fund administered by the Secretary of HUD to carry out the purposes of the Section 106 nonprofit sponsor loan program.

LOWER-INCOME FAMILIES As defined in the Housing and Community Development Act of 1974, families whose incomes do not exceed 80 percent of the median income for a given area, as determined by the Secretary of HUD, with adjustments for smaller and larger families—except that the Secretary may establish income ceilings higher or lower than 80 percent of the median for the area on the basis of findings that such variations are necessary because of prevailing levels of construction costs, unusually high or low family incomes, or other factors.

LOWER-INCOME HOUSING A term used in the Housing and Urban Development Act of 1968; refers to housing for persons and families whose income for the most part does not exceed 135 percent of the income limits established for admission to public housing and, for a limited part of the appropriations, not more than 90 percent of the limits established for occupants of projects insured under the Section 221(d)(3) program.

LOW-INCOME FAMILIES Families, including elderly and displaced families, who are in the lowest income group and who cannot afford to pay enough to cause private enterprise in their locality or metropolitan area to build an adequate supply of decent, safe, and sanitary dwellings for their use. (*See also* LOWER-INCOME FAMILIES, VERY LOW INCOME FAMILIES.)

LOW-INCOME HOUSING Housing units which, by reason of rental levels or amount of other charges, are available to families or individuals whose incomes do not exceed the maximum income limits established by the local housing authority (and approved by the HUD Secretary) for continued occupancy in federally assisted low-rent public housing.

LOW-INCOME HOUSING DEMONSTRATION PROGRAM (LRDP) HUD-administered program, repealed in 1971, that provided authority to HUD to contract for demonstration projects to develop improved public housing programs.

LOW-INCOME HOUSING PROJECT Any low-income housing developed, acquired, or assisted by a public housing agency. The improvement of any such housing.

LOW-RENT DEMONSTRATION PROGRAM (LRDP) (*See* LOW-INCOME HOUSING DEMONSTRATION PROGRAM.)

LOW-RENT HOUSING   Generally refers to low-rent public housing.

LOW-RENT HOUSING IN PRIVATE ACCOMMODATIONS [public housing] (*See* LEASED HOUSING.)

LOW-RENT PUBLIC HOUSING   Housing assisted under the provisions of the U.S. Housing Act of 1937 or under a state or local program having the same general purposes as the federal program.

LOW-RISE STRUCTURE   Garden apartment and other walk-up apartment structures in which upper stories are accessible by stairs only, as distinguished from buildings served by elevators, as in high-rise buildings.

LUMBER   (*See* FACTORY AND SHOP LUMBER, STRUCTURAL LUMBER, YARD LUMBER.)

LUXURY HOUSING   Housing units intended for renters or purchasers of substantial income, characterized by more and/or better amenities, services, and facilities available to the occupants, and larger living areas.

MAINTENANCE   (*See* EXTRAORDINARY MAINTENANCE, ORDINARY MAINTENANCE.)

MAJOR COMPLETION GRANT PAYMENT [urban renewal]   A payment from HUD to a local public agency at the time an urban renewal project is substantially completed. This payment, with progress payments, may equal 95 percent of the latest approved estimate of the total project capital grant.

MAJOR DISASTER [HUD]   Any hurricane, tornado, storm, flood, high water, wind-driven water, tidal wave, earthquake, drought, fire, or other catastrophe in any part of the United States which, in the determination of the President, is or threatens to be of sufficient severity and magnitude to warrant disaster assistance by the federal government to supplement the efforts and available resources of states, local governments, and relief organizations in alleviating the damage, loss, hardship, or suffering caused thereby, and with respect to which the governor of any state in which such catastrophe occurs or threatens to occur certifies the need for federal disaster assistance and gives assurance of the expenditure of a reasonable amount of the funds of such state, its local governments, or other agencies for alleviating the damage, loss, hardship, or suffering resulting from such catastrophe. (*See also* SECTION 203(H) DISASTER HOUSING MORTGAGE INSURANCE.)

MALL   Any area in a public place reserved for the use of pedestrians.

MANAGEMENT AGENT or MANAGING AGENT   A person or entity, such as a company, that manages and/or operates a property on behalf of its owner in accordance with a preestablished management plan.

MANAGEMENT AGREEMENT [FHA]   A formal contract between the owner of an FHA-insured project and the management agent or resident manager of a project; must be approved by HUD.

MANAGEMENT PLAN [FHA]   Formal or informal statement prepared by a project sponsor in which are outlined at least most of the following: the sponsor's view of his role and responsibility in the management of a project as well as his proposed relationship with the management agent, if any; discussion of the sponsor's and/or management agent's relationship with the on-site manager; personnel policy and organizational arrangements; marketing plan; admission procedures; equal employment opportunity plans; maintenance plan and program; rent collection arrangements; management-tenant relations plan; accounting system.

MANAGEMENT PROJECT   A project owned by a mortgagor nonprofit cooperative ownership housing corporation or trust which restricts permanent occupancy of the project to the members of the corporation or to the beneficiaries of the trust.

MANDATED PROJECT [urban renewal]   An urban renewal project which, at the time a request to HUD from a local public agency for a grant increase is submitted, had by virtue of a previous grant approval been placed on notice to complete a project within the grant approved. Only certain projects are excepted from the requirements of a mandate.

MANSARD ROOF A roof with two slopes on all four sides, the upper of which is flat or near flat while the lower is very steep.

MANUFACTURED HOUSING (*See* INDUSTRIALIZED HOUSING.)

MARGINALYSIS The study of the dollar differences between a first mortgage on a property and the price paid for similar property sold during the same period. (The term is derived from "price-mortgage margin analysis.")

MARKETABLE TITLE A good title about which there is no fair or reasonable doubt.

MARKET DATA APPROACH A method of appraisal through which the value of a property is established on the basis of prices for comparable property in a comparable market area and period.

MARKET INDICATORS Statistical measures of market activity—e.g., housing market indicators are the numbers of deeds recorded, mortgages placed, foreclosures, rents, lots recorded, building activity, construction costs, vacancies, and housing starts.

MARKET INTEREST RATE (*See* MARKET RATE.)

MARKET RATE (MR) The current rate of interest charged to borrow money in the open market. (On FHA-insured loans, the maximum MR that a lender can charge is fixed by HUD.)

MARKET RENT The highest price charged by owners for real property, based on current prices without consideration of subsidy.

In a Section 236 project: the rental rate necessary to cover vacancy and collection loss and to pay operating expenses, debt service, and mortgage insurance premium requirements on a level annuity mortgage at the market interest rate. (*See also* BASIC RENT.)

MARKET VALUE The price a property would bring from a willing, reasonably knowledgable buyer on the open market. Also called "actual cash value" or "fair cash value."

MASONRY [HUD] A construction of units of such materials as clay, shale, concrete, glass, gypsum, or stone, set in mortar. Plain concrete, because of its structural similarity to masonry, is often considered masonry.

MASONRY WALL [HUD] A bearing wall or nonbearing wall of hollow or solid masonry units.

MASS TRANSIT System of common carriers offering transportation to the public along established routes and on the basis of specific stops and schedules. Also called "public transportation."

MASS TRANSPORTATION The transportation of large numbers of people —usually by a mass transit or public transportation service, according to established schedules and along established routes.

MASTER COOPERATION AGREEMENT (*See* CONSOLIDATED COOPERATION AGREEMENT.)

MASTER DEED The basic document used in creating a condominium; includes a declaration of the rights and obligations of the owners of each unit relative to the condominium—particularly those pertaining to the responsibility for maintenance and repair. (*See also* ENABLING DECLARATION.)

MASTER METER [utilities] Utility meter used in projects where rent includes the cost of utilities. (*See also* CHECK METER.)

MASTER PLAN (*See* GENERAL PLAN.)

MAT FOUNDATION (*See* RAFT OR MAT FOUNDATION.)

MATURING INVESTMENTS Funds available from investments which are maturing at the time a financial statement or report is prepared.

MATURITY DATE The date on which a mortgage indebtedness is extinguished if paid in accordance with periodic payments provided for in the mortgage.

MAXIMUM LOAD POINT [transportation] Point on a mass transit route where the greatest number of passengers has been noted. It is usually quoted for twenty-four-hour periods in both directions. However, occasionally it is quoted for one direction only, or for the peak hour.

MAXIMUM LOAN-TO-VALUE RATIO [FHA] The maximum loan-value ratio that will be permitted in an FHA transaction; the maximum establishes the amount of equity or down payment required of the purchaser.

MECHANICAL SYSTEM The air conditioning and heating system of a building.

MECHANICS' LIEN A lien allowed by statute to contractors, laborers, and materialmen on buildings or other structures upon which work has been performed or materials supplied.

MEDALLION FINANCING   A second mortgage program promoted by the electrical industry to support the greater use of electricity in residential properties. Only new homes are eligible for such financing, and only such homes as include specified electrical appliances and equipment.

MEDICAL OR DENTAL GROUP [HUD]   A partnership or other association of persons licensed to practice dentistry, medicine, osteopathy, podiatry, or optometry in the state who, as their principal professional activity and as a group responsibility, engage in the coordinated practice of their profession in one or more group practice facilities. The group shares common overhead expenses, jointly establishes medical and other records, and jointly uses substantial portions of the equipment and services of professional, technical, and administrative staffs. It is composed of such types of professional personnel and makes available such health services as may be required to meet the standards prescribed by FHA. (*See also* GROUP PRACTICE FACILITY.)

MEGALOPOLIS   Clusters or concentrations of metropolitan areas in a geographic region.

MEMBER [construction]   One part of a unit of a structure.

MERCHANT BUILDER   A builder who builds housing units, usually of his own design and on his own land, for sale or rental to others.

METES AND BOUNDS   A description of land by courses and distances.

METROPOLITAN AREA   The area encompassed by a central city and surrounding municipal or political jurisdictions. (*See also* CENTRAL CITY, STANDARD METROPOLITAN STATISTICAL AREA.)

METROPOLITAN CITY   A city within a metropolitan area which is the central city of such area, as defined by the Office of Management and Budget. Or, any other city within a metropolitan area which has a population of 50,000 or more. (*See also* METROPOLITAN AREA.)

MEZZANINE FLOOR   A low, secondary story between two high stories; usually between the ground and first floors.

MILLWORK   Lumber shaped to a pattern or molded form, in addition to being dressed, matched, or shiplapped.

MINERAL-SURFACED ROLL ROOFING Roofing generally composed of an organic roofing felt, saturated and coated on both sides with asphalt, which may or may not contain fine mineral stabilizer.

MINIMUM FLOOR AREA REQUIREMENT Requirement, usually expressed in a local housing code, stated in terms of minimum floor area per occupant. The American Public Health Association's model housing code requires that a dwelling unit have a minimum floor space (limited to habitable room areas) of 150 square feet for the first occupant and 100 square feet for each additional occupant.

MINIMUM HOUSE SIZE REQUIREMENT Requirement, usually expressed in zoning regulations or deed restrictions, that a house contain a minimum floor area. Distinguished from minimum floor area requirement.

MINIMUM HOUSING CODE (*See* HOUSING CODE.)

MINIMUM HOUSING STANDARD (*See* HOUSING CODE.)

MINIMUM LOT A zoning regulation stipulating the minimum lot size on which construction will be permitted in a given area.

MINIMUM PROPERTY STANDARDS (MPS) [FHA] The overall minimum technical standards of construction acceptable to FHA.

MINIMUM STANDARDS OF OCCUPANCY Legal or socially accepted standards applied to the condition of housing units. (*See* HOUSING CODE.)

MIXED TRAFFIC [transportation] All forms of vehicular traffic, including buses.

MIXED-USE BUILDING A building in which commercial, warehousing, repair shops, and light industry divide space with upstairs or back-room tenants.

MIXED-USE PROPERTY [urban renewal] A property under a single ownership and legal description, including ownership as joint tenants or tenants in common, that after rehabilitation will be used in some part for residential purposes and in some part for nonresidential purposes as permitted under local law and the applicable urban renewal plan.

MOBILE HOME As defined in the Housing and Community Development Act of 1974, a structure, transportable in one or more sections, which is

8 body feet or more in width and is 32 body feet or more in length, which is built on a permanent chassis and designed to be used as a dwelling unit with or without a permanent foundation when connected to the required utilities, and which includes the plumbing, heating, air-conditioning, and electrical systems contained therein.

MOBILE HOME DEVELOPMENT   A development, site, parcel, or tract of land designed, equipped, maintained, or intended to be used to provide relatively long-term accommodations for mobile homes.

MOBILE HOME LOAN INSURANCE   (*See* TITLE I MOBILE HOME LOAN INSURANCE, SECTION 207 MORTGAGE INSURANCE FOR MOBILE HOME COURTS.)

MOBILE HOME PAD   (*See* PAD.)

MODAL SPLIT [transportation]   Statistical division of all traffic into private auto trips and transit trips of various types.

MODEL BUILDING CODE   (*See* NATIONAL CODE.)

MODEL CITIES PROGRAM (MC)   This program has been phased out and supplanted under provisions of Title I—Community Development of the Housing and Community Development Act of 1974. (*See also* DEMONSTRATION CITIES PROGRAM, MODEL CITIES SUPPLEMENTARY GRANTS.)

MODEL CITIES SUPPLEMENTARY GRANTS   Authorized by the Demonstration Cities and Metropolitan Development Act of 1966 and later amendments; authorizes HUD project grants to provide financial assistance to enable cities of all sizes to plan, develop, and carry out locally prepared and scheduled comprehensive demonstration programs containing new and imaginative proposals to rebuild and revitalize large slums and blighted areas.

Supplemental grants may be used for administrative costs related to the implementation of any approved Model Cities program; 100 percent of the cost of relocation may be approved.

Supplemental funds may not be used for costs related to general administration of local government, nor may they be used to replace nonfederal contribution obligated to projects or activities prior to applying for a planning grant.

Any municipality, county, or other public body having general governmental powers (or two or more public bodies jointly) is eligible to be a Model City. Limited to 150 cities which have already been selected.

Neighborhood residents, organizations, and other groups providing services or other assistance to a blighted target area (model neighborhood) located within a model city may benefit.

Applicant must show that the proposed model neighborhood contains serious physical, social, and economic problems and that the contemplated program can deal with these problems and make a substantial impact on the quality of urban life.

Allocations of supplemental grants have been developed through the utilization of a formula based on the population in the model neighborhood and the degree of poverty in the individual city. Section 105(c) of the Demonstration Cities and Metropolitan Development Act of 1966 authorizes the Secretary to make grants to city demonstration agencies "not to exceed 80 percent of the aggregate amount of non-federal contributions otherwise required to be made (by the city) to all projects or activities assisted by federal grant-in-aid programs . . . which are carried out in connection with such demonstration programs." The total eligible non-federal contribution is referred to as "base."

Monetary assistance is available in yearly program increments. A supplemental grant is released to a city in the form of a letter of credit. The city draws against the letter of credit on the basis of actual expenditures.

The phasing out and supplanting of this system is provided for in Title I—Community Development of the Housing and Community Development Act of 1974.

(*See also* DEMONSTRATION CITIES PROGRAM.)

MODEL CODE   (*See* NATIONAL CODE.)

MODEL LEASE [HUD]   A lease form embodying HUD's requirements and recommendations to be included in a lease between landlords and tenants.

MODEL NEIGHBORHOOD AREA (MNA) [Model Cities]   A geographical area in which funds are spent under a program authorized by the Demonstration Cities and Metropolitan Development Act of 1966.

MODERATE-INCOME HOUSING [HUD]   Housing units available at rentals or other charges comparable to those established in the community for housing insured under FHA's Section 221(d)(3) BMIR program.

MODERNIZATION [public housing]   Process of upgrading public housing projects when the local housing authority and HUD deem that the physical condition, location, and outmoded management policies in specific projects "adversely affect the quality of living of the tenants." To obtain HUD modernization funds, the housing authority must, in addition to submitting plans for modernization and rehabilitation of buildings and grounds, involve tenants in such planning and in changing management policies and practices, and in expanding services and facilities available to tenants. Further, to the degree possible, housing authorities are expected to employ tenants in modernization programs.

Modernization programs involve the sale of housing authority bonds and an adjustment in the annual contributions contract.

MODULAR CONSTRUCTION Construction method employing modular components.

MODULE A standardized unit of measurement according to which building materials are manufactured.

MONOLITHIC [construction] A concrete structure poured in one piece.

MONTHLY HOUSING EXPENSE [HUD] Includes payments by an owner for mortgage principal and interest, mortgage insurance premium, service charges, hazard insurance, real estate taxes and special assessments, maintenance and repairs, heating and utilities, and ground rent (where applicable).

MONTHLY TENANT A tenant whose lease provides that either the landlord or the tenant may terminate the lease at the end of a given month; such leases normally require that notice of termination be provided.

MONUMENT OF SURVEY Visible marks or indications left on natural or other objects indicating the lines and boundaries of a survey. May be posts, pillars, stones, cairns, and other such objects, but may also be fixed natural objects, blazed trees, roads, and even a water course.

MORTGAGE An instrument used to encumber real estate as security for a debt.

MORTGAGE [FHA] A first mortgage on real estate, in fee simple or on a leasehold, under a lease for not less than ninety-nine years which is renewable; or under a lease having a period of not less than seventy-five years to run from the date the mortgage is executed; or under a lease executed by a governmental agency for the maximum term consistent with its legal authority, provided such lease has a period of not less than fifty years to run from the date the mortgage is executed. The term "first mortgage" means such classes of first liens as are commonly given to secure advances on, or the unpaid purchase price of, real estate under the laws of the state in which the real estate is located, together with the credit instruments, if any, secured thereby.

MORTGAGE AMOUNT   The amount of a mortgage loan, distinguished from replacement cost or market value of a property against which the loan is obtained. The "principal."

MORTGAGE ASSIGNMENT   The selling of a mortgage by the mortgagee.

MORTGAGE ASSUMPTION   (*See* LOAN ASSUMPTION.)

MORTGAGE-BACKED SECURITIES PROGRAM   Program operated by the Government National Mortgage Association, through which mortgage lenders "pool" FHA- and VA-insured mortgages and sell securities or bonds against them. Such securities or bonds are guaranteed by GNMA with the full faith and credit of the federal government. Proceeds of the sales can be used by the issuers for further home financing.

MORTGAGE BOND OR NOTE   Evidence of the debt incurred through a mortgage.

MORTGAGEE   The original lender under a mortgage and its successors and assigns; includes the holders of credit instruments issued under a trust mortgage or deed of trust pursuant to which such holders act by and through a trustee therein named.

MORTGAGE GUARANTY INSURANCE CORPORATION (MGIC, MAGIC, or Magic)   One of several privately owned mortgage insurance companies that perform a function in the private sector similar to FHA's in the public sector.

MORTGAGE INSURANCE   Insurance of a lender against default by a mortgagor—issued by FHA, VA, or MGIC or other private companies engaged in the business.

MORTGAGE INSURANCE CERTIFICATE [FHA]   Certificate issued by FHA, serving as evidence that a contract of insurance has been executed.

MORTGAGE INSURANCE COMMITMENT [FHA]   (*See* CONDITIONAL COMMITMENT, CONTRACT OF INSURANCE, FIRM COMMITMENT.)

MORTGAGE INSURANCE PREMIUM (MIP) [FHA]   The amount that is paid to FHA for insuring the bank's mortgage loan to the sponsor; generally about 0.5 percent of the mortgage amount.

MORTGAGE PURCHASE   The acquisition of a mortgage by a permanent lender from an interim lender.

MORTGAGE RELIEF [FHA]   Any FHA-insured mortgage transaction which involves a modification of the mortgage forbearance agreement, or other similar relief.

MORTGAGE SERVICING OR MANAGEMENT   (*See* LOAN SERVICING.)

MORTGAGE TAKE-BACK   The issuance of a mortgage by the seller of a property.

MORTGAGE VALUE   The value of a property as established by a lender who would issue a mortgage upon it.

MORTGAGE WRITING   The process of securing financial arrangements between a buyer and seller through a lending institution.

MORTGAGING OUT   Borrowing 100 percent of the cost of a property through a mortgage.

MORTGAGOR   The original borrower under a mortgage and its successors and assigns.

MORTGAGOR CORPORATION   The corporation that has legal responsibility for repaying a mortgage loan.

MOTEL   Building(s) located near highways to provide lodging and other services and facilities to travelers.

MOVING EXPENSES [relocation]   Moving expenses for (1) individuals and families—costs of packing, storing (for a period of one year or less), carting, and insuring of property and incidental costs of disconnecting and reconnecting household appliances; (2) business concerns—costs of dismantling, crating, storing (for a period of one year or less), transporting, insuring, reassembling, reconnecting, and reinstalling of property (including goods or other inventory kept for sale), exclusive of the cost of any additions, improvements, alterations, or other physical changes in or to any structure in connection with effecting such reassembly, reconnection, or reinstallation.

MULTIFAMILY   Usually refers to a building containing more than two dwelling units, designed to be occupied by more than two families.

MULTIFAMILY DEVELOPMENT [HUD]   A development of more than two dwellings; usually associated with garden apartments, townhouses, and high-rises.

MULTIFAMILY PROJECT   Usually means a project containing five or more family units.

MULTIFAMILY RENTAL PROJECT   A project constructed for the purpose of providing rental housing accommodations for eligible tenants.

MULTIFAMILY SALES PROJECT   A project constructed under a blanket mortgage covering a group of not less than eight single-family dwellings constructed for eventual sale to individual purchasers.

MULTIPLE DWELLING   A building or portion of a building designed for occupancy usually by three or more families with independent living quarters for each.

MULTIPLE LISTING   A variation of an exclusive-right-to-sell listing under which a particular agent obtains a listing and distributes it to a number of other brokers—any of which can produce a purchaser; the commission is shared by the listing agent and the broker who produces the purchaser.

MULTIPLE-STAGE PROCESSING   [HUD/FHA] Procedure followed by a sponsor of a proposed multifamily housing project under which the sponsor submits his application for a firm commitment of mortgage insurance. There are three essential stages, each requiring varying exhibits: the first leads to the issuance by HUD of a feasibility letter; the second leads to a conditional commitment by HUD/FHA; the third leads to a HUD/FHA firm commitment. (*See also* SINGLE-STAGE PROCESSING.)

MUNICIPAL BOND   A bond issued by a municipality as a means of obtaining funds with which to finance a given project or activity.

MUNICIPALITY   A county, city, town, or other governmental body chartered by a state to govern itself.

MUTUAL MORTGAGE INSURANCE FUND   Fund used by the Secretary of HUD as a revolving insurance fund covering mortgages insured under Section 203 of the National Housing Act.

MUTUAL SELF-HELP PROGRAM   [HUD]   (*See* SELF-HELP AND MUTUAL SELF-HELP PROGRAMS.

NATIONAL ADVISORY COMMISSION ON LOW-INCOME HOUSING Commission established under provisions of Section 110 of the Housing and Urban Development Act of 1968 to conduct a comprehensive study and investigation of practical and effective ways of bringing decent, safe, and sanitary housing within the reach of low-income families.

NATIONAL BUILDING CODE Model building code published by the American Insurance Association. (*See also* NATIONAL CODE.)

NATIONAL BUREAU OF STANDARDS (NBS) NBS was established by act of Congress on March 3, 1901, as amended, to strengthen and advance the nation's science and technology and facilitate their effective application for public benefit. To this end, the Bureau conducts research and provides: (1) a basis for the nation's physical measurement system, (2) scientific and technological services for industry and government, (3) a technical basis for equity in trade, (4) technical services to promote public safety, and (5) technical information services.

NATIONAL CODE A model or uniform code issued by a national organization (federal or private).

NATIONAL COMMISSION ON URBAN PROBLEMS (*See* DOUGLAS COMMISSION.)

NATIONAL ENVIRONMENTAL POLICY ACT OF 1969 An act to establish a national policy for the environment, to provide for the establishment of a Council on Environmental Quality, and for other purposes. Approved January 1, 1970 and subsequently amended.

NATIONAL FLOOD INSURANCE PROGRAM (*See* FEDERAL INSURANCE ADMINISTRATION, FLOOD INSURANCE.)

"NATIONAL GOALS AND URBAN RENEWAL PRIORITIES" [urban renewal] The priority criteria used by HUD in considering new urban renewal project applications until enactment of Title I—Community Development of the Housing and Community Development Act of 1974. These applied to new survey and planning applications, general neighborhood renewal plans, and feasibility survey applications and intended to reflect the urgency of need for projects directed toward certain national goals, including projects that will provide: (1) more than 50 percent of the net acreage for low- and moderate-income family housing and related uses and (2) more than 50 percent of the housing units to be permitted by the Urban Renewal Plan for clearance sites for low- and moderate-income families.

NATIONAL HOMEOWNERSHIP FOUNDATION Corporation established by Section 107 of the Housing and Urban Development Act of 1968 to encourage private and public organizations at the national, community, and neighborhood levels to provide increased homeownership and housing opportunities in urban and rural areas for lower-income families.

NATIONAL HOUSING ACT Reference to this act usually refers to the National Housing Act of 1934 and its subsequent amendments.

NATIONAL HOUSING ACT OF 1934 Federal law that initiated the mortgage insurance programs of the Federal Housing Administration.

NATIONAL HOUSING AGENCY (NHA) Established by Executive Order No. 9070 of February 24, 1942, NHA held the responsibility for overseeing the operation of nearly all nonfarm housing programs of the federal government except housing located on military or naval reservations or bases. NHA's purview included the functions of the Federal Home Loan Bank Administration, the Federal Housing Administration, and the Federal Public Housing Authority. NHA was succeeded by the Housing and Home Finance Agency in 1947, in accordance with provisions of Reorganization Plan No. 3.

NATIONAL INDUSTRIAL RECOVERY ACT (NIRA) Law passed in 1933 to stimulate employment during the Depression and authorizing the use of federal funds to finance low-cost housing, slum clearance, and subsistence homesteads. The funds built 21,600 public housing units and 15,000 units in so-called greenbelt towns. In charge of the housing programs was a Federal Emergency Administrator of Public Works, appointed by the President.

NATIONAL SCIENCE FOUNDATION (NSF) The Foundation was established by the National Science Foundation Act of 1950 as amended and was given additional authority by the National Defense Education Act of 1958. The Foundation consists of the National Science Board of twenty-four members, a director, a deputy director, and four assistant directors, each appointed by the President with the advice and consent of the Senate. The director is the chief executive officer of the NSF and serves ex officio as a member of the board and as chairman of its executive committee.

The fundamental purpose of the NSF is to strengthen research and education in the sciences in the United States.

NATURAL GRADE The elevation of the original or undisturbed natural surface of the ground.

NECROPOLIS A city whose "life" is considered to be dying or dead.

NEGATIVE RENT Rental system under which certain very low income tenants pay no rent or are reimbursed for paying for their own utilities.

NEIGHBORHOOD A general or specific area within a city or community characterized by being bounded by rather definite (though not necessarily visible) enclosing boundaries, and/or by proximity to an institution or other landmark within the area—such as a school, shopping district, or park—and/or by a sameness of social or economic background of the residents, and/or by the style of architecture of the structures.

NEIGHBORHOOD DEVELOPMENT PROGRAM (NDP) Authorized by Title I of the Housing Act of 1949, as amended; provides HUD project grants, direct loans, and mortgage insurance to provide financial assistance for the rehabilitation or redevelopment of slum or blighted areas.

Provides funding on a two-thirds basis (population over 50,000) and three-fourths basis (population under 50,000) based on the amount of loan and grant funds needed over a twelve-month period in each urban renewal area contained in the community's program. Funding is on a three-fourths basis in areas, irrespective of population, designated as economic development areas by the Economic Development Administration.

On the basis of broad, flexible plans specifying major land uses, density of development, and the public facilities, the program permits urban renewal activities to be initiated in blighted areas with a minimum time lag between the recognition of the need for renewal and the actual start of physical improvement activities.

A contract for a loan or capital grant for the annual increment of a renewal program could cover activities in several contiguous or noncontiguous areas. Funds may not be used for the construction of buildings.

Local public agencies—which can be a local or county renewal agency or housing authority or a local or county department of government—depending upon state enabling legislation are eligible to participate.

The locality must have a currently certified Workable Program for Community Improvement, and the area (or areas) to be assisted must be a slum, blighted, deteriorated, or deteriorating area or a vacant, unused, underused, or inappropriately used area and otherwise acceptable to the Secretary.

The Housing and Community Development Act of 1974 provides for the phasing out of the NDP and for its supplanting through Title I—Community Development block grants.

(*See also* TITLE I URBAN RENEWAL PROJECTS.)

NEIGHBORHOOD FACILITIES GRANTS (*See* SECTION 703 NEIGHBORHOOD FACILITIES GRANTS.)

NEIGHBORHOOD FACILITIES PROGRAM (NF) [HUD] Provides grants to help local public bodies finance development of neighborhood centers to serve low- and moderate-income communities.

Such grants are supplanted by block grants available through Title I—Community Development of the Housing and Community Development Act of 1974.

(*See also* SECTION 703 NEIGHBORHOOD FACILITIES GRANTS.)

NEIGHBORHOOD REHABILITATION The rehabilitation of neighborhoods under the provisions of an Urban Renewal Plan or of a Neighborhood Development Program. Distinguished from a clearance project. (*See also* CLEARANCE PROGRAM, REHABILITATION.)

NET EFFECTIVE INCOME [FHA] A mortgagor's earning capacity, after deductions for federal income taxes that is likely to prevail during the first third of the mortgage term.

NET INCOME Gross income remaining after the payment of operating expenses.

NET LEASE A lease providing for the tenant to pay all costs pertinent to the use of the leased property except the debt service, including utilities, real estate taxes, repairs, maintenance, and insurance.

NET PROJECT COST [urban renewal] The expense involved in acquiring land for an urban renewal project, the cost of preparing it for resale, minus the resale (or "disposition") price received. Net project cost includes all administrative costs, including planning costs but not relocation costs. (*See also* GROSS PROJECT COST, TITLE I URBAN RENEWAL PROJECTS.)

NETWORK [transportation] A sum total of all links of a transit or highway system in a given area for traffic analysis purposes. Its characteristics are described and fed into a computer.

NET WORTH TEST   Guideline employed by the IRS in recognizing the existence of a limited partnership, which provides essentially that when the capital derived by the limited partnership is $2.5 million or less, its corporate general partner's net worth (as defined by IRS) must be at least 15 percent; if the capital amount exceeds $2.5 million, the corporate general partner's net worth must be 10 percent or more of the capital amount.

NEW COMMUNITY   (*See* NEW TOWN. NEW TOWN IN TOWN. TITLE IV NEW COMMUNITIES ASSISTANCE, TITLE VII NEW COMMUNITIES LOAN GUARANTEES, TITLE X MORTGAGE INSURANCE FOR LAND DEVELOPMENT AND NEW COMMUNITIES.)

NEW COMMUNITY DEVELOPMENT CORPORATION   Corporation established within HUD to administer HUD's loan functions and other functions of the New Community Development Program. (Originally named the Community Development Corporation.) (*See also* TITLE VII NEW COMMUNITIES LOAN GUARANTEES.)

NEW COMMUNITY DEVELOPMENT PROGRAM   A program under Section 711 of the Housing and Urban Development Act of 1970 and later amendments intended to result in a newly built community or a major addition to an existing community and meeting the economic, social, environmental, and other standards established by federal statutes, including: (1) economically balanced new communities within metropolitan areas as alternatives to urban sprawl; (2) additions to existing smaller towns and cities which can be economically converted into growth centers to prevent decline and accommodate increased population; (3) major new-town-in-town developments to help renew central cities, including the development of areas adjacent to existing cities for an increase in their tax base; (4) freestanding new communities where there is a clear showing of economic feasibility, primarily built to accommodate population growth. (*See also* TITLE IV NEW COMMUNITIES ASSISTANCE, TITLE VII NEW COMMUNITIES LOAN GUARANTEES, TITLE X MORTGAGE INSURANCE FOR LAND DEVELOPMENT AND NEW COMMUNITIES.)

NEW COMMUNITY LOAN GUARANTY ASSISTANCE   (*See* NEW COMMUNITY DEVELOPMENT PROGRAM, TITLE IV NEW COMMUNITIES ASSISTANCE, TITLE VII NEW COMMUNITIES LOAN GUARANTEES, TITLE X MORTGAGE INSURANCE FOR LAND DEVELOPMENT AND NEW COMMUNITIES.)

NEW TOWN   A new municipality built in an undeveloped area (however close to an existing municipality), intended to be self-governing, relatively self-contained, containing the residential and nonresidential facilities and institutions required to achieve such goals.

Also, large developments on the outskirts of metropolitan areas that are very large subdivisions or planned unit developments served by shopping facilities, schools, churches, and other services and facilities available in most suburban areas.

NEW TOWN IN TOWN   Concept of a new town implemented within a city area, such as in an urban renewal clearance area or a former military installation area.

NONASSISTED PROJECT OR NONASSISTED URBAN RENEWAL PROJECT [urban renewal]   An urban renewal project undertaken by a local public agency for which federal financial assistance is not required but HUD certification of the Urban Renewal Plan is necessary to make the provisions of Section 220 apply to the urban renewal area. An Urban Renewal Plan approved by the local governing body and HUD is necessary.

NONBEARING WALL [HUD]   A wall which supports no vertical load other than its own weight.

NONCASH CREDIT   (*See* NONCASH GRANT-IN-AID.)

NONCASH GRANT-IN-AID   Credits allowed by the federal government for public improvements built with local funds that directly benefit a project receiving federal grant funds. Also called "noncash credit" and "local grant-in-aid." The investment by the city or other local governing body substitutes for a cash payment of the cost of a given federally assisted project.

NONCOMPENSATIVE REGULATIONS   Regulations affecting the use of given land areas that do not provide for compensation of property owners.

NONCONFORMING USE   Use of a building or of land that does not conform with officially established governing regulations.

NONDWELLING FACILITIES [HUD]   Includes site development improvements and facilities located outside building walls, including streets, sidewalks, and sanitary, utility, and other facilities.

NONPROFIT COOPERATIVE HOUSING CORPORATION OR TRUST An organization initiated and organized by bona fide members or stockholders who are the ultimate consumers or by a consumer group or sponsor, the members and organizers of which do not have an identity of interest with the builder or landowner and which conducts all transactions between it and the builder and the landowner on an arm's-length basis.

NONPROFIT MORTGAGOR [FHA] A corporation or association organized for purposes other than the making of a profit or gain for itself or persons identified therewith and which FHA finds is in no manner controlled by or under the direction of persons or firms seeking to derive profit or gain therefrom.

NONPROFIT ORGANIZATION A corporation, association, foundation, trust, or other organization no part of the net earnings of which inures, or may lawfully inure, to the benefit of any private shareholder or individual.

NONPROFIT SPONSOR (NP) (*See* NONPROFIT MORTGAGOR, NONPROFIT ORGANIZATION.)

NONRECOURSE DEBT A debt for which none of the principals is personally liable.

NONWHITE A non-Caucasian, so defined by the Bureau of the Census.

NOTE A promise of payment of a certain sum of money at a specified time.

NOTE [FHA] A note or other evidence of indebtedness executed, upon a form approved by FHA, for use in the jurisdiction where the loan is disbursed.

NOTICES [HUD] HUD statements used to disseminate information of a temporary or "throwaway" nature to categorical program participants. (*See also* CIRCULARS, GUIDES, HANDBOOK.)

NUCLEAR FAMILY The husband, wife, and children; the immediate family. (*See also* EXTENDED FAMILY.)

NUISANCE [code] Anything that unlawfully annoys or does damage to another, including everything that endangers life or health, gives offense to the senses, or obstructs the reasonable and comfortable use of property.

NURSING HOME   A facility operated by a proprietary or nonprofit corporation or association, licensed or regulated by a state or other governmental entity, for the accommodation of convalescents or other persons who are not acutely ill and not in need of hospital care but who require skilled care and related medical services.

NURSING HOME AND INTERMEDIATE CARE FACILITIES MORTGAGE INSURANCE   (*See* SECTION 232 MORTGAGE INSURANCE FOR NURSING HOMES.)

OBSOLESCENCE   The state of having outgrown usefulness—whether because of age, technological change, or whatever.

OCCUPANCY AGREEMENT   Agreement between a buyer and seller under which the buyer is permitted to occupy a property prior to settlement or closing.

OCCUPANCY LIMITATIONS [HUD]   Standard requirements limiting the number of persons who can occupy a dwelling unit, as follows:

Number of bedrooms	Minimum number of persons	Maximum number of persons
0	1	2
1	1*	2
2	2	4
3	4	6
4	6	8

* Only if efficiency unit is not available.

OCCUPANCY STANDARDS [HUD]   To avoid overcrowding, occupancy standards have been established as follows:

Number of of bedrooms	Minimum number of persons	Maximum number of persons
0	1	1
1	1	2
2	2	4
3	4	6
4	6	8
5	8	10
6	10	12

Dwellings should be so designed that: (1) except in the case of infants and very young children, persons of opposite sex (except parents) should not occupy the same bedroom; (3) the living room not be required for sleeping purposes; (3) every member of a family regardless of age should be considered as a person. Large families may be permitted to occupy two units (preferably adjoining) if sufficiently large units are not available (in such instances, the two units are considered as a single accommodation for rent purposes). In certain instances, doubling up of elderly single persons or remaining members of tenant families is permitted.

OCCUPANT CAR RATIO (OCR) [HUD] The number of parking and garage spaces, without time limits, required or available for each living unit on a site.

OCCUPANT MORTGAGOR A mortgagor who occupies the property covered by a mortgage.

OCCUPATIONAL SAFETY AND HEALTH ADMINISTRATION (OSHA) OSHA develops and promulgates occupational safety and health standards, develops and issues regulations, conducts investigations and inspections to determine the status of compliance with safety and health standards and regulations, and issues citations for noncompliance with safety and health standards and regulations.

The Assistant Secretary for Occupational Safety and Health has responsibility for the occupational safety and health activities in the Department of Labor.

OSHA has regional offices established in ten areas throughout the United States.

OFFER TO BUY An expression of willingness in a contract to buy a property on specified terms; an offer results in a contract when a seller accepts an offer without qualification prior to withdrawal of the offer by the prospective buyer.

OFFICE OF ECONOMIC OPPORTUNITY (OEO)   OEO was established within the Executive Office of the President by the Economic Opportunity Act of 1964 as amended. The act provides for the establishment of the National Advisory Council on Economic Opportunity, composed of twenty-one members appointed by the President. The Advisory Council advises the OEO director with respect to policy matters arising in the administration of the act; reviews the effectiveness and operation of programs under the act; and makes recommendations concerning the improvement of such programs, the elimination of duplication of effort, and the coordination of such programs with other federal programs designed to assist low-income individuals and families.

The purpose of OEO is to strengthen, supplement, and coordinate efforts to further the policy of the United States to "eliminate the paradox of poverty in the midst of plenty in this nation by opening to everyone the opportunity for education and training, the opportunity to work, and the opportunity to live in decency and dignity."

Consists of a Headquarters Office in Washington, D.C., and ten regional offices. It is headed by a director, who is assisted by a deputy director and five assistant directors, all of whom are appointed by the President by and with the consent of the Senate.

OFFICE OF EMERGENCY PREPAREDNESS (OEP)   OEP, so designated by act of October 21, 1968, is a redesignation of the Office of Emergency Planning. The basic responsibilities of the Office are prescribed by Executive Order No. 11051 of September 27, 1962. The purpose of OEP is to assist and advise the President in the coordination and determination of policy for all emergency preparedness activities.

OEP is concerned with the following areas of preparedness for a national emergency: use of resources such as manpower, materials, industrial capacity, transportation, and communications; the civil defense program; the organization of government; stabilization of the civilian economy; rehabilitation after enemy attack; continuity of federal, state, and local governments; and administration and coordination of the National Defense Executive Reserve Program.

This Office also determines the kinds and quantities of strategic and critical materials to be acquired and stockpiled against a war emergency under the Strategic and Critical Materials Stock Piling Act of 1946.

It investigates the importation of commodities to determine whether the rate of circumstances of such importation threaten to impair the national security within the terms of Sec. 232 of the Trade Expansion Act of 1962.

This Office coordinates federal assistance to states in coping with major disasters under the Disaster Relief Act of 1970.

OFFICE OF INTERSTATE LAND SALES REGULATIONS (OILSR) [HUD]   (*See* INTERSTATE LAND SALES ADMINISTRATOR.)

OFFICE OF MANAGEMENT AND BUDGET (OMB)   Formerly the Bureau of the Budget, OMB was established in the Executive Office of the President pursuant to Reorganization Plan 2 of 1970, effective July 1, 1970. By Executive Order No. 11541 of July 1, 1970, all functions transferred to the President of the United States by Part I of Reorganization Plan 2 of 1970 were delegated to the Director of OMB. Such functions are carried out by the director under the direction of the President. The Office's functions include aiding the President to bring about more efficient and economical conduct of government service; assisting in developing efficient coordinating mechanisms to implement government activities and to expand interagency cooperation; assisting the President in the preparation of the budget and the formulation of the fiscal program of the government; and controlling the administration of the budget.

OFFICE OF MINORITY BUSINESS ENTERPRISE (OMBE)   The U.S. Department of Commerce OMBE (1) coordinates all federal programs which can be of assistance to minorities who seek to establish or expand business, (2) encourages and assists the minority enterprise efforts of the private sector and coordinates them with federal efforts, (3) assists the development of state and local minority enterprise programs, (4) maintains a national clearinghouse for information on minority business enterprise, (5) stimulates the development of new areas of assistance for minority business development both in public and private sectors, and (6) provides assistance to minority businessmen on a local level through OMBE-affiliated business development organizations. OMBE is the focal point and catalyst in the development of resources which assist minority businessmen. There are no federal grants or loans available from this office.

"OFFICIAL MAP"   Map prepared by an official planning body and adopted by a governing entity as a designation in advance of areas for later public acquisition of land for use as streets, parks, or other public facilities.

OFF-SITE   Something located or occurring outside of a property line, distinguished from on-site.

OFF-SITE CONSTRUCTION   Construction or fabrication of housing units or components at a location away from the building site, usually in a factory. (*See also* PREFABRICATED HOUSING.)

OFF-SITE IMPROVEMENTS   Construction activities that take place off of an actual building lot, such as the installation of streets, curbs, sidewalks, and sewers needed by the building under construction.

OFF-STREET PARKING   Parking spaces located on private property, usually in an area provided especially for such use.

OLDER AMERICANS ACT OF 1965   An act to provide assistance in the development of new or improved programs to help older persons through grants to the states for community planning and services and for training; through research, development, or training project grants; and to establish within the Department of Health, Education, and Welfare an operating agency to be designated the Administration on Aging. Approved July 14, 1965, and subsequently amended.

OMNIBUS CRIME CONTROL AND SAFE STREETS ACT OF 1968   An act to assist state and local governments in reducing the incidence of crime, to increase the effectiveness, fairness, and coordination of law enforcement and criminal justice systems at all levels of government, and for other purposes. Approved June 19, 1968, and subsequently amended.

ON-SITE   Something located or occurring within a property line, distinguished from off-site.

OPEN-END ADVANCE [FHA]   An insured advance of funds made by an approved mortgagee in connection with a previously insured mortgagee pursuant to an open-end provision in the mortgage.

OPEN-END FINANCING   Financing provided in such a manner as to permit the borrower and the lender to increase the amount of a loan for such purpose as to cover the cost of improvements to the property after the initial loan is made.

OPEN-END INSURANCE CHARGE [HUD]   The charge paid by the mortgagee to FHA in consideration of the insurance of an open-end advance.

OPEN-END MORTGAGE   (*See* OPEN-END FINANCING.)

OPEN HOUSING   (*See* OPEN-OCCUPANCY HOUSING.)

OPEN LAND AREA [urban renewal]   An area that has not been developed with buildings or public improvements other than incidental buildings or structures.

OPEN LAND EXCEPTION [urban renewal]　A feature of the urban renewal program designed to provide loans and advances to carry out urban renewal activities on predominantly open land and to provide limited grants to dispose of the land for the development of housing units for persons of low and moderate income.

OPEN LISTING　A listing with any number of real estate brokers.

OPEN-OCCUPANCY HOUSING　Housing units and areas the occupancy of which is unrestricted to any ethnic, racial, economic, or religious group—usually as a matter of conscious management policy.

OPEN SPACE LAND PROGRAM　(*See* TITLE IV OPEN SPACE LAND PROGRAM.)

OPEN SPACE RATIO (OSR) [HUD]　The minimum or available square foot amount of open space which is provided for each square foot of floor area. The OSR is calculated by dividing the open space by the total floor area. For calculating purposes, "open space" is the total land area minus the building area (adjusted for building mass) plus the usable roof area. (*See also* LAND-USE INTENSITY.)

OPEN SPACES　Areas that are not built up; usually intended for recreational or agricultural uses or even scenic purposes.

OPERATING EXPENSES [HUD]　The amounts necessary to meet the normal costs of, and to provide for, operating and maintaining a project and to establish and maintain reasonable and proper reserves for repairs, maintenance, replacements, and other necessary reserves during an operating year; includes mortgage insurance, taxes, premium charges, utilities, special assessments, administrative expenses, insurance charges, and similar expenses.

OPERATING INCOME OR RECEIPTS　Income derived from the operation of a project, from dwelling rental, utility surcharges, nondwelling rental, interest on investments, and sales and services to tenants.

OPERATING SUBSIDY [public housing]　Subsidy paid by the federal government to a local housing authority to compensate for the limitation on rent of 25 percent of a tenant's adjusted monthly income, as a result of the Housing and Urban Development Act of 1970. The operating subsidy funds the amount of the deficit between rents and expenses up to the difference between the annual contributions paid to the authority by the federal government.

OPERATING YEAR [HUD]   The period of twelve consecutive calendar months following the initial occupancy date and each succeeding period of twelve consecutive calendar months.

OPERATION [public housing]   Any or all undertakings appropriate for management, operation, services, maintenance, security (including the cost of security personnel), or financing in connection with a low-income housing project. Includes the financing of tenant programs and services for families residing in such projects, particularly where there is maximum feasible participation of the tenants in the development and operation of such programs and services.

OPERATION BREAKTHROUGH   Program initiated by HUD in 1969, under provisions of Section 108 of the Housing and Urban Development Act of 1968, to stimulate innovations applicable to housing production in construction, land-use costs, management, financing, marketing, user satisfaction, appearance, and the overall environment—through research and development activities financed in large part by HUD.

OPTION AGREEMENT OR CONTRACT   The right acquired, for a consideration, to buy or sell property at a fixed price within a specified time.

ORDINARY MAINTENANCE   Work which, regardless of scope, is a continuing function, performed by the regularly employed staff, seasonal or part-time personnel, or by maintenance contract, and the expenditures for which follow a level trend year after year. (*See also* EXTRAORDINARY MAINTENANCE, PREVENTIVE MAINTENANCE.)

ORGANIZATIONAL EXPENSE [FHA]   (*See* LEGAL AND ORGANIZATIONAL EXPENSES.)

ORIGINATING FEE [FHA]   (*See* LOAN ORIGINATION FEE.)

ORIGIN-DESTINATION SURVEY (O&D or O-D)   Study of the origin and destination of persons, vehicles, or goods—together with identification of their purposes, methods, habits, travel time, etc.

ORTHOGRAPHIC PROJECTION   A drawing in which the projections from the object are perpendicular to the plane of the projection.

OUTER COURT [HUD]   An open, outdoor space enclosed on at least two sides by exterior walls of a building or by exterior walls and property lines on which walls are allowable, with one side open to a street, drive-way, alley, or yard. (*See also* COURT, INNER COURT.)

OUTLYING AREA HOMES MORTGAGE INSURANCE [*See* SECTION 203(I) MORTGAGE INSURANCE FOR HOMES IN OUTLYING AREAS.]

OUTSTANDING INDEBTEDNESS RELATING TO THE PROPERTY The total out-standing amount of unsecured obligations of the borrower incurred in connection with improving, repairing, or maintaining a property and out-standing mortgages or obligations constituting liens on the title to the property to be improved.

OVERALL ECONOMIC DEVELOPMENT PROGRAM (OEDP) Program which, when approved by the Administrator of the Economic Development Ad-ministration, entitles an area to assistance from the Economic Develop-ment Administration.

OVERCROWDING The occupancy of dwellings, buildings, or neighbor-hoods by more persons than such facilities were designed to shelter or to a degree that imperils the health, safety, and welfare of such occupants. (*See also* EXTENT OF HOUSING OVERCROWDING, OCCUPANCY STANDARDS.)

OVERFINANCING The result of an investment which does not produce a positive cash flow after amortization, or if the amount of a loan exceeds the value of the property financed.

OVERIMPROVEMENT An improvement too elaborate or expensive in its locale in relation to other improvements in the immediate vicinity.

OVERINCOME TENANTS Tenants whose income is beyond the point which permits them to occupy certain housing or which entitles them to an amount of subsidy.

OWNER-ARCHITECT AGREEMENT Contract between an architect and the owner of a project stipulating the services to be performed and the fee to be paid to the architect.

OWNER-BUILDER Person acting as his own general contractor in building housing for his own use.

OWNER-OCCUPANT Property owner who occupies a property. Distin-guished from absentee landlord or owner.

OWNERSHIP The right to possess and use property to the exclusion of others.

P

PACKAGER (*See* CONSULTANT.)

PAD The area in a mobile home park allocated for the placement of a mobile home unit.

PANELIZED HOUSE House built with components assembled in a factory—such as floor, wall, and roof system.

PANEL SYSTEM [construction] (*See* SLAB SYSTEM.)

PARAPET A wall or barrier at the edge of a bridge, top of a building, retaining wall, cliff, or other steep descent for the protection of pedestrians.

PARAPET WALL [HUD] That part of any wall entirely above the roof of a building.

PARCEL Any tract or contiguous tracts of land in the same ownership, whether one or more platted lots or parts of lots.

PARK A geographically delineated area, usually but not necessarily owned and maintained by a governing body, intended to serve the recreational or leisure-time needs of a certain population.

PARKWAY An arterial highway designed to serve only noncommercial vehicles, generally characterized by its location within a park, or bordered by grass and trees to create a parklike setting.

PART I APPLICATION [urban renewal] The portion of a formal application from a local public agency for loan and grant contract submitted to

HUD which includes the detailed documentation of the renewal project plans and evidence of their legal sufficiency.

PART II APPLICATION [urban renewal]   That portion of a formal application for loan and grant to HUD which contains the local project approval data in connection with a proposed urban renewal project. This approval data includes formal evidence of local governmental approval of and co-operation with the project plans perfected by the local public agency and accepted by HUD.

PARTERRE   Ornamental bed of flowers in a formal garden, intended for viewing from walks through a garden.

PARTIAL TAKING   The condemnation of only a part of a property for a public purpose.

PARTICIPATIONS   Loans in which investors, usually lending institutions with excess investment funds, purchase an interest in mortgages held by other investors with excess loan demands.

PARTITION ACTION   The legal separation of real estate interests between or among parties holding an interest in such real estate.

PARTNERSHIP   (*See* GENERAL PARTNERSHIP, LIMITED PARTNERSHIP, TWO-TIER PARTNERSHIP.)

PARTY WALL [HUD]   A wall, used jointly by two parties under easement agreement, erected upon a line separating two parcels of land, each of which is a separate real estate entity.

PASSIVE INVESTOR   An investor who invests only equity capital and does not take any active role in the packaging, building, or managing of a project. Distinguished from active investor.

PASS-THROUGH   Tax advantage of a limited partnership which permits income, profit, loss, and deductions to pass through the legal structure of the organization of the respective limited partners for their benefit rather than the partnership's. Also called "flow-through."

PATENT [real estate]   A document issued for the purpose of granting public lands to an individual.

PATIO   A surfaced outdoor living space designed to supplement the basic indoor living area.

PAYBACK PERIOD The number of months needed to completely return an initial investment.

PAYMENT BOND A bond conditioned upon the payment of money by a principal to persons under contract with him.

PAYMENT IN LIEU OF TAXES [PILOT] Payments of a sum of money by a tax-exempt or tax-excused property owner to a taxing authority in amounts presumably commensurate with the cost of public services provided to such owner.

PEAK HOUR [transportation] A sixty-minute period on an average week-day when the greatest number of people travel past a given point.

PENTHOUSE [HUD] A structure located on the roof of a building to pro-vide living accommodations or to house mechanical systems equipment. When the area of the penthouse exceeds 20 percent of the roof area or when the penthouse is to serve as living accommodations, the penthouse is considered as another story (or half story, depending on its dimensions).

PERCENTAGE LEASE Lease arrangement under which the tenant's rent is based on a percentage of the tenant's gross or net income.

PERCENTAGE RENT (*See* PERCENTAGE LEASE.)

PERFORMANCE BOND A surety bond guaranteeing the performance of a specific act under a contract.

PERFORMANCE CODE A building code establishing design and engineer-ing criteria without reference to specific methods of construction—as dis-tinguished from a specification code.

PERFORMANCE STANDARD REGULATIONS OR ZONING Regulations limit-ing the amount of smoke, noise, or odor that commercial or industrial facilities may produce.

PERGOLA Open garden structure enclosing part of a path or walk, with vines or pleached trees often trained overhead.

PERIOD OF OWNERSHIP BY SERVICEMAN [FHA] That period of time during which a military service is required to pay mortgage insurance premiums to FHA, commencing with the date FHA endorses a mortgage for insurance and terminating when the Secretary of Defense furnishes

FHA with a certificate indicating that the military service will no longer be liable for payment of such insurance premiums.

PERMANENT FINANCING [FHA]   Mortgage loan which covers a stipulated percentage of total development cost, including the interim loans, construction loan, financing expenses, marketing, administrative costs, legal costs, and other expenses attributable to the development; this loan differs from the construction loan in that this financing takes place after the project is constructed and open for occupancy.

PERMANENT LOAN AGREEMENT OR CONTRACT [public housing]   Loan from HUD to a local housing authority to finance the costs of preparing feasibility studies and other costs incidental to the advance planning of a public housing project.

PERRON   A stepped ramp, usually 6 feet 3 inches between risers.

PERSONAL LIVING UNIT SYSTEM (PLUS) [construction]   An American building system that features the stacking and/or steel frame support of steel-faced modular box-type construction units.

PERSPECTIVE DRAWING   The drawing of an object showing the three dimensions that appear to the eye.

PG-46   (*See* HUD PG-46.)

PHILLIPS AMENDMENT   A proviso in federal statutes that, unless the governing body of a locality agrees to its completion, no public housing can be built or completed in a community where the people, by their elected officials or by referendum, have indicated they do not want it; the amendment also provides for the disposition of such projects and the liability for costs. Also called "Los Angeles Amendment." (*See also* ROANOKE AMENDMENT.)

PHYSICAL ASSET   (*See* TANGIBLE ASSET.)

PHYSICAL COMPLETION DATE [HUD]   The last day of the calendar month in which the construction of a project is substantially completed and substantially all of the dwellings or space are available for occupancy.

PHYSICAL PLANT   The grounds, buildings, and equipment, both movable and stationary, of a project.

PHYSICAL SECURITY   The land and all improvements within the boundaries of a lot.

PIECE OF THE ACTION   A sharing of the profits or other disbursements of a profit-making enterprise.

PIER   A masonry or concrete column supporting foundations or the floor structure in crawl spaces. May be freestanding or bonded at its sides to other masonry or concrete.

PILASTER [HUD]   A pier forming part of a masonry or concrete wall, partially projecting therefrom and bonded thereto.

PILE FOUNDATION [HUD]   A building foundation system composed of timber, concrete, or steel members driven vertically to a hard soil or rock strata which will support the design load.

PILING   Wood or concrete posts driven into the earth to provide adequate footing for heavy loads.

"PIPELINE"   Figuratively, the place where applications, usually for federal financial assistance, wait to be processed or approved by appropriate federal agencies.

PLACE   An open, unoccupied space, other than a street or alley, usually at least 10 feet wide, permanently reserved as the principal means of access to abutting or adjacent property.

PLACEMENT FEE   (*See* DISCOUNT POINTS.)

PLACEMENT IN INELEGIBILITY STATUS [HUD]   A disqualification from participation in HUD programs pending the elimination of the circumstances which constitute the basis for imposition of the disqualification.

PLANNED DEVELOPMENT ZONING   An extension of the concept of planned unit development, in which no intensive use of land is permitted except as part of a large-scale planned development; development of small tracts is permitted only if they are planned as an integral part of the overall development of a larger area.

PLANNED UNIT DEVELOPMENT [PUD]   Zoning classification permitting flexibility of site design by combining building types and uses in ways that would be prohibited by the detailed predeterminations of traditional zoning standards—e.g., instead of lot-by-lot requirements, some such requirements are applied to an entire zoned area. Discretionary public review of proposed site plans or designs is required. (*See also* PLANNED DEVELOPMENT ZONING.)

PLANNED VARIATIONS A demonstration conducted by the Department of Housing and Urban Development in sixteen cities participating in the Demonstration Cities Program to develop the special revenue sharing concept.

PLANNING In the simplest terms, the identification of short- and long-term needs and problems relating to a given effort and the identification of resources existing or needed to meet such needs or to solve such problems. (*See also* CITY PLANNING.)

PLANNING [urban renewal] (*See* URBAN RENEWAL PLANNING.)

PLANNING ADVANCE [urban renewal] A repayable advance of federal funds to a local public agency to finance surveys and planning for an urban renewal project. Repayable with interest out of any funds which become available to the local public agency for the actual execution of the project.

PLANT (*See* PHYSICAL PLANT.)

PLANTING PLAN Map showing building outlines and existing and new trees, planting, lawn areas, etc.

PLAT [real estate] (*See* PLOT.)

PLAT OF SURVEY A scaled drawing identifying a parcel of real estate, prepared by a registered surveyor, including a legal description of the property and the dimensions of the physical improvements. (*See also* LOAN SURVEY, SPOTTED SURVEY.)

PLINTH [HUD] A solid concrete or masonry block at the base of a column.

PLOT [real estate] A map representing a tract of land subdivided into lots, with streets shown thereon. Also, the act of preparing a plat or plot. Used interchangeably with "plat."
[HUD] A parcel of land consisting of one or more lots or portions thereof, which is described by reference to a recorded plat or by metes and bounds. (*See also* METES AND BOUNDS.)

PLOTTAGE (*See* ASSEMBLAGE.)

POINTING The filling and finishing of joints in a masonry wall as a preventive measure against the deterioration of such wall.

POINTS (*See* DISCOUNT POINTS.)

POLICE POWER The authority of a political jurisdiction to establish and to enforce its laws, ordinances, and other regulations.

POLICY [real estate] A written contract of title insurance.

POPULATION IMPLOSION The concentration of people on relatively small portions of land.

PORTLAND CEMENT Common gray cement; called "portland" because it resembles the gray limestone from the Isle of Portland.

POST-AND-BEAM BUILDING A method of building characterized by the cross beams resting on vertical posts.

POTENTIAL VALUE Value anticipated for a property if certain specific occurrences affecting its value should occur.

POVERTY According to the Social Security Administration, poverty exists when a family must spend more than a third of its income on food. (*See also* EXTENT OF POVERTY.)

POVERTY AREA Group of census tract areas that ranks relatively low in terms of a composite index covering family incomes, educational background, family stability, employment, and housing conditions.

POWER OF SALE [real estate] A clause inserted in a will, deed, or trust or trust agreement authorizing the sale or transfer of land in accordance with the terms of the clause.

PREDETERMINED PRICES FOR SUBDIVISIONS OF SMALL PARCELS [urban renewal] Method of offering urban renewal project land in which the local renewal agency establishes the schedule of prices for a subdivision of small parcels of similar character and proposed uses and then offers the parcels primarily to separate purchasers.

PREDOMINANTLY OPEN LAND AREA [urban renewal] An area developed at least to the extent of having deteriorated or obsolete improvements, such as buildings, surfaced streets, sidewalks, or utilities.

PREDOMINANTLY RESIDENTIAL AREA [urban renewal] The present character of an area is predominantly residential if 51 percent or more of the land, exclusive of land used for streets, alleys, or public rights-of-way, consists of:

1. Improved parcels occupied by any of the following: (*a*) dwellings or institutional facilities used for dwelling purposes; (*b*) public, semipublic, or institutional residential neighborhood facilities which are incidental to, are necessary for, and directly serve and support dwelling facilities in the residential neighborhood of the urban renewal areas; (*c*) buildings which are residential in character both as to exterior design and interior arrangement, notwithstanding present temporary nonresidential uses.

2. Improved parcels used for both residential and nonresidential purposes if 51 percent or more of floor space is devoted to residential use.

3. Unimproved parcels which, on the basis of the circumstances, are considered to be residential in character, including (*a*) parcels used for residential purposes (e.g., private parking, house gardens); (*b*) parcels intermingled with improved residential parcels or with residential-type site improvements in an area that is appropriate for continued residential use. Such a determination must be supported by evidence that prevailing conditions in the area, such as land-use planning or zoning, make residential development the expected type of use of the land.

4. Parcels clearly in excess of the needs of (*a*) the buildings on them and (*b*) the appurtenant uses, and the excessive portion meets the criteria for unimproved parcels in (3) above.

When the residential or nonresidential character of a particular parcel is uncertain, it is considered nonresidential in character.

PREENTRY LOSSES   Tax deductible expenses that occur prior to the beginning of construction of a project; that is, prior to initial closing.

PREEXISTING USE   In zoning, a certain land use that existed prior to the establishment of a different zoning classification; usually implies that the preexisting use does not comply with the zoning classification.

PREFAB BELT   An area, comprised essentially of Illinois, Indiana, Michigan, Ohio, and Wisconsin, where a concentration of prefab, sectionalized housing, mobile home, and industrial housing plants is located.

PREFABRICATED HOUSING (prefab)   Housing with structural and/or mechanical components assembled off-site. (*See also* OFF-SITE CONSTRUCTION.)

PREFEASIBILITY CONFERENCE [HUD]   Conference held between the principals of a project and HUD Area Office or Insuring Office personnel prior to submitting an application or a proposal for development under a HUD program.

PRELIMINARY LOAN [public housing]   A loan by HUD to a local housing authority to cover the costs of preliminary surveys, optioning of sites, and planning and preparation of a development program for a low-rent public housing project.

PRELIMINARY RESERVATION [FHA]   An advance commitment to a builder or seller of Section 235 housing that funds will be available for assistance payments when homes are sold to families who qualify for such assistance.

PREPAYMENT PENALTY [HUD]   A mortgage prepayment penalty cost is any cost incurred by a seller, in connection with the prepayment of a mortgage in good standing, in excess of the unpaid principal plus accrued interest thereon on the date title to the property transfers to a purchaser. (*See also* LOCK-IN.)

PREPAYMENT PRIVILEGE   The provision in a mortgage permitting the mortgagor to prepay the mortgage in whole or in part upon any interest payment date after giving the mortgagee (usually) thirty days advance notice, (usually) in writing, of intention to prepay, without charge for such prepayment. (*See also* LOCK-IN.)

PRESENT VALUE RATE OF RETURN   (*See* DISCOUNTED RATE OF RETURN.)

PRESIDENT'S DOMESTIC COUNCIL   (*See* DOMESTIC COUNCIL.)

PREVAILING WAGE RATES   Wage ratio determined by the Department of Labor to be those prevalent in a given project area. (*See also* DAVIS-BACON ACT.)

PREVENTIVE MAINTENANCE   The maintenance action taken, on the basis of regular methodical inspections, to avoid or minimize costly measures at some future time. (*See also* EXTRAORDINARY MAINTENANCE, ORDINARY MAINTENANCE.)

PRINCIPAL   The amount of a debt.

PRINCIPAL [bonding]   In the case of a bid bond, a person bidding for the award of a contract or the person primarily liable to complete a contract for the obligee, or to make payments to other persons in respect of such contract, and for whose performance of his obligation the surety is bound under the terms of a payment or performance bond.

PRINCIPAL [FHA]   Individuals, corporations, joint ventures, and partnerships having any interest in a project or participating as a sponsor, owner, general contractor, project manager or management agent, and packager or consultant. Includes architects and attorneys who have any interest in a project other than arms-length fee arrangements for professional services. If the principal is a corporation or partnership, the term includes general partners, corporate officers, and directors and all stockholders and limited partners having 10 percent or more interest in the organization.

PRINCIPAL OBLIGATION   The amount owed by a mortgagor.

PRIVATE GARAGE [HUD]   A garage building designed for the storage of not more than four motor vehicles. (*See also* COMMERCIAL GARAGE, COMMUNITY GARAGE, PUBLIC GARAGE.)

PRIVATE MORTGAGOR—NONPROFIT   A corporation or association organized for purposes other than the making of profit or gain for itself or persons identified therewith and which FHA finds is in no manner controlled by or under the direction of persons or firms seeking to derive profit or gain therefrom. Such a mortgagor is regulated or supervised under federal or state laws or by political subdivisions of states or agencies thereof, or FHA, as to rent charges and methods of operation. The regulation or supervision of the mortgagor is in such manner as prescribed by FHA. (*See also* NONPROFIT MORTGAGOR, NONPROFIT ORGANIZATION.)

PRIVATE MORTGAGOR—PROFIT [FHA]   Any mortgagor approved by FHA which, until the termination of all obligations of FHA under the insurance contract and during such further period of time as FHA remains the owner, holder, or reinsurer of the mortgage, may in FHA's discretion be regulated or restricted as to rents or sales, charges, capital structure, rate of return, and methods of operation.

PRIVATE NEW COMMUNITY DEVELOPER   Any private entity organized in a form satisfactory to HUD for carrying out one or more new community development programs.

PROCEED ORDER   A written order to a general contractor to proceed with a change in contract requirements, subject to a later equitable adjustment of the contract price and/or time for completion as provided in the contract. The order must state a limiting amount. (*See also* CHANGE ORDER.)

PROCLAIMER [urban renewal]   A procedure instituted by HUD on December 15, 1970, through which a local public agency may "proclaim" to HUD that certain local agency program actions were carried out or that given program determinations were made in compliance with existing statutory and HUD administrative requirements.

Through this procedure, the local agency presumably saves the time required to obtain certain HUD approvals and to submit certain documents otherwise required by HUD. (A local agency's proclaimer procedures are subject to HUD audit.)

PROFIT MORTGAGE [FHA]   A mortgage which is or has been insured under any of the FHA multifamily housing programs other than Sections 213(a)(1) and 213(a)(2) of the act.

PRO FORMA   In form only; not necessarily official.

PROGRAM RESERVATION [public housing]   The reservation by HUD of funds for the development of a public housing project by a local housing authority.

PROGRESS PAYMENTS   Periodic payments from a construction loan made to a general contractor, based upon the progress in the completion of his contract; such payments earn interest to the lender as of the day the funds are disbursed. Also called "draw" or "take down."

PROJECT   (*See* HOUSING PROJECT.)

PROJECT AREA COMMITTEE (PAC) [urban renewal]   Committee comprised of residents of an urban renewal project area, representative of a cross-section of area residents, to assist the local renewal agency to carry out its responsibility to allow citizen participation in the renewal process.

PROJECT BOUNDARIES [urban renewal]   Official boundary of an urban renewal project, outside of which a local public agency has no specific administrative powers or jurisdiction.

PROJECT CAPITAL GRANT PROGRESS PAYMENTS [urban renewal]   Periodic payments from HUD to a local renewal agency during project execution; the payments may aggregate up to 75 percent of the latest approved estimate of the grant payable.

PROJECT EXECUTION [urban renewal]   The actual carrying out of an urban renewal project, after the Urban Renewal Plan and other basic plans have been approved and a loan and grant contract entered into. A project reaching the execution stage has passed from the planning to the "doing" phase. Basic execution stage activities are land acquisition and clearance, relocation of displacees, site improvements, disposition of cleared land, and the accomplishment of voluntary rehabilitation activities by property owners.

PROJECT GRANT   Grant approved for a particular project or activity according to established criteria and regulations. Distinguished from formula grant.

PROJECT IMPROVEMENT [urban renewal]   A street, utility, park, playground, or other public improvement exclusive of any building that is installed, constructed, or reconstructed within the boundaries of an urban renewal project area. It also must qualify under HUD criteria as necessary for carrying out the objectives of the Urban Renewal Plan. A project improvement may be financed with Title I loan funds or it may be provided as a noncash local grant-in-aid.

PROJECT INITIATION DATE [public housing]   The date of the first contract for federal financial assistance for a public housing project between the federal government and a local housing authority.

PROJECT LOAN NOTE [urban renewal]   Note issued by a local public agency at the time a contract is executed with the federal government, for deposit with the government, to evidence the local public agency's obligation for loans or advances made by the government pursuant to the contract.

PROJECT NOTE   Short-term notes to be sold on the private market by the local issuing agency, which are secured by a pledge by the local issuing agency of its loan rights under the contract with the federal government.

PROJECT NOTIFICATION AND REVIEW SYSTEM (PN&R or PNRS) (A-95 Review)   Requirement, established in the Office of Management and Budget's circular number A-95, that state and local public bodies applying for federal financial assistance for given purposes coordinate applications for such assistance through established state, metropolitan, and regional clearinghouses (such as planning agencies) prior to approval of the applications by the federal agencies administering the given programs. The procedure was established pursuant to provisions of Title IV of the Intergovernmental Corporation Act of 1968, Section 204 of the Demonstration Cities and Metropolitan Development Act of 1966, and Section 102(2)(c) of the National Environmental Policy Act of 1969.

PROJECT REHAB   A HUD effort initiated in July 1969 to encourage large-scale rehabilitation as an approach to providing standard housing for low- and moderate-income residents of central cities as well as for meeting a portion of the nation's housing production goals established in the Housing and Urban Development Act of 1968; the program was intended to be primarily an FHA undertaking.

PROJECT SELECTION CRITERIA   Criteria established by HUD for the approval of sites on which are to be built subsidized housing projects. Under the criteria, sites are rated according to the degree to which they comply with court decisions that have blocked construction of new subsidized housing in areas of minority concentration unless such housing is also built in outlying nonminority neighborhoods.

PROPERTY [HUD]   A lot or plot including all buildings and improvements thereon.

PROPERTY BETTERMENT EXPENSES   Expenditures for extraordinary replacements which result in a substantial betterment of structures, sites, or nonexpendable equipment. Distinguished from repair and maintenance expenses.

PROPERTY LINE   A recorded boundary of a lot or plot.

PROPERTY MANAGEMENT [urban renewal]   Functional responsibility of a local public agency to:

1. Provide maximum assistance, advice, and counsel to project residents until their relocation is completed.

2. Provide a high level of security and protection to project residents and private property.

3. Maintain occupied property in a safe, habitable condition and cleared land in a neat, orderly manner that will have a positive influence on the project area. Supplementary maintenance services must be provided to the extent necessary to eliminate health, safety, and fire hazards, to promote the dignity of the residents, and to improve the neighborhood environment.

4. Make maximum use of project residents and other persons in the locality to perform property management services to reduce unemployment and to upgrade the earnings of the underemployed.

5. Charge fair and equitable rents, taking into consideration the condition of the property, the condition of the project area, and the terms and conditions of occupancy.

6. Coordinate property management services with social service and public assistance programs to the fullest extent practicable.

7. Complete property management activities, consistent with the above, at the earliest possible time to avoid delays in project completion.

PROPERTY REHABILITATION STANDARDS (PRS) [urban renewal] The combination of local code standards and rehabilitation requirements which are established by a local public agency for properties to be retained in a rehabilitation area.

PROPERTY TAX A tax on real estate.

PROPRIETARY LEASE Lease issued by a cooperative to purchasers of shares in the corporation providing the purchaser with the right to occupancy for a long term and with a restricted right to sell his shares to a third party.

PRO-RATE [real estate] To allocate between seller and buyer their proportionate share of an obligation paid or due.

PROTECTED PASSAGEWAY [HUD] An exit passage such as from interior stairs to the outside of a building or tunnels discharging to the outside of the building.

PROTOTYPE COST LIMITS Generally refers to the maximum loan amount permitted for the construction of assisted housing units, based upon HUD's interpretation of the cost of constructing similar units in a similar market area. However, certain prototype cost limits are established by statutory regulation. (*See also* STATUTORY ROOM COST.)

PUBLIC AUCTION [urban renewal] Method of offering urban renewal project land in which land is offered at public auction, with a publicly announced minimum bid. A variation provides for execution, prior to announcement of the auction, of a firm agreement with a potential redeveloper that agrees to make a specified minimum bid which the local public agency agrees to accept if there are no higher bids.

PUBLIC BOND A bond issued by a public agency such as a federal, state, or local governmental entity.

PUBLIC CORPORATION A corporation established by a governmental entity to perform a certain function—usually because such function can be better performed outside of the governmental entity.

PUBLIC DOMAIN Land owned by government.

PUBLIC GARAGE [HUD]   A garage building designed for the storage of five or more motor vehicles, for the use of the residents of a multifamily project or their visitors. (*See also* COMMERCIAL GARAGE, COMMUNITY GARAGE, PRIVATE GARAGE.)

PUBLIC HEALTH SERVICE (PHS)   The Service had its origin in an act of July 16, 1798, authorizing marine hospitals for the care of American merchant seamen. Subsequent legislation has vastly broadened the scope of its activities.

PHS consists of three operating agencies: the Health Services and Mental Health Administration, the National Institutes of Health, and the Food and Drug Administration. Unified direction of these agencies is the responsibility of the Assistant Secretary for Health of HEW.

PHS is specifically charged with promoting and assuring the highest level of health attainable for every individual and family. It is also responsible for collaborating with governments of other countries and with international organizations in world health activities.

The major functions of the Service are (1) to identify health hazards in products and services which enter man's life, to develop and promulgate, and assure compliance with, standards for control of such hazards; (2) to support the development of, and improve the organization and delivery of, comprehensive and coordinated physical and mental health services for all Americans, and provide direct health care services to limited federal beneficiary populations; and (3) to conduct and support research in the medical and related sciences, promoting the dissemination of knowledge in these sciences, and further the development of health education and training to ensure an adequate supply of qualified health manpower.

PUBLIC HEARING [urban renewal]   A hearing required by statute before land may be acquired for an urban renewal project by the local governing body. Provides an opportunity for interested persons and organizations to present their views concerning an urban renewal project.

PUBLIC HOUSING   Housing assisted under the provisions of the United States Housing Act of 1937 or under a state or local program having the same general purposes as the federal program. Distinguished from privately financed housing, regardless of whether federal subsidies or mortgage insurance are features of such housing development.

PUBLIC HOUSING ACQUISITION   (*See* ACQUISITION—WITH REHABILITATION. ACQUISITION—WITHOUT REHABILITATION.)

PUBLIC HOUSING ADMINISTRATION (PHA)   Federal agency that succeeded the U.S. Housing Authority and operated as a constituent of the Housing and Home Finance Agency until the establishment of the Department of Housing and Urban Development in 1965, when HUD assumed responsibility for PHA operations, including the administration of the provisions of the U.S. Housing Act of 1937.

PUBLIC HOUSING AGENCY   (*See* LOCAL HOUSING AUTHORITY.)

PUBLIC HOUSING MODERNIZATION   (*See* MODERNIZATION.)

PUBLIC HOUSING PROJECT   A housing project owned and operated by a local housing authority. Should not be confused with housing projects owned and operated by nonprofit organizations or limited-distribution mortgagors receiving federal subsidies through the Federal Housing Administration.

PUBLIC INTEREST GROUPS (PIGS)   Trade, professional, and other private associations and groups that singly or in concert attempt or purport to represent the public interest in dealings with Congress or federal agencies.

PUBLIC LAND ASSEMBLY   The assembly by a governmental unit of development tracts under which the power of eminent domain or acquisition through negotiation is used as a means of assuring orderly private development.

PUBLIC MORTGAGOR   A corporation or trust approved by the FHA, which is also a federal or state instrumentality, a municipal corporate instrumentality of one or more states, or a limited dividend or redevelopment or housing corporation formed under and restricted by federal or state laws or regulations of a state banking or insurance department as to rents, charges, capital structure, rate of return, or methods of operation.

PUBLIC OFFICIAL   An appointed, elected, or employed representative of a public body or agency.

PUBLIC PURPOSE   A purpose that will benefit the general public welfare.

PUBLIC SERVICE GRANTS   Grants made by HUD pursuant to Title VII of the Housing and Urban Development Act of 1970 to help defray the initial costs of essential public services (including schools) with respect to the development of new communities. (*See also* TITLE VII COMMUNITY DEVELOPMENT TRAINING GRANTS.)

PUBLIC TRANSPORTATION   (*See* MASS TRANSIT.)

PUBLIC USE   Use that will serve the general public, as distinguished from only certain individuals.

PUBLIC UTILITY   A private or public corporation operating under a more or less exclusive franchise, regulated by governments, to provide a certain service or product to the general public—e.g., gas, electricity, telephone, transportation.

PUBLIC WATER OR SEWER SYSTEM   [HUD]   One which is owned and operated by a local government authority or by a local public utility company adequately controlled by a government authority. Distinguished from community water or sewer system.

PUBLIC WORKS AND ECONOMIC DEVELOPMENT ACT OF 1965   An act to provide grants for public works and economic development facilities, other financial assistance, and the planning and coordination needed to alleviate conditions of substantial and persistent unemployment and underemployment in economically distressed areas and regions. Approved Aug. 26, 1965, and subsequently amended. (*See also* ECONOMIC DEVELOPMENT ADMINISTRATION.)

PUNCH LIST   A record of incomplete or unsatisfactory items of work covered by a contract.

PURCHASE MONEY MORTGAGE   Mortgage in which the seller becomes the mortgagee.

PURCHASING COOPERATIVE   [HUD]   The mortgagor of a management project which has purchased the project from the mortgagor of an investor project.

QUADROMINIUM   A variation of a condominium ownership in which each of four owners has it available for only three months a year and each is responsible for only his share of the cost.

QUALIFIED PROJECT   A housing project providing rental or cooperative housing for low-income persons under the provisions of Section 221(d)(3) or Section 236.

QUASI-PUBLIC   Almost public.

QUICK ASSET   (*See* CURRENT ASSET.)

QUICK-TAKE   The acquisition of a property under the power of eminent domain, prior to the completion or condemnation proceedings, to avoid loss of the time required to complete such proceedings. (*See also* BLANKET CONDEMNATION.)

QUIET ENJOYMENT   A provision in a lease or deed certifying that the tenant or purchaser will be permitted to enjoy the premises in peace and without disturbance by the landlord or seller.

QUIET TITLE [real estate]   An action in a district court to remove recorded defects in a title.

QUITCLAIM DEED   A deed transferring only such title as the seller possesses, without warranty as to the status of the title.

R

RACE [HUD]   The racial identity of the head of the family determines the racial grouping of the family.

RACIAL COVENANT   Covenant restricting members of certain races from ownership of certain property, which the U.S. Supreme Court ruled in 1946 is an illegal covenant.

RADIAL STREET SYSTEM   A street layout in which streets "radiate" from a certain center point or area. Distinguished from a gridiron plan.

RAFT OR MAT FOUNDATION [HUD] A foundation system where the building structure is supported upon a system of continuous concrete beams or slabs arranged to reduce unit soil pressures and differential settlement.

RAMP [HUD] A sloping walkway providing access to and from floors having different elevations.

RANDOM SAMPLE [statistics] A sample selected by chance, usually at selected intervals.

RANGE [real estate] A part of the government survey, being a strip of land 6 miles in width and numbered east or west of the principal meridian.

RAPID BUS SERVICE Bus service whose route includes freeways.

RAPID DEPRECIATION A rate of depreciation for tax purposes in excess of straight-line depreciation. (*See also* STRAIGHT-LINE DEPRECIATION.)

RATE OF RETURN The percentage of income returned from an investment in relation to the amount invested.

RAW LAND Unimproved land, distinguished from improved area or land.

REAL ESTATE (*See* REAL PROPERTY.)

REAL ESTATE EQUITY TRUST A real estate investment trust which invests directly in real property and derives its income primarily from rents.

REAL ESTATE INVESTMENT TRUST (REIT) An unincorporated business trust or association which owns real property or mortgages. A REIT cannot manage directly the properties it owns—it must be a passive investor; nor can it develop or sell land. (*See also* REAL ESTATE EQUITY TRUST, REAL ESTATE MORTGAGE TRUST.)

REAL ESTATE MORTGAGE TRUST A real estate investment trust which invests in mortgages and derives its income mainly from loan fees and the interest received during the amortization period of the mortgages owned.

REAL PROPERTY Land and that which is affixed to it.

REALTOR A real estate agent or broker who is a member of the National

Association of Realtors (formerly National Association of Real Estate Boards). The term "Realtor" is copyrighted and nonmembers of the Association cannot use it.

REALTY   A brief term for "real property."

RECAPTURE   The application of ordinary income tax rates to gains reflecting prior excess or rapid depreciation.

RECEIVER   A person or an entity, court-appointed, that assumes control of a property when the court finds that such a qualified and impartial person or entity should be so designated in the interest of justice.

RECERTIFICATION OF INCOME [HUD]   HUD requirement that, in all assisted housing, all tenants' incomes be checked periodically to determine their eligibility for occupancy; changes in income result in recomputation of rental rates and subsidy payments.

RECLAMATION   The process of converting waste natural resources (such as land) into productive use.

RECORDING   Placing a change in the ownership of real estate on public record—usually in a courthouse.

RECREATION FACILITY LOANS [rural]   (*See* SECTION 304 RECREATION FACILITY LOANS.)

REDEEM [real estate]   To buy back. The act of buying back lands after a mortgage foreclosure, tax foreclosure, or other execution sale.

REDEMPTION   A buying back; repurchase.

REDEVELOPER   A person, group, or other entity engaged in the business of developing land made available through a slum clearance program.

REDEVELOPER'S STATEMENT OF PUBLIC DISCLOSURE [urban renewal]   Form completed by redevelopers of land in urban renewal areas, outlining the nature of the redeveloper's project and his naming principals and disclosing information about the scope and development cost of the proposed project.

REDEVELOPER'S STATEMENT OF QUALIFICATIONS AND FINANCIAL RESPON-

SIBILITY [urban renewal]   Form outlining the qualifications and financial capacity of a redeveloper of land in an urban renewal area; used by the local public agency and by HUD to evaluate the competence of the redeveloper.

REDEVELOPMENT   The development or improvement of cleared or undeveloped land, usually in an urban renewal area. In technical usage, this term includes erection of buildings and other development and improvement of the land by private or public redevelopers to whom the land has been made available, but it does not include site or project improvements installed by a local public agency in preparing the land for disposition by sale or lease. The distinction between the popular and the technical meanings is significant in that necessary expenses of a local public agency in preparing land for disposition to a redeveloper may be considered part of gross project cost for federally assisted financing purposes. The expenses incurred by the redeveloper in the reuse of the acquired land, however, are entirely his obligation.

REDEVELOPMENT AREA [EDA]   (*See* ECONOMIC DEVELOPMENT ADMINISTRATION.)

RED-LINING   Practice of some lenders, insurance companies, and others involving the refusal to make or guaranty loans or to issue insurance policies on property in areas that they deem to be bad risks.

REEXAMINATION DATE   (*See* DATE OF REEXAMINATION.)

REFERRAL SYSTEM [urban renewal]   Procedure developed by a local public agency for calling on resources outside the agency to provide the special skills and services needed to assist families and individuals residing in a project area, or relocated from a project area, in overcoming social and economic problems which interfere with adequate rehousing opportunities, increase the hardship of displacement, or make it difficult to obtain the financing necessary to undertake rehabilitation activities.

REGION   As defined in the Housing and Community Development Act of 1974, all or part of the area of jurisdiction of one or more units of general local government, and one or more metropolitan areas.

REGIONAL ADMINISTRATOR (RA) [HUD]   (*See* HUD REGIONAL ADMINISTRATOR.)

REGIONAL INTERAGENCY COORDINATING COMMITTEE (RICC) [Model

Cities] Committee formed of representatives of the regional offices of the federal agencies involved in the Model Cities program.

REGIONAL OFFICE OF HUD   One of ten offices of HUD located across the country to oversee the operations of HUD Area and Insuring Offices.

REGULATORY AGREEMENT [FHA]   Document setting forth HUD's requirements for project accounting, rental schedules, management agent transfers, etc.—to which the sponsor agrees.

REHABILITATION (rehab)   The restoration to good condition of deteriorated structures, neighborhoods, and public facilities. Structural and facility rehabilitation may involve repair, renovation, conversion, expansion, remodeling, or reconstruction. Rehabilitation is undertaken to achieve a physical quality approaching—or even sometimes exceeding—a quality comparing favorably with that of other well-maintained older properties and with new ones. Rehabilitation increases the useful life of the property. Neighborhood rehabilitation encompasses structural rehabilitation and, in addition, may extend to street improvements and a provision of such amenities as parks and playgrounds. (*See also* NEIGHBORHOOD REHABILITATION.)

REHABILITATION EXPENDITURES [IRS]   Amounts chargeable to capital accounts relating to property or additions or improvements to property with a useful life or five years or more. Such expenditures must be incurred in connection with the rehabilitation of an existing structure for low-income rental housing. (The cost of acquiring property to be rehabilitated is not counted as a rehabilitation expenditure.)

REHABILITATION GRANT PAYMENT [urban renewal]   Periodic reimbursements, in full, made to a local renewal agency by HUD for rehabilitation grants made to property owners, properly made. (*See also* SECTION 115 GRANTS.)

REHABILITATION LOAN   (*See* SECTION 312 HOUSING REHABILITATION LOANS.)

REHABILITATION REQUIREMENTS [HUD]   The criteria established by a local public agency, omitted or not adequately covered in local regulations, which are established for properties in a rehabilitation area to assure their restoration to a sound condition. Generally, rehabilitation requirements are the minimum performance provisions of HUD publication, PG-50, Rehabilitation Guide for Residential Properties, which are (1) omitted or not adequately covered in local regulations, (2) requirements which properties must meet to be at least eligible for direct federal rehabilitation loans.

RELATED FACILITIES [HUD]   New structures suitable for use by elderly or handicapped families, such as cafeterias or dining halls, community rooms or buildings, workshops, infirmaries or other inpatient or outpatient health facilities, or other essential service facilities, and structures suitable for such uses provided by rehabilitation, alteration, conversion, or improvement of existing structures which are otherwise inadequate for such uses.

RELOCATION   The process by which a public agency fulfills the statutory requirement that decent, safe, and sanitary dwellings within their financial means be made available to families or businesses displaced by public programs.

RELOCATION ADJUSTMENT PAYMENT (RAP)   An allowance paid for a specified period of time after relocation, to help a family or an elderly individual meet the expense of relocation, based upon a formula established by federal law.

RELOCATION ADVISORY ASSISTANCE PROGRAM   The relocation assistance provided by state highway agencies, as required by the Federal-Aid Highway Act.

RELOCATION ASSISTANCE PROGRAM   A local public agency's documented program for the provision of measures, facilities, and services required to relocate families or businesses from an urban renewal project area.

RELOCATION GRANT PAYMENT [urban renewal]   Periodic reimbursements, in full, to the local public agency by HUD for relocation payments to relocatees, properly made.

RELOCATION PAYMENT   The cash amount paid by a local public agency to individuals, families, and business concerns for their reasonable, necessary moving expenses and any direct loss of personal property resulting from their displacement from property purchased by a renewal agency in an urban renewal project area. The public agency is reimbursed for these expenditures through a relocation grant from the federal government.

RELOCATION SETTLEMENT COSTS   Settlement costs and related charges which are incurred by an owner in connection with the acquisition of his property as part of a relocation plan and for which reimbursement or compensation would not otherwise be made.

RELOCATION SURVEY   A study of an area in which relocation of persons and/or businesses is to be conducted to determine the requirements for new shelter of those to be displaced; includes a rather precise analysis of such factors as family or business size, income, age, social composition, health conditions, and need for relocation assistance or adjustment payments.

RELOCATION WORKLOAD   Families and individuals interviewed or listed by a relocation agency as eligible for relocation services and payments.

RENDERING   A drawing showing how a proposed construction project will appear after its completion.

RENEWAL AGENCY   (*See* LOCAL PUBLIC AGENCY.)

RENT   The amount paid, usually regularly and at fixed amounts, to an owner for the use of real property.

RENT ADVISORY BOARD   This Board was established by Executive Order No. 11632 of November 22, 1971, and is continued under Executive Order No. 11640 of January 26, 1972. The Rent Advisory Board is composed of such members as the President may from time to time appoint and a designated chairman. The Board provides advice to the Price Commission and Cost of Living Council concerning special considerations involved in the stabilization of rents and assists in the performance of the Commission by making technical analyses of specific matters.

The Board is composed of fifteen members, including the chairman, and equally represents consumers, industry, and the public.

The Rent Advisory Board first convened November 23, 1971, to formulate rent stabilization policy recommendations for the Economic Stabilization Program. First issuance of the rent regulations for Phase II became effective December 29, 1971.

The Board acts as principal adviser to the Price Commission on matters of rent policy. The Board examines and deliberates rent issues that are either requested by the Commission, deemed important by Board members, or brought to its attention by the Board staff. Decisions and recommendations are forwarded to the Price Commission.

The Board staff coordinates, with the Price Commission, the development of rent stabilization policies, ensures implementation of rent policy, and serves as rent staff to the Price Commission.

RENTAL GAP REQUIREMENT [public housing]   (*See* TWENTY PERCENT GAP.)

RENTAL HOUSING [HUD]   Housing, the occupancy of which is permitted by the owner thereof in consideration of the payment of agreed charges, whether or not, by the terms of the agreement, such payment over a period of time will entitle the occupant to the ownership of the premises or space in a mobile home court or park properly arranged and equipped to accommodate mobile homes.

RENT CERTIFICATE   A subsidy given by a public body, such as the federal government, to families occupying substandard housing to permit them to rent acceptable housing; the amount is the difference between the contract rent and the amount established as what the family can afford from its normal income. Similar to direct housing allowance. (*See also* INCOME MAINTENANCE SUBSIDY, INCOME TRANSFER FOR HOUSING.)

RENT CONTROL   Regulation by a governmental entity of rental rates; frequently also addresses itself to tenant-landlord relations and arrangements.

RENT FORMULA RATE   The rental rate at which total project replacement cost must earn basic net income.

RENT SUPPLEMENT PROGRAM (RS)   A direct subsidy program in which the family pays 25 percent of its income toward the rent, with this amount supplemented by the government to cover the difference between the amount paid by the family and the market rate rent.

The Housing and Community Development Act of 1974 consolidates this program within the Section 236 interest subsidy program, requiring rent supplements for up to 20 percent of families in all new Section 236 projects who cannot afford to pay the basic rent within 25 percent of their incomes.

(*See also* SECTION 101 RENT SUPPLEMENT PROGRAM.)

RENT-UP PERIOD [FHA]   A period of time beginning on the date permission to occupy a project is granted and ending, usually, on the date sustaining occupancy is reached, as determined according to the program involved.

REPLACEMENT COST [FHA]   The FHA's estimate of the construction cost of a property or project when the proposed improvements are completed. The replacement cost may include the land, the proposed physical improvements, utilities within the boundaries of the land, architect's fees, taxes, interest during construction, and other miscellaneous charges incident to construction and approved by FHA.

REPLACEMENT HOUSING [urban renewal]   Housing units constructed or rehabilitated to replace, on a one-to-one basis, housing units demolished or removed by urban renewal activities.

REPLACEMENT PAYMENTS   Payment for nonexpendable equipment purchased as a replacement of equipment.

REPLACEMENT RESERVES   Funds set aside through accounting procedures to assure that funds are available to replace installed items in a project, covering such items as ranges, refrigerators, water heaters, air conditioners, floor tile, and bathroom tile.

REPRODUCTION COST   The cost to replicate a property at current costs with materials used when the property was originally constructed.

RESERVE   An amount allocated from income for use if needed, such as an operating reserve, a replacement reserve, or a depreciation reserve.

RESIDENT MANAGER   Person assigned the responsibility for leasing apartments and managing a project on a day-to-day basis. (Such a person may or may not actually reside in the project.)

RESIDUAL RECEIPTS   Funds remaining at the end of an accounting year after all operating and other costs and payments have been paid.

RESIDUALS   The profit on the sale or the cash generated by a refinancing of an investment.

RESOURCE RECOVERY ACT OF 1970   An act to amend the Solid Waste Disposal Act to provide federal financial assistance for the construction of solid waste disposal facilities, to improve research programs pursuant to such act, and for other purposes. Approved October 26, 1970, and subsequently amended.

RESTRICTED COMMON AREAS AND FACILITIES [HUD]   Those areas and facilities restricted to a particular family unit or number of family units. (*See also* COMMON AREAS AND FACILITIES.)

RESTRICTIVE COVENANT   Usually, a covenant restricting the occupancy of real property by certain racial, ethnic, religious, and other minority groups. Such a covenant may also restrict the use of real property.

RETAIL PURCHASE [utilities]   Purchase of energy by tenants from supplying public utility companies and billed to tenants by the utility, as distinguished from a wholesale purchase.

REUSE APPRAISAL   An appraisal of reuse value. (*See also* DISPOSITION APPRAISAL.)

REUSE VALUE [urban renewal]   The price a local public agency places on land, cleared through the urban renewal process, to be sold to a redeveloper, based upon a disposition or reuse appraisal.

REVALUATION   The reestablishment of the assessed value of real estate.

REVENUE BOND   Bond issued to finance revenue-producing facilities, which revenue is expected to repay the bonds.

REVENUE SHARING   Concept of federal financial assistance involving the allocation of a portion of the receipts of the federal government to states and local governments. Intended as a substitute for certain federally assisted categorical programs and project grant systems. (*See also* GENERAL REVENUE SHARING, HELLER-PECHMAN PLAN, SPECIAL REVENUE SHARING, URBAN COMMUNITY DEVELOPMENT SPECIAL REVENUE SHARING.)

REVENUE STAMPS   Stamps sold by the federal or a state government and affixed to certain documents, such as stocks, bonds, and deeds, upon their issuance, sale, or transfer.

REVERSION   The return of real estate to its or an original owner, as upon the expiration of a lease. Also, the legal right of a property owner to regain use and occupancy of real estate, such as upon the expiration of a lease.

REZONING   Action by a governing body changing the zoning classification of a land area to another classification.

RIGHT-OF-WAY   The right which one has to pass across the lands of another. An easement. Also refers to the area itself.

RING CELL SYSTEM [construction]   A German building system that features the assembly of box modules by successively attaching in precast concrete "ring" sections.

RIOT INSURANCE   (*See* CRIME INSURANCE, FEDERAL INSURANCE ADMINISTRATION, URBAN PROPERTY PROTECTION AND REINSURANCE.)

RIPARIAN RIGHTS   The rights of an owner of land abutting a water body.

RIPENING COST   The cost of waiting for an investment to provide a return—as the cost of waiting for a tract of land to increase in value or to be suited to development.

RIPRAP   Stones or rocks of indiscriminate dimensions placed so as to form a foundation or wall, usually along the banks of a stream of water to prevent erosion.

RISER   The vertical face of a step or stepped ramp.

RISK FACTOR   The percentage or portion of income established as the amount intended to cover the risks of a given investment.

ROANOKE AMENDMENT   [public housing]   A proviso in the federal statutes which states that the Public Housing Administration cannot authorize the construction of any projects rejected by a local governing body or by referendum unless such projects are subsequently approved by the same procedure through which they were rejected. It was superseded by the "Los Angeles" or Phillips Amendment. (*See also* PHILLIPS AMENDMENT.)

ROLLOVER   Provision of the Internal Revenue Code permitting the owners of Section 221(d)(3) or 236 housing to sell such projects to their tenants or to an organization of such tenants (as in a cooperative organization) and thereby defer taxes on any gains realized if the proceeds of the sale are then invested in equity in similar projects.

ROOM   (*See* COMBINED ROOMS, HABITABLE ROOM.)

ROTUNDA   A dome-covered room or building.

ROW HOUSE   A row of three or more attached, one-family dwellings, each built with similar architectural treatment, separated by vertical divisions termed party or lot-line walls, and each having private entrances (usually both front and rear). Often called a "town house," which is a more modern term for a row house.

ROYALTY   [real estate]   Sum(s) paid to a landowner for the right of taking certain natural resources from his property, such as oil, minerals, gravel, and timber.

RURAL AREA Any open country, or any place, town, village, or city which is not part of or associated with an urban area and which has a population not in excess of 2,500 inhabitants, or has a population in excess of 2,500 but not in excess of 10,000 if it is rural in character, or has a population in excess of 10,000 but not in excess of 20,000 and is not contained within a standard metropolitan statistical area and has a serious lack of mortgage credit as determined by the Secretary of HUD.

RURAL HOUSING LOANS Authorized by Title V of the Housing Act of 1949 and later amended; provides direct loans or guaranteed or insured loans obtained through the Farmers Home Administration for construction, repair, or purchase of housing; to provide necessary and adequate sewage disposal facilities for the applicant and his family; to purchase or install essential equipment, which upon installation becomes part of the real estate; to buy a minimum adequate site on which to place a dwelling for the applicant's own use. Housing debts under certain circumstances may be refinanced. (*See also* FARMERS HOME ADMINISTRATION.)

Restrictions on the use of the loans are that a dwelling financed for a family with a low or moderate income must be modest in size, design, and cost. An applicant must be without sufficient resources to provide on his own account the necessary housing, buildings, or related facilities and be unable to secure the necessary credit from other sources upon terms and conditions which he reasonably could be expected to fulfill.

RURAL HOUSING SITE LOANS (*See* SECTION 524 AND 525 SITE LOANS.)

RURAL RENTAL HOUSING LOANS (*See* SECTION 515 AND 521 RURAL RENTAL HOUSING LOANS.)

RURAL SELF-HELP HOUSING TECHNICAL ASSISTANCE (*See* SECTION 523 TECHNICAL ASSISTANCE.)

RURAL-URBAN FRINGE (rurban) The area around an urban area where urban land uses meet rural land uses.

RURBAN (*See* RURAL-URBAN FRINGE.)

S

SADDLE   A small indenture in a sloping roof intended to carry water away from the back of a chimney.

A section of wood or metal across a doorway, a threshold, or a sill, forming the base of such a framing.

SAFE STREETS ACT   (*See* OMNIBUS CRIME CONTROL AND SAFE STREETS ACT OF 1968.)

SALE-LEASEBACK   Transaction in which an investor-owner of a property sells the land only to another investor, then leases the land back for a long term; the original investor maintains ownership of the improvements.

SALES-ASSESSMENT RATIO   The ratio of the assessed value of real property to its selling price.

SALES PRICE [FHA]   The price stated in a sales agreement, adjusted to exclude any portion of closing costs, prepayable expenses, or costs of non-real estate items excluded from the mortgage which the agreement indicates will be assumed by the seller.

SALES PROJECT [FHA]   A project owned by a mortgagor nonprofit housing corporation or trust which is organized for the purpose of construction of homes for members of the corporation or for beneficiaries of the trust.

SALVAGE VALUE   Usually, the value of a building minus the cost of demolition.

SAMPLE [statistics]   A limited number of items or persons sufficient to be representative of the complete number, such as a percentage of a total. (*See also* RANDOM SAMPLE.)

SANDWICH LEASE   Lease arrangement in which a principal is the lessee of one party's property and lessor of that property to another.

SANITARY SEWER   A sewer that carries only sewage, as distinguished from a storm sewer.

SASH   The framework that encloses the glass in a window.

SATELLITE CITY   Incorporated city located outside of a central city upon which its economic and social functions depend.

SAVINGS AND LOAN ASSOCIATION (S&L)   A financial institution which promotes thrift and savings and which provides mortgage financing. As a segment of the so-called lending industry, S&L's are the largest source of funds for residential home financing. S&L's are regulated either by federal or state agencies or by both, depending upon the nature of their charter. S&L's can be classed either as mutual or stock associations. (*See also* FEDERAL SAVINGS AND LOAN ASSOCIATION.)

SCATTERED-SITE HOUSING   Housing units dispersed, usually by a local housing authority, in small numbers on numerous, noncontiguous sites throughout a community. The concept is intended to minimize the institutional appearance of large projects located on single sites and to foster economic and/or racial integration. (*See also* IN-FILL HOUSING.)

SCENIC EASEMENT   Easement granted by a landowner, usually to a public highway agency, to provide scenic enhancement of a road.

SCHEMATIC DRAWINGS   Architectural plans drawn to scale, including: (1) a site plan showing lot lines and dimensions, adjacent buildings, project buildings outlined and their overall dimensions, parking areas and number of parking spaces, driveways, adjacent streets and utilities and their sizes, patios and other recreation areas, off-site improvements, unit types and room composition, contours, north point, site and gross floor areas; (2) dimensioned plan of each typical unit; (3) elevations for typical buildings (for elevator and complex construction types also); (4) lobby floor; (5) typical floor; (6) mechanical, service, storage, and other nonrent facilities; (7) commercial use areas.

SCHOOL ASSISTANCE IN FEDERALLY AFFECTED AREAS   Authorized in the Federally Impacted Areas Act, Titles I and III of Public Law 81-874 and later amendments; provides formula grants to eligible local educational agencies bearing financial burdens as when the tax base of a district is reduced through the federal acquisition of real property or when there is a sudden and substantial increase in school attendance as the result of federal activities. Also provides major disaster assistance by replacing or repairing damaged or destroyed supplies, equipment, or facilities.

SCIENTIFIC WILD-ASS GUESS (SWAG) Frequently used term denoting that while an estimate is "educated," it is not to be interpreted as necessarily a good one.

S CORPORATION (*See* SUBCHAPTER S CORPORATION.)

SCRAP VALUE The worth of the part(s) of an item(s) of property if it is sold for a use other than its existing use.

SEALED BIDS [urban renewal] [HUD] Method for offering urban renewal project land in which sealed bids are invited by the local public agency under specific provisions as to the place and cutoff date, time for the receipt of proposals, and time for opening and reading of bids.

SEASONAL HOUSING Housing units designed for seasonal rather than year-round occupancy.

SECONDARY MORTGAGE MARKET That section of the market for mortgages in which original mortgages are bought and sold by investors. (*See also* FEDERAL NATIONAL MORTGAGE ASSOCIATION, GOVERNMENT NATIONAL MORTGAGE ASSOCIATION.)

SECOND MORTGAGE A mortgage representing a second lien on property, subordinated to the claim of the holder of the first mortgage. Also called "second trust."

SECOND TRUST (*See* SECOND MORTGAGE.)

SECRETARY [HUD] The Secretary of the Department of Housing and Urban Development, the Secretary of Defense, or, in the case of the U.S. Coast Guard, the Secretary of Transportation and any officer or employee designated by either the Secretary of Defense or the Secretary of Transportation to issue certificates of eligibility and certificates of termination.

SECTION [architecture] A drawing showing the details of a cross section of a building.

SECTION 8 HOUSING ASSISTANCE PAYMENT PROGRAM (HAP program) (leased housing) [public housing] Originally known as "Section 23 leased housing" when it was established by the 1965 housing act. Section 8 was established in the Housing and Community Development Act of 1974, under Title II—Assisted Housing.

The program is essentially the same as Section 23; however, the 1974 act enables HUD to enter into contracts directly with owners of eligible housing and to perform certain functions otherwise assigned to a local housing authority in areas where a public housing agency is unable to implement the program.

Eligible sponsors (or owners) of Section 8 housing include private builder-developers, cooperatives, and public agencies. Owners of Section 8 housing assume all ownership, management, tenant selection, and maintenance responsibilities—which functions may be contracted to any entity (including a local housing authority) approved by HUD.

(*See also* SECTION 23 LEASED HOUSING.)

SECTION 23 LEASED HOUSING [public housing] Program established by the 1965 housing act enabling local housing authorities to provide public housing by leasing existing private housing from private owners for occupancy by public housing tenants. Federal legislation passed in 1970 expanded Section 23 to permit housing authorities to lease newly constructed housing as well as existing structures. The maximum term of a lease for existing housing is 15 years; for new housing, the term is 20 years.

Public housing tenants in leased housing pay the same rent that would be paid for authority-owned housing; the difference is made up by the authority with federal contributions and special subsidies, called "housing assistance payments." (*See also* HOUSING ASSISTANCE PAYMENT.)

The Housing and Community Development Act of 1974 renamed the program "Section 8 housing assistance payment program" under Title II—Assisted Housing. (*See also* SECTION 8 HOUSING ASSISTANCE PAYMENT PROGRAM.)

SECTION 101 RENT SUPPLEMENT PROGRAM Authorized by the Housing and Urban Development Act of 1965 and later amendments; provides direct payments by FHA, to make good-quality rental housing available to low-income families at prices they can afford; FHA makes payments to owners of approved multifamily rental housing projects to supplement the partial rental payments of eligible tenants. Rental projects must be part of an approved Workable Program for Community Improvement or approved by local government officials. Most rent supplement projects are financed through mortgages insured under the Section 221(d)(3) market interest rate program.

Assistance covers the difference between the tenant's payment and the market rental, but it may not exceed 70 percent of the market rental.

The Section 236 Rent Supplement Program can be used to further supplement the rental charges for tenants in up to 40 percent of the units in Section 236 projects. Section 106 and Appalachian Housing Assistance grants are available to nonprofit sponsors of rent supplement projects to help defray planning and development costs.

Eligible sponsors include nonprofit, cooperative, builder-seller, investor-sponsor, and limited-distribution mortgagors. Public bodies do not qualify as mortgagors under this program.

Families must be within the income limits (as determined by locality on a case-by-case basis) prescribed for admission to public housing to qualify for benefits under this program. Others may occupy family units in a rent supplement project but must pay the full rent and may not benefit from subsidies.

FHA makes monthly payments to project owners to make up the difference between the partial rentals paid by assisted tenants and the market rent. Assisted tenants must pay at least 25 percent of their adjusted monthly income (after certain deductions) for rent.

The Housing and Community Development Act of 1974 consolidates this program within the Section 236 interest subsidy program, requiring rent supplements for up to 20 percent of families in all new Section 236 projects who cannot afford to pay basic rent within 25 percent of their incomes.

SECTION 106 AND 106(b) NONPROFIT SPONSOR "SEED MONEY" AND PLANNING LOANS

Authorized by the Housing and Urban Development Act of 1968 and later amendments; provides direct loans and grants to assist and stimulate prospective nonprofit sponsors of FHA-insured low- and moderate-income housing to develop sound housing projects.

FHA may make interest-free loans to nonprofit sponsors to cover 80 percent of preconstruction expenses for planning low- and moderate-income housing projects to be developed under Sections 236, 221(d)(3) BMIR, rent supplement housing, and 235(i). Eligible expenses include organization expenses, legal fees, consultant fees, architect fees, preliminary site engineering fees, land options, FHA and FNMA application fees, and construction loan fees. If the repayment of the loan is not recoverable from mortgage proceeds, the loan may be converted to a grant.

Nonprofit organizations wishing to sponsor low- and moderate-income housing projects are eligible.

These loans, which are interest-free, may not exceed 80 percent of the eligible development costs incurred in planning the housing proposal. The entire loan, or a partial amount, may be converted to a grant when, for an acceptable reason, the proceeds of an insured mortgage do not become available to repay the loan. Hence, loans are converted to grants if the loan is not recoverable from the mortgage proceeds.

The loan term is normally six months but may extend for up to two years, depending upon the timing of the disbursement of mortgage funds.

SECTION 107 NATIONAL HOMEOWNERSHIP FOUNDATION (*See* NATIONAL HOMEOWNERSHIP FOUNDATION.)

SECTION 112 CREDITS [urban renewal]   Credits as local grants-in-aid to urban renewal projects for expenditures by educational institutions and hospitals conducting activities that contribute to the objectives of an Urban Renewal Plan.

The system is to be phased out under provisions of Title I—Community Development of the Housing and Community Development Act of 1974, which supplants the urban renewal program with a system of block grant financing. However, certain Section 112 credits are allowable and maintained for certain purposes during the transition period in accordance with Section 116(b) of the 1974 act.

SECTION 112 PROJECT [urban renewal]   Urban renewal project financed in whole or in part with Section 112 credits.

SECTION 115 HOUSING REHABILITATION GRANTS Authorized by the Housing and Urban Development Act of 1965 and later amendments; provides HUD grants, to provide funds to individuals and families who own and occupy one-to-four dwelling unit residential properties in Neighborhood Development Program, urban renewal, and federally assisted code enforcement areas.

Grants assist in the rehabilitation of property located in federally assisted code enforcement areas, urban renewal areas where there is a rehabilitation or code enforcement plan, certified areas, and for properties in areas under a statewide Fair Access to Insurance Requirements (FAIR) plan determined to be uninsurable because of physical hazards.

When grantee's income exceeds $3,000 per year, the grant may be reduced if the housing expense is less than 25 percent of his income.

Grants may be in amounts up to $3,500 (however, this maximum is subject to change, as enabling statutes are amended by the Congress).

Such grants are supplanted by block grants provided in Title I—Community Development of the Housing and Community Development Act of 1974.

SECTION 116 DEMOLITION GRANT PROGRAM Program administered by HUD under provisions of Section 116 of the Housing Act of 1949 as amended by the Housing and Urban Development Act of 1965, which provides grants to municipalities to cover a part of the cost of demolishing structures found unsafe.

This program is supplanted by block grants provided in Title I—Community Development of the Housing and Community Development Act of 1974.

SECTION 117 CONCENTRATED CODE ENFORCEMENT PROGRAM This program is supplanted by block grants provided through Title I—Community Development of the Housing and Community Development Act of 1974. (*See also* FEDERALLY ASSISTED CODE ENFORCEMENT.)

SECTION 118 INTERIM ASSISTANCE PROGRAM [HUD] Authorized by Section 118 of the Housing Act of 1949 as amended, the program provides limited and short-term funding assistance to help cities, other municipalities, and counties plan and carry out programs to alleviate harmful conditions in areas where urban renewal is planned but in which some immediate public action is required.

This program is supplanted by block grants provided through Title I—Community Development of the Housing and Community Development Act of 1974.

SECTION 202 ELDERLY HOUSING Housing program resulting from the Housing Act of 1959, authorizing fifty-year direct loans at a 3 percent interest rate to finance the development of housing for elderly persons of moderate income.

The Housing and Community Development Act of 1974 reestablished the interest rate to be the current average yield on outstanding marketable obligations of the federal government (which, in 1974, was approximately 8.5 percent).

The 1974 act also permits HUD to make Section 8 housing assistance payments on behalf of low-income elderly families residing in projects financed under Section 202.

SECTION 203(b) HOME MORTGAGE INSURANCE Authorized by the National Housing Act as amended to help families undertake home ownership, provides FHA mortgage insurance; FHA insures lenders against loss on mortgage loans. These loans may be used to finance the purchase of proposed, under construction, or existing one-to-four family housing units, as well as to refinance indebtedness on existing housing. The maximum insurable loan is subject to change.

The maximum amount of the loan is altered periodically by Congress. The down payment would be the difference between the maximum loan amount and the purchase price of the home. In addition to the down payment, the purchaser must pay for all items of prepaid expense. The maximum interest rate is established by the HUD Secretary, to which is added $\frac{1}{2}$ percent for mortgage insurance premium. The FHA application fee is $40 for existing and $50 for proposed housing. The service charge by the mortgagees varies, but normally it may not exceed 1 percent of the total mortgage.

The mortgage term may extend for thirty years or three-fourths of the remaining economic life, whichever is less, except thirty-five years if the mortgagor is unacceptable under a thirty-year term and the property was constructed subject to FHA or VA inspection.

SECTION 203(h) DISASTER HOUSING MORTGAGE INSURANCE Authorized by the Housing Act of 1954 and later amendments; provides FHA mortgage insurance to help victims of a major disaster undertake home ownership; FHA insures lenders against loss on mortgage loans. These loans may be used to finance the purchase of proposed, under construction, or existing single-family housing for the occupant-mortgagor who is a victim of a major disaster. The maximum insurable loan for such an occupant-mortgagor is subject to change. To qualify for assistance the home must be in an area designated by the President as a disaster area.

Any family which is a victim of a major disaster as designated by the President is eligible to apply.

The maximum amount of the loan is 100 percent of the FHA estimated value. No down payment is required. The maximum interest rate is established by the HUD Secretary, to which is added $\frac{1}{2}$ percent for mortgage insurance premium. The FHA application fee is $40 for existing and $50 for proposed housing. The service charge by the mortgagee varies, but it may not normally exceed 1 percent of the total mortgage.

The mortgage term may extend for thirty years or three-fourths of the property's remaining economic life, whichever is less, except thirty-five years if the mortgagor is unacceptable for a thirty-year term and the property was constructed subject to FHA or VA inspection.

SECTION 203(i) MORTGAGE INSURANCE FOR HOMES IN OUTLYING AREAS Authorized by the Housing Act of 1959 and later amendments; provides FHA mortgage insurance to help families purchase homes in outlying areas; FHA insures lenders against loss on mortgage loans. These loans may be used to finance the purchase of proposed, under construction, or existing one-family nonfarm housing or new farm housing on 5 or more acres adjacent to a highway. The maximum insurable loan for an occupant mortgagor on a one-family home is subject to change. All families are eligible to apply.

For most families, the maximum loan is 97 percent of the estimated value. The down payment is the difference between the maximum loan and the purchase price of the home. In addition to the down payment, the purchaser must pay for all items of prepaid expense. The maximum interest rate is established by the HUD Secretary, to which is added ½ percent for mortgage insurance premium. The FHA application fee is $40 for existing and $50 for proposed housing. The service charge by the mortgagee varies, but it may not normally exceed 1 percent of the total mortgage.

The mortgage term may extend for thirty years or three-fourths of remaining economic life, whichever is less, except thirty-five years if the mortgagor is unacceptable under a thirty-year term and the property was constructed subject to FHA and VA inspection.

SECTION 203(k) MAJOR HOME IMPROVEMENT LOAN INSURANCE   Authorized by the Housing Act of 1961 and later amendments; provides mortgage insurance through FHA to help families repair or improve existing residential structures outside urban renewal areas. FHA insures lenders against loss on loans. These loans may be used to finance the alteration, repair, or improvement of existing one- to four-family housing not within urban renewal areas. The housing must be at least ten years old unless the loan is primarily to make major structural improvements.

The loan term may extend for twenty years or three-fourths of the remaining economic life of the property, whichever is less.

SECTION 207 MORTGAGE INSURANCE FOR MOBILE HOME COURTS   Authorized by the Housing Act of 1955 and later amendments; provides FHA mortgage insurance to make possible the financing of construction or rehabilitation of mobile home parks; FHA insures lenders against losses on mortgages. Insured mortgages may be used to finance the construction or rehabilitation of mobile home courts. The maximum mortgage limit is subject to change. In areas where cost levels so require, limits may be increased.

Eligible mortgagors include investors, builders, developers, and others who meet FHA requirements for mortgagors. For most mortgagors, the maximum amount of the loan may not exceed 90 percent of the estimated value. The maximum interest rate permissible is established by the HUD Secretary, to which is added ½ percent for mortgage insurance premium. The FHA application and commitment fee is $3 per $1,000 of the mortgage amount. The FHA-inspection fee may not exceed $5 per $1,000 of the mortgage amount.

The maximum mortgage term is forty years or not appreciably in excess of three-fourths of the remaining economic life, whichever is less.

SECTION 207 MORTGAGE INSURANCE FOR RENTAL HOUSING Authorized by the National Housing Act as amended in 1938 and in later amendments; provides FHA mortgage insurance for rental housing; FHA insures lenders against losses on mortgages. Insured mortgages may be used to finance the construction or rehabilitation of rental detached, semidetached, row, walkup, or elevator-type structures with eight or more units. The unit mortgage limits for nonelevator apartments are subject to change according to the number of bedrooms in the units. Limits per family unit are somewhat higher for elevator apartments. In areas where cost levels so require, limits per family unit may be increased up to 45 percent.

Eligible mortgagors include investors, builders, developers, and others who meet FHA requirements for mortgagors. All families are eligible to occupy a dwelling in a structure whose mortgage is insured under the program, subject to normal tenant selection. The maximum amount of the loan would be equal to 90 percent of the estimated value in most cases. The maximum permissible interest rate is established by the HUD Secretary, to which is added $\frac{1}{2}$ percent for mortgage insurance premium.

The mortgage term is forty years or not appreciably in excess of three-fourths of the remaining economic life, whichever is less.

SECTION 212 CONTRIBUTION OR SUBSIDY [public housing] Amendment to the U.S. Housing Act of 1937 in the Housing Act of 1969, authorizing HUD to pay annual contributions to local housing authorities in excess of debt service requirements up to the statutory annual maximum.

SECTION 213 COOPERATIVE SALES Authorized by the Housing Act of 1950; provides FHA mortgage insurance to make it possible for housing cooperatives to sponsor the development of new housing that will be sold to individual cooperative members. FHA insures lenders against losses on mortgages. Insured mortgages may be used to finance construction of single-family detached, semidetached, or row housing consisting of five or more units.

Eligible mortgagors include nonprofit cooperative sponsors intending to sell individual units to cooperative members.

Members of the cooperative are eligible to purchase individual units in the project from the nonprofit cooperative sponsor with the aid of FHA-insured financing.

The maximum amounts of the loans to the individual purchasers are 100 percent of estimated value up to a statutory maximum, which changes according to amendments by Congress. The down payment would be the difference between the maximum loan amount and the purchase price of the home, but would in no case be less than $200. This $200 may be applied to closing costs and prepaid items. The amount of the project loan cannot exceed the sum of the individual loans. The maximum interest rate is established by the HUD Secretary, to which is added ½ percent for mortgage insurance premium. The FHA application and commitment fee is $3 per $1,000 for the mortgage amount.

The mortgage term is thirty-five years or not appreciably in excess of three-fourths of the remaining economic life, whichever is less.

SECTION 213 INVESTOR-SPONSORED COOPERATIVE HOUSING Authorized by the Housing Act of 1956 and later amendments; provides FHA mortgage insurance to provide good-quality multifamily housing to be sold to nonprofit cooperatives; FHA insures lenders against losses on mortgages. Insured mortgages may be used to finance the construction or rehabilitation of detached, semidetached, row, walkup, or elevator-type structures with five or more units. The unit mortgage limits for nonelevator apartments vary according to size of the units. Limits per family unit are somewhat higher for elevator apartments. In areas where cost levels so require, limits per family unit may be increased up to 45 percent.

Eligible mortgagors include investors, builders, developers, public bodies, and others who meet FHA requirements for mortgagors.

Members of the nonprofit cooperative which organizes the project are eligible to occupy dwellings in the project on a cooperative ownership basis.

The maximum amount of the loan may be equal to 90 percent of the estimated replacement cost for proposed construction and 90 percent of the appraised value after rehabilitation for rehabilitated structures. The maximum interest rate is established by the HUD Secretary, to which is added ½ percent for mortgage insurance premium.

The mortgage term is forty years or not appreciably in excess of three-fourths of the remaining economic life, whichever is less.

SECTION 213 LIMIT [public housing] Amendment to the U.S. Housing Act of 1937 in the Housing Act of 1969, providing that the rent of a public housing tenant may not exceed 25 percent of the family's adjusted income.

SECTION 213 MORTGAGE INSURANCE FOR PURCHASE OF SALES-TYPE COOPERATIVE HOUSING Authorized by the Housing Act of 1950 and later amendments; provides FHA mortgage insurance to provide good-quality new housing available for purchase by individual members of a housing cooperative.

FHA insures lenders against losses on mortgages. Insured mortgages may be used to finance purchase by a cooperative member of single-family detached, semidetached, or row housing, constructed under the sponsorship of a nonprofit cooperative, with five or more units. The unit mortgage limits vary according to unit sizes.

Eligible mortgagors include members of a nonprofit cooperative which sponsor such housing.

For most families, the maximum amount of the loan would be equal to 97 percent of estimated value, up to a maximum amount.

The down payment would be the difference between the maximum loan amount and the purchase price of the home. The maximum interest rate is established by the HUD Secretary, to which is added $1/2$ percent for mortgage insurance premium.

The mortgage term is thirty years, but it may be thirty-five years if the mortgagor is unacceptable under a thirty-year term.

SECTION 220 MORTGAGE INSURANCE FOR HOMES IN URBAN RENEWAL AREAS

Authorized by the Housing Act of 1954 and later amendments; provides FHA mortgage insurance to help families purchase or rehabilitate homes in urban renewal areas; all families are eligible to apply; FHA insures lenders against loss on mortgage loans. These loans may be used to finance acquisition or rehabilitation of one- to eleven-family housing in approved urban renewal or code enforcement areas. Maximum insurable loans for the occupant mortgagor vary according to the size of the units. Properties must be constructed or rehabilitated pursuant to an approved Urban Renewal Plan.

For most families, the maximum amount of the loan would be equal to 97 percent of estimated replacement cost, up to a maximum amount. The down payment would be the difference between the maximum loan amount and the purchase price of the home or the estimated value, whichever is less. In addition, the purchaser must pay all items of prepaid expense. Special terms are available for qualified veterans. The maximum interest rate is established by the HUD Secretary, to which is added $1/2$ percent for mortgage insurance premium. The FHA application fee is $40 for existing and $50 for proposed housing. The service charge by the mortgagee varies but may not normally exceed 1 percent of the total mortgage.

The mortgage terms may extend for thirty years or three-fourths of remaining economic life of the property, whichever is less, but it may be thirty-five years if the mortgagor is unacceptable under a thirty-year term and the property was constructed subject to FHA and VA inspection.

SECTION 220 MORTGAGE INSURANCE FOR RENTAL HOUSING IN URBAN RENEWAL AREAS

Authorized by the Housing Act of 1954 and later amendments; provides FHA mortgage insurance to provide good quality rental housing in urban renewal areas; FHA insures lenders against loss on mortgages. Insured mortgages may be used to finance proposed construction or rehabilitation of detached, semidetached, row, walkup, or elevator-type rental housing or to finance purchase of properties which have been rehabilitated by a local public agency. Property must consist of two or more units and must be located in an urban renewal area, urban redevelopment project, code enforcement program area, or urban area receiving rehabilitation assistance as a result of natural disaster. Unit mortgage limits for nonelevator apartments vary according to the size of the units. Limits per family unit are somewhat higher for elevator apartments. In areas where cost levels so require, limits per family unit may be increased up to 45 percent.

Eligible mortgagors include investors, builders, developers, public bodies, and others who meet FHA requirements for mortgagors.

All families are eligible to occupy a dwelling in a structure whose mortgage is insured under the program, subject to normal tenant selection.

For most mortgagors, the maximum amount of the loan may not exceed 90 percent of the estimated replacement cost. The maximum interest rate is established by the HUD Secretary, to which is added $\frac{1}{2}$ percent for mortgage insurance premium.

The mortgage term is forty years or not appreciably in excess of three-fourths of the remaining economic life, whichever is less.

SECTION 220(h) HOME IMPROVEMENT LOAN INSURANCE [urban renewal]
Authorized by the Housing Act of 1961 and later amendments; provides mortgage insurance through FHA to help families repair or improve existing residential structures in official urban renewal or concentrated code enforcement areas.

FHA insures lenders against loss on loans. These loans may be used to finance the alteration, repair, or improvement of existing one- to eleven-family structures. Property must be located in an approved urban renewal, redevelopment, or code enforcement program area or urban area receiving rehabilitation assistance as a result of natural disaster. The structure must be at least ten years old unless the loan is to make major structural improvements.

The loan terms may extend for twenty years or three-fourths of the remaining economic life of the property, whichever is less.

SECTION 220(h) IMPROVEMENT LOANS FOR RENTAL HOUSING IN URBAN RENEWAL AREAS
Authorized by the Housing Act of 1961 and later amendments; provides mortgage insurance through FHA to make possible the financing of improvements for rental housing in urban renewal areas.

FHA insures lenders against loss on loans. Insured loans may be used to finance alteration, repair, or improvement of existing detached, semidetached, row, walkup, or elevator-type rental housing consisting of five or more units. Housing must be at least ten years old, unless the loan is primarily to make structural improvements. Property must be located in an approved urban renewal area, urban redevelopment project, or code enforcement program area or urban area receiving rehabilitation assistance as a result of natural disaster.

Public and private mortgagors who meet FHA requirements as determined on a case-by-case basis for mortgagors are eligible.

The loan term is twenty years or not appreciably in excess of three-fourths of the remaining economic life, whichever is less.

SECTION 221 RELOCATION HOUSING   [*See* SECTION 221(D)(2) MORTGAGE INSURANCE FOR FAMILIES OF LOW AND MODERATE INCOME.]

SECTION 221(d)(2) MORTGAGE INSURANCE FOR FAMILIES OF LOW AND MODERATE INCOME   Authorized by the Housing Act of 1954 and later amendments; provides FHA mortgage insurance, to make homeownership more readily available to families displaced by urban renewal or other government action as well as other low-income and moderate-income families.

FHA insures lenders against loss on mortgage loans. These loans may be used to finance the purchase of proposed or existing low-cost one- to four-family housing units or the rehabilitation of such housing. Maximum insurable loans for an occupant-mortgagor vary according to the size of the unit and economic conditions in the area. Higher mortgage limits are available for two- to four-family housing units.

All families are eligible to apply. Displaced families qualify for special terms. Certification of eligibility as a displaced family is made by the appropriate local government agency.

For most families, the maximum amount of the loan is the appraised value of the property or 97 percent of the appraised value plus prepaid expenses such as taxes or insurance, whichever is less. The down payment is the difference between the maximum loan amount and the purchase price of the home plus prepaid expenses. For displaced families the down payment required would be somewhat smaller but in no event less than $200. The maximum interest rate is established by the HUD Secretary, to which is added $1/2$ percent for mortgage insurance premium. The FHA application fee is $40 for existing and $50 for proposed housing. The service charge by mortgagees varies, but it may not normally exceed 1 percent of the total mortgage.

The mortgage term may extend for thirty years, but it may be thirty-five or forty years if the mortgagor is unacceptable under a thirty-year term.

SECTION 221(d)(3) MORTGAGE INSURANCE FOR RENTAL HOUSING FOR LOW- AND MODERATE-INCOME FAMILIES AT MARKET INTEREST RATE

Authorized by the Housing Act of 1954 and later amendments; provides FHA mortgage insurance, with rent supplements to low-income tenants, to provide good quality rental or cooperative housing within the price range of low- and moderate-income families.

FHA insures lenders against loss on mortgages. Insured mortgages may be used to finance construction or rehabilitation of rental or cooperative detached, semidetached, row, walkup, or elevator structures or to finance the purchase of properties which have been rehabilitated by a local public agency. Such housing must have five or more units. The unit mortgage limits for nonelevator apartments vary according to the size of the units. Unit mortgage limits are somewhat higher for elevator-type structures. In areas where cost levels so require, limits per family unit may be increased up to 45 percent. Most rent supplement projects are built under this program, although this program is also used independently of rent supplement.

Eligible sponsors include public, nonprofit, cooperative, builder-seller, investor-sponsor, and limited distribution mortgagors.

A nonprofit sponsor must receive from FHA certification of eligibility prior to submission of a formal project application.

All families are eligible to occupy a dwelling in a structure whose mortgage is insured under the program, subject to normal tenant selection requirements for private rental housing. Low-income families may qualify for rent supplement benefits when the mortgagor has qualified for this assistance. A preference must be given to displacees.

For limited distribution mortgagors, the maximum amount of the loan would be equal to 90 percent of the estimated replacement cost in most cases. For other mortgagors the maximum amount of the loan would be equal to 100 percent of the estimated replacement cost in most cases.

The mortgage term is forty years or not appreciably in excess of three-fourths of the remaining economic life, whichever is less.

SECTION 221(d)(3) MR   [*See* SECTION 221 (D)(3) MORTGAGE INSURANCE FOR RENTAL HOUSING FOR LOW- AND MODERATE-INCOME FAMILIES AT MARKET RATE INTEREST.]

SECTION 221(d)(4) MORTGAGE INSURANCE FOR RENTAL HOUSING FOR FAMILIES OF MODERATE INCOME

Authorized by the Housing Act of 1959 and later amendments; provides FHA mortgage insurance to provide good-quality rental housing within the price range affordable by moderate-income families; profit-motivated sponsors are eligible; FHA insures lenders against loss on mortgages. Insured mortgages may be used to finance construction or rehabilitation of detached, semidetached, row, walkup, or elevator-type rental housing containing five or more units. The unit mortgage for nonelevator apartments vary according to unit sizes. Unit mortgage limits are somewhat higher for elevator-type structures. In areas where cost levels so require, limits per family unit may be increased up to 45 percent. Rental rates must permit occupancy by moderate-income families.

The maximum amount of the loan would be equal to 90 percent of the estimated replacement cost in most cases. The maximum permissible interest rate is established by the HUD Secretary, to which is added ½ percent for mortgage insurance premium.

The mortgage term is forty years or not appreciably in excess of three-fourths of the remaining economic life, whichever is less.

SECTION 221(h) MORTGAGE INSURANCE FOR LOW-INCOME REHABILITATION HOUSING Authorized by the Demonstration Cities and Metropolitan Development Act of 1966 to finance the acquisition by low-income purchasers of individual rehabilitated units. Supplanted by the Section 235 program.

SECTION 221(i) CONDOMINIUM CONVERSION Authorized by the Housing and Urban Development Act of 1968 and later amendments; provides mortgage insurance and/or direct loans and/or interest subsidies through FHA to help low- and moderate-income families purchase a home under a condominium plan of family unit ownership at a below-market rate of interest. FHA insures lenders against loss on mortgage loans. These loans may be used by families to finance the purchase of a dwelling unit in a Section 221(d)(3) BMIR project which is converted to a condominium plan of family-unit ownership. Families can have the benefit of a below-market rate of interest on the mortgage loans for the purchase of the dwellings.

Families eligible to apply must fall within certain income limits as determined by a local HUD office on a case-by-case basis. In most cases, families are required to make a down payment equal to 3 percent of the purchase price of the home, including certain prepaid expenses. Eligible families are required to make monthly mortgage payments at a rate of interest between 3 and 6 percent, depending upon the family's financial capacity. In most cases there is no application fee.

The mortgage terms may extend for forty years or three-fourths of the remaining economic life of the property, whichever is less.

SECTION 221(j) CONVERSION OF MULTIFAMILY RENTAL HOUSING TO COOPERATIVE HOUSING Authorized by the Housing and Urban Development Act of 1968 and later amendments; provides FHA mortgage insurance and direct payments to help low- and moderate-income families benefit from housing under a cooperative plan of ownership at a below-market rate of interest. FHA insures lenders against loss on mortgage loans. These loans may be used to finance the conversion of a 221(d)(3) BMIR rental project to a cooperative. Mortgage amounts insurable are 100 percent of appraised value for continued use as a cooperative.

Cooperatives composed of families whose incomes are within the limits prescribed by Section 221(d)(3) may apply; special provisions for tenants with incomes above limits to become cooperators.

Members of the cooperative are eligible to occupy dwellings in the structure whose mortgage is insured under the program.

The maximum amount of the loan would be equal to 100 percent of the value for continued use as a cooperative. The current maximum interest rate is 3 percent. The FHA application and commitment fee is $3 per $1,000 of the mortgage amount.

The mortgage term is forty years or not appreciably in excess of three-fourths of the remaining economic life, whichever is less.

SECTION 222 MORTGAGE INSURANCE FOR SERVICEMEN'S HOUSING Authorized by the Housing Act of 1954 and later amendments to finance the purchase of proposed or existing one-family housing for mortgagors certified by the Secretary of Defense or Secretary of Transportation. Mortgage insurance on one-family dwelling or condominium unit insured under any other section of the National Housing Act is eligible for transfers to Section 222 if assumed by eligible servicemen. Property must meet criteria of Section 203(b) or 234(c).

SECTION 223(e) MORTGAGE INSURANCE FOR HOUSING IN DECLINING AREAS Authorized by the Housing and Urban Development Act of 1968 and later amendments; provides FHA mortgage insurance to help families purchase or rehabilitate housing in declining urban areas; all families are eligible to apply; FHA insures lenders against loss on mortgage loans. These loans may be used to finance the purchase, repair, rehabilitation, and construction of housing in older, declining urban areas where conditions are such that certain normal eligibility requirements for mortgage insurance under a particular program cannot be met. The property must be an acceptable risk, giving consideration to the need for providing adequate housing for low- and moderate-income families.

Mortgages for housing eligible under the special program may be insured under any one of several FHA programs. The maximum amount of the loan, the down payment, and other mortgage terms vary according to the FHA program under which the mortgage is insured. The maximum interest rate is established by the HUD Secretary, to which is added ½ percent for mortgage insurance premium. Fees are established under the applicable FHA program.

SECTION 231 MORTGAGE INSURANCE FOR RENTAL HOUSING FOR THE ELDERLY Authorized in the Housing Act of 1959 and later amendments; provides FHA mortgage insurance with rent supplements to certain eligible sponsors to provide rental housing for the elderly; FHA insures lenders against loss on mortgages. Insured mortgages may be used to finance construction or rehabilitation of detached, semidetached, walkup, or elevator-type rental housing designed for occupancy by elderly or handicapped individuals and consisting of eight or more units. The unit mortgage limits for nonelevator apartments vary according to the size of the unit. Limits per family unit are somewhat higher for elevator apartments. In areas where cost levels so require, limits per family unit may be increased up to 45 percent.

Eligible mortgagors include investors, builders, developers, public bodies, and nonprofit sponsors—nonprofit sponsors and public bodies can obtain rent supplement contracts.

All elderly or handicapped persons are eligible to occupy apartments in the structure whose mortgage is insured under the program.

For nonprofit and public mortgagors, the maximum amount of the loan would be equal to 100 percent of the estimated replacement cost in most cases. For all other mortgagors, the maximum amount of the loan would be equal to 90 percent of the replacement cost in most cases. The maximum interest rate is established by the HUD Secretary, to which is added ½ percent for mortgage insurance premium. In addition to mortgage insurance nonprofit sponsors and public bodies may receive rent supplements on behalf of low-income elderly.

The mortgage term is forty years or not appreciably in excess of three-fourths of the remaining economic life, whichever is less.

SECTION 232 MORTGAGE INSURANCE FOR NURSING HOMES Authorized by the Housing Act of 1959 and later amendments; provides FHA mortgage insurance to make possible the financing of nursing homes and related facilities; FHA insures lenders against loss on mortgages. Insured mortgages may be used to finance construction or rehabilitation of facilities accommodating twenty or more patients requiring skilled nursing care and related medical services or those who, while not in need of nursing home care, are in need of minimum but continuous care provided by licensed or trained personnel. Nursing home and intermediate care services may be combined in the same facility covered by an insured mortgage or may be in separate facilities. Eligible mortgagors include investors, builders, developers, and private nonprofit corporations or associations licensed or regulated by the state for the accommodation of convalescents and persons requiring skilled nursing care or intermediate care. Documentation regarding the characteristics of the property and the qualifications of the mortgagor are assembled by the mortgagee and submitted with the application. Approval by the state agency designated by the Public Health Service Act for the state in which the facility is to be located is required.

The maximum amount of the loan would be equal to 90 percent of the estimated value of the physical improvements and major movable equipment. Maximum interest rate is established by the HUD Secretary, to which is added $\frac{1}{2}$ percent for mortgage insurance premium.

The mortgage term is twenty years or not appreciably in excess of three-fourths of the remaining economic life, whichever is less.

SECTION 233 MORTGAGE INSURANCE FOR EXPERIMENTAL HOUSING AND OTHER PROJECTS Authorized by the Housing Act of 1961 and later amendments; provides FHA mortgage insurance to help finance the development or rehabilitation of homes, including rental multifamily housing that incorporates new or untried construction concepts designed to reduce housing costs, raise living standards, and improve neighborhood design; also to finance the construction or rehabilitation, using new techniques, of facilities, including major movable equipment, for group practice of dentistry, medicine, or optometry; also to finance the purchase of land and the development of building sites for subdivisions or new communities, including water and sewer systems and streets, where new technologies are incorporated.

The type of construction, mortgage limit, down payment, term, interest rate, and fees are governed by eligibility requirements of the applicable home mortgage or improvement loan insurance program.

SECTION 234(c) MORTGAGE INSURANCE FOR PURCHASE OF CONDO-MINIUM UNITS Authorized by the Housing Act of 1961 and later amendments; provides FHA mortgage insurance to enable families to purchase units in condominium projects; FHA insures lenders against loss on mortgage loans. These loans may be used to finance the acquisition of individual units in proposed or existing condominium projects containing four or more units. The maximum insurable loan for an occupant mortgagor is subject to change. If the condominium project contains more than eleven units, the project mortgage must be or have been insured under an FHA multifamily housing insurance program other than its Section 213 cooperative housing program. A mortgagor may not own more than four units.

For most families the maximum amount of the loan would be equal to

97 percent of the estimated value, depending on the amount of the loan. The down payment would be equal to the difference between the maximum loan amount and the purchase price of the unit. Servicemen are eligible for a smaller down payment. The maximum interest rate is established by the HUD Secretary, to which is added $\frac{1}{2}$ percent for mortgage insurance premium. The FHA application fee is $40, but when an application is filed before an issuance of a commitment to insure the project mortgage there is no fee. The service charge by the mortgagee varies, but it may not normally exceed 1 percent of the total mortgage amount.

The mortgage term may extend for thirty years, but it may be thirty-five years if the mortgagor is unacceptable under a thirty-year term.

SECTION 234(d) CONDOMINIUM MORTGAGE INSURANCE   Authorized by the Housing Act of 1964 and later amendments; provides mortgage insurance through FHA to enable sponsors to develop condominium projects in which individual units will be sold to home buyers.

FHA insures lenders against loss on mortgage loans. These loans may be used to finance the construction or rehabilitation of multifamily housing structures by a sponsor intending to sell individual units as condominiums, which also would be eligible for the benefits of mortgage insurance under this program. Eligible sponsors include investors, builders, developers, public bodies, and others who meet FHA requirements for mortgagors. All families are eligible to purchase condominium units whose mortgage is insured under this program. Servicemen are eligible for more liberal mortgage terms. For most mortgagors, the maximum amount of the loan is 90 percent of the replacement cost or sum of the unit mortgage amounts, whichever is less.

The mortgage term is forty years or not appreciably in excess of three-quarters of the remaining economic life, whichever is less.

SECTION 235(i) INTEREST SUBSIDY   Authorized by the Housing and Urban Development Act of 1968 and later amendments; provides mortgage insurance and interest subsidies through the Federal Housing Administration to make homeownership more readily available to lower-income families by providing monthly payments to lenders of FHA-insured mortgage loans on behalf of the lower-income families. FHA insures lenders against losses on mortgage loans.

These loans may be used to finance the purchase of a single-family dwelling, a two-family house, or a unit in a multifamily project. Families eligible to receive the benefits of the subsidies and the mortgage insurance must fall within certain income and asset limits (as determined by locality on a case-by-case basis) as explained in program literature.

For eligible families, the down payment is 3 percent of acquisition cost.

Assistance payments are made monthly to the lender and may reduce the effective interest rate paid by the homeowner to as low as 1 percent. Assisted families are required to pay at least 20 percent of their adjusted income (gross income after certain allowable deductions) for mortgage payment. Interest-reduction payments may extend for the full mortgage term, but they cease when the assisted family's income exceeds the maximum allowable for receiving the benefits of the subsidy.

The mortgage term may extend for thirty years, but it may be thirty-five to forty where the purchaser is unacceptable under a thirty-year term.

SECTION 235(j) INTEREST SUBSIDY HOME   Authorized by the Housing and Urban Development Act of 1968 and later amendments; provides mortgage insurance and subsidies through the Federal Housing Administration to assist lower-income families to purchase rehabilitated homes from nonprofit sponsors at prices they can afford. Other provisions are similar to the Section 235(i) program.

SECTION 235(j) PROJECT MORTGAGE   Authorized by the Housing and Urban Development Act of 1968, and later amendments; provides mortgage insurance and subsidy payments through the Federal Housing Administration to make it possible for a nonprofit organization or public body to finance the acquisition and the rehabilitation of housing that will be sold to lower-income families. FHA insures lenders against loss on mortgage loans. These loans may be used to finance the purchase and rehabilitation of housing for subsequent resale to lower income families. Nonprofit sponsors as well as the home purchasers can receive the benefits of interest-reduction payments. The project must consist of four or more single-family or two-family dwellings or dwelling units in a multifamily structure for which a plan of family unit ownership is approved.

Purchasers of the rehabilitated dwelling units must have incomes within specified limits (as determined by locality on a case-by-case basis) and be recommended by the nonprofit sponsoring organization. Interest assistance payments are paid to the mortgagee on behalf of the nonprofit sponsor/mortgagor on the outstanding loan balance starting with the final endorsement of the project.

SECTION 236 INTEREST REDUCTION (OR SUBSIDY) PROGRAM   Authorized by the Housing and Urban Development Act of 1968 and later amendments; provides direct payments of subsidies to mortgage lenders and provides mortgage insurance for nonprofit, cooperative, builder-seller, investor-sponsor, and limited-distribution sponsors for the construction of rental and cooperative housing for persons of low and moderate income by providing interest-reduction payments to lower their housing costs. Families and individuals, including the elderly and handicapped, who are eligible to receive the benefits of the subsidies must fall within certain income limits as determined locally on a case-by-case basis. Families with higher incomes may occupy apartments but may not benefit from subsidy payments.

Assistance payments are made monthly by FHA to the mortgagee and may bring the effective interest rate paid by the mortgagor to as low as 1 percent. Benefits received in this way are passed on to those families qualifying for assistance. Assisted families are required to pay for rent at least 25 percent of their adjusted income (income after certain allowable deductions). The mortgage term normally extends for forty years. Interest-reduction payments may extend for the full term of the mortgage. For individual families, assistance ceases when their income exceeds the maximum allowable for receiving the benefits of subsidy.

The Housing and Community Development Act of 1974 provides for up to 20 percent of families in Section 236 projects whose incomes will not permit them to afford to pay basic rent to receive "rent supplements" in addition to receiving the benefits of the interest subsidy. (*See also* SECTION 101 RENT SUPPLEMENT PROGRAM.)

The 1974 act also establishes a minimum rental equal to utility costs.

SECTION 237 MORTGAGE INSURANCE FOR SPECIAL CREDIT RISKS Authorized by the Housing and Urban Development Act of 1968 and later amendments; provides mortgage insurance with interest subsidies to eligible applicants to make homeownership possible for low- and moderate-income families who cannot meet normal FHA requirements.

FHA insures lenders against loss on mortgage loans. These loans may be used to finance the purchase of new or existing single-family homes or the purchase and rehabilitation of existing single-family homes. The maximum insurable mortgage varies according to economic conditions.

Only families that qualify for homeownership under regular FHA credit standards are eligible. Families qualifying for mortgage insurance under this program must have a gross monthly income at least four times the families' required payment to the mortgage.

Counseling assistance must be obtained by the applicant mortgagor from a HUD-approved Section 237(e) counseling agency before his application may be submitted by the mortgagee. Information regarding availability of counseling assistance is available through HUD-FHA Area and Insuring Offices.

The down payment required is determined by the requirements for the FHA program under which the application originates. Application may be originated under most FHA home mortgage programs. Buyers whose mortgages are to be insured under Section 237 may also qualify for assistance payments under Section 235(b). Assistance payments are made monthly by FHA to the mortgagee and may bring down the effective interest rate paid by the homebuyer to as low as 1 percent. The application fee is $45 for proposed and $35 for existing housing.

The term of the mortgage is determined by the program under which the application originates.

SECTION 240 MORTGAGE INSURANCE FOR PURCHASERS OF LEASED HOUSING   Authorized by the Housing and Urban Development Act of 1968; provides FHA mortgage insurance to help homeowners obtain fee-simple title to property which they hold under long-term leases.

For one- to four-family residences, the maximum amount insurable is the cost of purchasing fee-simple title or $10,000 per family unit, whichever is less. All homeowners whose homes are located on property which is held under long-term ground leases are eligible to apply. The maximum amount of the loan is equal to the difference between the maximum amount prescribed under FHA's Section 203(b) program of mortgage insurance and current indebtedness on the property subject to the $10,000 loan limitation. The current maximum interest rate is established by the HUD Secretary, to which is added $\frac{1}{2}$ percent for mortgage insurance premium. The FHA application fee is $20. The service charge by the mortgagee varies but may not normally exceed 1 percent of the total loan.

The mortgage term may extend for twenty years or three-fourths of the remaining economic life of the dwelling, whichever is less.

SECTION 241 SUPPLEMENTAL LOAN INSURANCE FOR MULTIFAMILY HOUSING   Authorized by the Housing and Urban Development Act of 1968 and later amendments to finance 90 percent of the cost of alteration, repair, additions, and improvements of any multifamily project insured under any section of the act; loan proceeds may be used to finance the purchase of equipment to be used in the operation of a nursing home or group practice facility.

SECTION 242 MORTGAGE INSURANCE FOR HOSPITALS   Authorized by the Housing and Urban Development Act of 1968 and later amendments; provides FHA mortgage insurance to enable the financing of hospitals; FHA insures lenders against loss on mortgages.

The loans may be used to finance the construction or rehabilitation of nonprofit hospitals including major movable equipment. The program is not yet operational for proprietary facilities. Eligible applicants are proprietary facilities or facilities of private nonprofit corporations or associations licensed or regulated by the state, municipality, or other political subdivision.

An applicant is required to furnish detailed information about the proposed hospital including state certification to a regional office of the Public Health Service which is responsible for determining the feasibility of all proposals. The sponsor submits a formal application through an FHA-approved mortgagee to the FHA-insuring office after first applying to the Department of Health, Education, and Welfare. The maximum mortgage amount may not exceed 90 percent of the estimated replacement cost. The current maximum interest rate is established by the HUD Secretary, to which is added $\frac{1}{2}$ percent for mortgage insurance premium. The mortgage term may extend for twenty-five years.

SECTION 304 RECREATION FACILITY LOANS [rural]   Authorized by the Consolidated Farmers Home Administration Act of 1961 and later amendments; provides guaranteed or insured loans through the Farmers Home Administration to assist eligible farm and ranch owners or tenants, through the extension of credit and supervisory assistance, to convert all or a portion of the farms they own or operate to outdoor income-producing recreational enterprises which will supplement or supplant farm or ranch income and permit carrying on sound and successful operations.

Funds may be used to (1) develop land and water resources; (2) repair and construct buildings; (3) purchase land, equipment, livestock, and related recreation items; and (4) pay necessary operating expenses.

Recreation enterprises that may be financed include camp grounds, horseback riding stables, swimming facilities, tennis courts, shooting preserves, vacation cottages, lodges and rooms for visitors, lakes and ponds for boating and fishing, docks, nature trails, hunting facilities, and winter sports areas.

SECTION 312 HOUSING REHABILITATION LOANS   Authorized by the Housing Act of 1964 and later amendments; provides direct loans from HUD at below-market interest rate to provide funds to individuals and families who own residences and to owners and tenants of nonresidential properties in Neighborhood Development Program, urban renewal, and code enforcement areas.

These loans may be used to rehabilitate property located in federally assisted code enforcement areas, urban renewal areas where there is a rehabilitation or code enforcement plan, certified areas, and for properties in areas under a statewide Fair Access to Insurance Requirements (FAIR) plan determined to be uninsurable because of physical hazards.

Coverage extends to an owner or tenant of any property in the above-described areas except in a certified area where it only extends to an owner-occupant of residential property.

Loans are issued at 3 percent interest and have a term of up to twenty years.

SECTION 314 DEMONSTRATION PROJECT GRANT   Supplanted by block grants provided through Title I—Community Development of the Housing and Community Development Act of 1974. (*See also* DEMONSTRATION PROJECT GRANT.)

SECTION 314(b) GRANTS [health planning]   Authorized by Title III of the Public Health Service Act as amended by the Comprehensive Health Planning and PHS Amendments of 1966 and the Partnership for Health Amendments of 1967 and later amendments. Provides grants through the Health Services and Mental Health Administration of the U.S. Department of Health, Education, and Welfare to public agencies and nonprofit organizations to provide financial support for areawide comprehensive health planning, including assessing health needs and alternatives, determining gaps and overlaps in existing health programs, and recommending courses of action that may be taken to achieve the targeted priority health goals.

SECTION 501 AND 502 [small business]   (*See* SMALL BUSINESS ADMINISTRATION.)

SECTION 502 RURAL HOUSING LOANS   Authorized by Title V of the Housing Act of 1949 and later amendments. Section 502 provides loans to residents of rural areas to build, buy, or improve homes and farm service buildings and related facilities and to buy building sites.

SECTION 504 HOUSING LOANS [rural]   Authorized by the Housing Act of 1949 and later amendments; provides direct loans through the Farmers Home Administration to assist owner-occupants in rural areas who do not qualify for Section 502 loans to repair or improve their dwellings, to make such dwellings safe and sanitary, and to remove hazards to the health of the occupants, their families, or the community. This includes repairs to the foundation, roof, or basic structure as well as water and waste disposal systems. Termed "very low income housing repair loans."

SECTION 515 AND 521 RURAL RENTAL HOUSING LOANS   Authorized by the Housing Act of 1949 and later amendments; provides direct loans or guaranteed or insured loans through the Farmers Home Administration to provide for rural residents in economically designed and constructed rental and cooperative housing and related facilities suited for independent living.

Applicants may be individuals, cooperatives, nonprofit organizations, or corporations unable to finance the housing either with their own resources or with credit obtained from private sources. However, applicants must be able to assume the obligations of the loan, furnish adequate security, and have sufficient income for repayment. They must also have the ability and intention of maintaining and operating the housing for purposes for which the loan is made.

SECTION 523 TECHNICAL ASSISTANCE [rural]   Authorized by the Housing Act of 1949 and later amendments; provides project grants through the Farmers Home Administration to states, counties, or other political subdivisions or to nonprofit organizations to provide financial assistance for the promotion of programs of technical and supervisory assistance which will aid needy low-income individuals and their families in carrying out mutual self-help efforts in rural areas.

SECTION 524 AND 525 SITE LOANS [rural]   Authorized by the Housing Act of 1949 and later amended; provides direct loans and/or guaranteed or insured loans obtained through the Farmers Home Administration to assist public or private nonprofit organizations interested in providing sites for housing, to acquire and develop land in rural areas to be subdivided as adequate building sites and sold on a nonprofit basis to eligible low- and moderate-income families and cooperatives and nonprofit applicants.

Loans may be used for the purchase and development of adequate sites, including necessary equipment which becomes a permanent part of the development; for water and sewer facilities if not available; payment of necessary engineering, legal fees, and closing costs; for needed landscaping and other necessary facilities related to buildings such as walks, parking areas, and driveways.

SECTION 608a   Inactive program that provided mortgage insurance for World War II veterans' rental housing.

SECTION 701 COMPREHENSIVE PLANNING ASSISTANCE   Authorized by the Housing Act of 1954 and later amendments; provides HUD project grants to strengthen the decision-making capabilities of state and local governments and thereby promote the more effective use of the nation's physical, economic, and human resources.

A broad range of subjects may be addressed under programs supported by these grants, including patterns of land use, the provision of public services, and the effective development and utilization of human and natural resources.

Types of activities which may be undertaken include preparing development plans, policies, and strategies; programming capital investments, governmental services, and implementation measures; and coordinating related activities carried on by other levels of government.

Eligible applicants include state agencies designated by the governor: areawide planning agencies including councils of governments; counties; cities; local development districts; economic development districts; Indian tribal bodies not being funded; localities which have suffered a major disaster; and official government planning agencies for areas where a substantial reduction in employment has occurred as a result of a decline in federal purchase or closing of a federal installation.

Type of grant: project grants are available, normally for two-thirds of the cost of the assisted project. Grants for three-fourths of project cost may be given in cases involving redevelopment areas, economic development districts, areas with a substantial reduction in federally related employment, the Appalachian Regional Commission and local development districts within its jurisdiction, and various interstate regional commissions.

SECTION 701(b) URBAN PLANNING RESEARCH AND DEMONSTRATION GRANTS   Authorized by the Housing Act of 1954 and later amendments; provides HUD grants to develop and improve methods and techniques for comprehensive planning, to advance the purpose of the comprehensive planning assistance program, and to assist in the conduct of research related to needed revisions of state statutes which create, govern, or control local governments or local government operations.

Funds are used for studies, research, and demonstration activities that meet research needs determined by the Department of Housing and Urban Development.

Public agencies, public and private universities, profit-making and non-profit organizations are eligible applicants. Grants may be up to 100 percent, but cost sharing is encouraged.

SECTION 702 BASIC WATER AND SEWER FACILITIES GRANTS   Authorized by the Housing and Urban Development Act of 1965; provides HUD project grants to construct water and sewer facilities.

Types of eligible projects include facilities to store, supply, treat, purify, or distribute water; sanitary sewer systems for the collection, transmission, and discharge of liquid wastes (excluding sewage treatment works); and storm sewer systems for the collection, transmission, and discharge of storm water caused by rainfall or groundwater runoff. Building or household connections and local distribution and collection laterals are not eligible for assistance. The facility system must be part of the comprehensively planned development of the area.

Cities, towns, counties, Indian tribes, or public agencies or instrumentalities of one or more states or one or more municipalities which have the legal authority to plan, finance, construct, and operate the facility are eligible applicants.

Program grants are not to exceed 50 percent of eligible land and construction costs for new water and sewer facilities. Under certain circumstances, communities having a population of less than 10,000 are eligible for 90 percent grant assistance. The applicant must provide sufficient funds in cash to complete funding of the project.

Grant assistance is available for a reasonable length of time as required by project completion. Such funds are not disbursed until after the grantee's portion of project funds has been substantially expended. Federal funds are dispensed only in amounts estimated to meet project obligations for the ensuing three months.

Such grants are supplanted by block grants provided through Title I—Community Development of the Housing and Community Development Act of 1974.

SECTION 703 NEIGHBORHOOD FACILITIES GRANTS Authorized by the Housing and Urban Development Act of 1965; provides HUD project grants to aid in the construction and/or rehabilitation of community service centers which offer a wide range of community services.

Construction of centers or the acquisition, expansion, or rehabilitation of existing structures to be used as multipurpose neighborhood centers are eligible activities. Funds may not be used for any other purpose.

Eligible development costs include architectural and engineering services, land acquisition and related costs (appraisals, etc.), and construction.

Local public bodies, agencies, or Indian tribes possessing authority under state or local law are eligible.

Priority is given to projects benefiting low-income families.

Proposed facilities must be (1) needed to carry out a program of community service (including a community action program under Title II, Economic Opportunity Act of 1964) in the area; (2) consistent with comprehensive planning for the community; and (3) accessible to a significant proportion of the area's low- or moderate-income residents.

Eligible applicants must provide one-third of the total development cost except in those areas designated as redevelopment areas under Section 401 or 403 of the Public Works and Economic Development Act of 1965, in which case the local share is one-fourth.

For approved projects, assistance is available from the time of a grant agreement with HUD until closeout of the project (no time limits). Disbursements are made as required but not more frequently than once a month.

Such grants are supplanted by block grants available through Title I—Community Development of the Housing and Community Development Act of 1974.

SECTION 706 URBAN BEAUTIFICATION AND IMPROVEMENT PROGRAM
(*See* URBAN BEAUTIFICATION AND IMPROVEMENT PROGRAM.)

SECTION 803 MORTGAGE INSURANCE FOR MILITARY (CAPEHART) HOUSING
(*See* CAPEHART-WHERRY HOUSING.)

SECTION 809 HOUSING   Inactive program that provided mortgage insurance for civilian employees at a research or development installation of a military department, NASA or AEC, or a contractor thereof.

SECTION 810   Inactive program that provided mortgage insurance for single- and multifamily rental housing for military personnel and essential civilian personnel serving or employed in connection with a defense installation.

SECTIONALIZED HOUSE   House constructed in a factory in two halves. Plumbing, wiring, bathroom fixtures, carpeting, kitchen cabinets and equipment, and flooring are all installed in the factory. The halves are shipped to and joined at the construction site on a completed foundation.

SECTION OR SECTION OF LAND [real estate]   A parcel of land comprising 1 square mile or 640 acres.

SECTRA SYSTEM [construction]   A French industrialized building system involving an on-site construction process as well as the use of prefabricated components. Demountable site framework units with integral hot-water curing and aligning mechanisms are used for floor slabs and exterior walls, while interior partitions, staircases, ductwork, and plumbing are prefabricated.

SECULAR TREND [statistics]   The long-term trend indicated by a body of data, usually for a period of over ten years.

SECURITY   (*See* COLLATERAL.)

SECURITY DEPOSIT   Sum of money, the amount of which is stipulated in a lease agreement, deposited by tenant with a manager to cover the cost of tenant-caused damages, possible delinquent rent upon vacation of the unit, etc.

SEED MONEY (*See* FRONT MONEY.)

SEED MONEY LOANS [*See* SECTION 106 AND 106(B) NONPROFIT SPONSOR "SEED MONEY" AND PLANNING LOANS.]

SEEPAGE PIT A covered pit with open-jointed lining through which septic tank effuent may seep or leach into surrounding porous soil.

SELF-HELP AND MUTUAL SELF-HELP PROGRAM [HUD] Any plan through which a person or group of persons provides some portion of the initiative (including labor in lieu of cash investment—sweat equity and other such concepts) in producing low- and moderate-income housing for himself or itself. (*See also* SWEAT EQUITY.)

SELLER'S MARKET A market condition characterized by an excess of demand, resulting in prices favoring the seller, as contrasted with a buyer's market.

SELLER'S REIMBURSEMENT AGREEMENT [FHA] Agreement executed by a seller of a Section 235 dwelling that is more than one year old on the date of an FHA mortgage insurance commitment, when the seller has not been occupying the property as an owner-occupant (other than a seller that is a nonprofit organization or public body or public agency), agreeing to reimburse HUD for any payments made by HUD to correct deficiencies or to compensate the buyer for structural or other defects which seriously affect the use and livability of the dwelling. In executing the agreement, the seller deposits in escrow for one year an amount equaling 5 percent of the sales price of the property to be used to reimburse HUD or to compensate the buyer for correcting the defects.

This agreement is mandatory on affected transactions occurring after April 9, 1971.

SEMIANNUAL DETERMINATION [urban renewal] Determination by HUD, issued semiannually, of the interest rate specified by local urban renewal agencies in original contracts for project advances and loans and in contract amendments authorized during the six-month period following the determination.

SEMIDETACHED HOUSE A dwelling structure containing two dwelling units separated vertically by a party wall. Also called "double house."

SENIOR CITIZEN   (*See* ELDERLY PERSON.)

SENIOR OPPORTUNITIES AND SERVICES PROGRAM (SOS)   Program funded by the Office of Economic Opportunity, focusing on employment opportunities and volunteer services for persons aged over fifty-five.

SEPTIC TANK   A covered, watertight sewage settling tank intended to retain the solids in the sewage flowing through the tank long enough for satisfactory decomposition of settled solids by bacterial action to take place.

SERVICE BRANCH [FHA]   The Department of Defense or the Department of Transportation. Certificates of eligibility are normally issued by a field commander, acting for the secretary of the appropriate department.

SERVICE INDUSTRY   An industry representing the sale of services, rather than the sale of goods—e.g., laundries, teachers, lawyers, repair shops.

SERVICE LINE   A gas, water, or other utility pipeline that connects the main pipeline to a property.

SERVICEMAN [HUD]   A member of the armed forces or the Coast Guard whose service branch has certified that he is eligible for participation in the Section 222 program.

SERVICE ROAD   A road running parallel to a limited access highway, providing access to abutting properties and serving vehicles entering or leaving the limited access highway. Also called "frontage road."

SET ASIDE   The portion of a Congressional appropriation that is reserved or "set aside" for use in conjunction with other government programs.

SETBACK LINES   Those lines which delineate the required distances for the location of a structure in relation to the perimeter of a property.

SETTLEMENT   (*See* CLOSING.)

SETTLEMENT COSTS [HUD]   Recording fees, transfer taxes, and similar expenses incidental to conveying real property; penalty costs for prepayment of any mortgage encumbering such real property; and the pro rata portion of real property taxes allocable to a period subsequent to the date of vesting of title or the effective date of the acquisition of such real property, whichever is earlier. Loan discount payments. Sales commissions. Distinguished from closing costs.

SETTLEMENT HOUSE (*See* COMMUNITY CENTER.)

SEVERANCE DAMAGES Loss resulting from a partial taking.

SEWER A system of underground pipes designed to carry sewage or surface water from one point to another.

SHALL In official or governmental terminology, indicates that which is required. (*See also* SHOULD.)

SHELTER RENT Rental cost of or income from apartments, less the cost of utilities.

SHOP LUMBER (*See* FACTORY AND SHOP LUMBER.)

SHORT-TERM LOAN [construction] (*See* CONSTRUCTION LOAN.)

SHOULD In official or governmental terminology, indicates that which is recommended but not required. (*See also* SHALL.)

"SHOW-UP TIME" RULE Rule requiring a general contractor to pay his hourly employees for a minimum of hours once they have reported to work, regardless of the weather.

SIGN-OFF POWER [Model Cities] Authority vested in a City Demonstration Agency to approve or disapprove certain other HUD-funded programs proposed to be undertaken in a Model Cities area not necessarily related to the model cities program.

SIMULTANEOUS SETTLEMENT Transaction through which a seller obtains mortgage financing on behalf of a buyer and the buyer assumes the seller's loan at settlement.

SINGLE-FAMILY HOUSING Housing units provided in detached, duplex, row-house, or town-house units.

SINGLE-STAGE PROCESSING [HUD/FHA] Procedure followed by the sponsor of a proposed multifamily housing project under which the sponsor provides, at the first submission of an application for a firm commitment of mortgage insurance, all exhibits necessary to meet all FHA's requirements. The sponsor's complete case submission may be processed in one stage and a firm commitment issued—eliminating the steps involved in a review of project feasibility and the issuance of a conditional commitment. (*See also* ACCELERATED MULTIFAMILY PROCESSING, MULTIPLE-STAGE PROCESSING.)

SINGLE TAX SYSTEM   Theoretical revenue-producing system under which all governmental revenue would be derived through the taxation only of land.

SINKING FUND   A fund intended to receive regular payments of equal amounts of money to be used for the payment of a debt or as a replacement reserve.

SITE ANALYSIS   (*See* ANALYSIS OF LOCATION.)

SITE APPROVAL   (*See* ANALYSIS OF LOCATION.)

SITE-CLEARANCE ACTIVITIES [urban renewal]   Includes the following in urban renewal areas:

1. Demolition of structures, removal of slabs on grade, removal of foundations to required elevations, breaking up basement slabs to prevent seepage, and filling of basements with suitable material

2. Breaking up and removing of abandoned street paving, curbs, gutters, and sidewalks

3. Necessary removal of abandoned utility mains and adjustments to facilities which are to remain

4. Moving of acquired structures on their present lots or on other lots within the project area, except that expenditures for improving the structures, providing new foundations or utility connections, landscaping, and similar items involved in preparing the property for resale are ineligible

5. Relocating underground of overhead utility distribution lines

SITE CONTROL   Any legal document that establishes one's rights to a site, such as a deed, option, or contract.

SITE COSTS   The cost of land acquisition and site improvement. (*See also* SITE IMPROVEMENT COSTS.)

SITE-IMPROVEMENT COSTS   Costs incurred in preparing a site for construction or erection of a building and providing required facilities for servicing the building once erected. The costs include clearance, excavation, grading, landscaping, connecting utility lines, and installation of streets, curbs, sidewalks, gutters, street lighting, and sewers.

SITE OFFICE [urban renewal]   Office established in an urban renewal area by the local public agency for the following kinds of activities (to the extent that they are related to or concerned with the problems of displacement and relocation of site occupants or rehabilitation of their properties):

1. As a center for furnishing families and individuals with information, counseling, and aid by appropriate social welfare agencies and other community resources

2. As a center for furnishing business concerns with information, counseling, and referral services

3. As a meeting place for neighborhood organizations and groups which will encourage the participation of site occupants and help establish lines of communication between site occupants, public officials, and community leaders with respect to project activities to be undertaken

4. As a place where staff of other agencies may work with the LPA to develop coordinated social welfare services to be made available to families and individuals in the project area

SKETCH PLAN   Initial, preliminary, rough plan to show only a conceptual representation of a proposed project, used primarily for discussion purposes.

SKID ROW   The locale, usually in an urban area, of concentration of homeless and often aimless persons—characterized by unusually inexpensive lodging, provided either privately or by religious "missions."

SKIP-PAYMENT PRIVILEGE   Provision in a mortgage, or policy of a lender, permitting the mortgagor to skip monthly payments at any time his payment total is ahead of the schedule provided in the mortgage.

SLAB SYSTEM [construction]   Building system in which slabs or panels are almost universally made of reinforced concrete, the variations occurring primarily in the degree to which other components and assemblies are integrated into the slab and its structural functions. Also called "panel system."

SLOPE RATIO [HUD]   Relation of horizontal distance to vertical rise or fall—e.g., 2 feet horizontal to 1 foot vertical would be expressed as "two to one" (2:1).

SLUM   A predominantly residential area where, by reason of dilapidation, overcrowding, faulty arrangement or design, lack of ventilation, light, or sanitation facilities, or any combination of these factors, living conditions are considered to be detrimental to safety, health, and morals.

SLUM CLEARANCE   The demolition and removal of buildings from any slum area, usually under the provisions of the federally assisted urban renewal program. (*See also* SITE-CLEARANCE ACTIVITIES.)

SLURBS   Suburban slums or suburban areas verging on or seemingly destined to become slums.

SMALL BUSINESS   According to the Small Business Act, "one which is independently owned and operated and which is not dominant in its field of operation." The SBA is permitted by the act to define a small business according to number of employees and dollar volume of business, with both criteria varying from industry to industry. (*See also* SMALL BUSINESS ADMINISTRATION.)

SMALL BUSINESS ADMINISTRATION (SBA)   SBA was created by the Small Business Act of 1953 as amended. It also derives its authority from the Small Business Investment Act of 1958 as amended; from Section 213(a) of the War Claims Act of 1948 as amended; from Title IV of the Economic Opportunity Act of 1964 as amended; and from the Disaster Relief Act of 1970. The Secretary of the Department of Housing and Urban Development, by authority in Section 312(f) of the Housing Act of 1964, has delegated to SBA certain responsibilities and functions under the loan program for rehabilitation of nonresidential property. The Secretary of Commerce has delegated to SBA certain responsibilities and functions under Section 202 of the Public Works and Economic Development Act of 1965.

The fundamental purposes of SBA are to aid, counsel, assist, and protect the interests of small business; to ensure that small business concerns receive a fair proportion of government purchases, contracts, and subcontracts as well as of the sales of government property; to make loans to small business concerns, state and local development companies, and the victims of floods or other catastrophes; to license, regulate, and make loans to small business investment companies; to improve the management skills of small business owners, potential owners, and managers; and to conduct studies of the economic environment.

SMALL TOWN   As defined in the Housing and Community Development Act of 1974, any town, village, or city with a population of not more than 10,000 according to the most recent available data compiled by the U.S. Bureau of the Census.

SOCIAL AND ECONOMIC STATISTICS ADMINISTRATION (SESA)   SESA was established on January 1, 1972, by the Secretary of Commerce. It brought together the Bureau of the Census and the former Office of Business Economics to form a single organization for carrying out statistical programs of the Department.

SESA was established to serve as a center for collecting, compiling, analyzing, and publishing a broad range of general-purpose statistics dealing with economic, social, and demographic data; to be responsible for the preparation, interpretation, and projection of measures of aggregate economic activity; and, as requested, to analyze the significance and meaning of changes in social statistics.

In cooperation with business and industry, government, and other public or private organizations, SESA conducts censuses and surveys and otherwise collects, processes, and analyzes statistical data relating to the social and economic activities and characteristics of the population and enterprises of the United States or other areas prescribed by law. SESA publishes and disseminates the resulting statistics for use by business, government agencies, and the public.

SOCIAL SERVICES   Any of a combination of services provided on a reasonably formal basis to a certain group of persons (usually low-income, elderly, or youths), including economic and social counseling, organizing and assisting tenant organizations, operating day-care centers and child-related programs, maintaining recreational facilities, and acting as liaison between tenants and various community agencies.

SOCIAL SURVEY [urban renewal]   Survey conducted by a local public agency to obtain information on the nature, extent, and range of socioeconomic problems of project area residents; covers such basic elements as age, income and its source, record of employment and unemployment, past welfare history and present welfare needs, degree of participation in formal and informal community groups, educational achievements, past residential mobility, health, and similar characteristics.

In addition, the social survey may be used to obtain information on project residents' attitudes on factors related to urban renewal activities—for example, their feelings about moving or leaving the neighborhood, attitudes and suggestions about specific renewal action, aspirations and desires for rehousing, and perception of their own socioeconomic problems.

SOFFIT   The underside of parts extending from a building—e.g., the underside of a cornice, arch, or roof overhang.

SOFT DOLLARS   The amount of an investment which is tax deductible during the construction period of a project and which result in tax savings. The term "soft dollars effect" refers to the fact that every dollar of tax deduction incurred during the first taxable year results in a reduction of tax during that year; thus, in effect, reducing the amount of equity invested by the amount of the tax shelter.

SOFT DOLLARS EFFECT   (*See* SOFT DOLLARS.)

SOLAR ENERGY SYSTEM   As defined in the Housing and Community Development Act of 1974, any addition, alteration, or improvement to an existing or new structure designed to utilize solar energy to reduce the energy requirements of that structure from other energy sources and which is in conformity with such criteria as are prescribed by the Secretary of HUD in consultation with the National Bureau of Standards.

SOLE SECURITY CLAUSE   Clause in a mortgage relieving the mortgagor of personal responsibility for repayment of the debt beyond the value of the mortgaged property.

SOUND HOUSING   Housing units with no defects or only slight defects which are normally corrected during the course of regular maintenance. Examples of slight defects are lack of paint; slight damage to porch or steps; small cracks in walls, plaster, or chimney; broken gutters or downspouts. Distinguished from deteriorating housing and dilapidated housing. (*See also* STANDARD HOUSING UNIT.)

SOUTHERN STANDARD BUILDING CODE   Model building code, used prominently especially in the South. (*See also* NATIONAL CODE.)

SPECIAL ASSESSMENT   A tax on property in a specific district that will benefit specifically from the improvements to be paid for by the tax, such as sewer or water facilities and streets.

SPECIAL ASSESSMENT BOND   Bond issued by a governmental entity to finance special improvements to be repaid from special assessment revenues.

SPECIAL ASSISTANCE FUNDS [FHA]   Funds made available to the Government National Mortgage Association for the purchase of mortgages financing low- or moderate-income housing under certain FHA mortgage insurance programs; purchase is financed by Treasury borrowings.

SPECIAL CONDITIONS The section in a contract document where are placed provisions covering situations peculiar to the transaction involved.

SPECIAL CREDIT RISK (*See* SECTION 237 MORTGAGE INSURANCE FOR SPECIAL CREDIT RISKS.)

SPECIAL FAMILY SUBSIDY [public housing] A subsidy paid by HUD to a local housing authority on behalf of certain categories of families (including the elderly and unusually large, low-income families displaced by public action) to assist in housing such families and still operate a project on a solvent basis. The subsidy cannot exceed $10 per unit per month.

SPECIAL-PURPOSE DISTRICT School, water, highway, and sewer districts and other units of government with power to tax and spend for particular purposes; their boundaries are seldom identical with the political boundaries of cities, townships, or counties.

SPECIAL-PURPOSE PROPERTY A combination of land and improvements with only one highest and best use because of the special design of the building(s) and equipment it houses—e.g., church, school, theater, hospital, gas station, bowling alley.

SPECIAL REVENUE SHARING Proposal by the Nixon administration to substitute the concept of revenue sharing for certain categorical grant programs, eliminating the latter and providing discretionary authority to states and units of local government for allocating funds to functions rather than programs. (*See also* GENERAL REVENUE SHARING, HELLER-PECHMAN PLAN, URBAN COMMUNITY DEVELOPMENT SPECIAL REVENUE SHARING.)

SPECIAL RISK INSURANCE FUND A revolving fund used by the Secretary of HUD to insure mortgages under Sections 223(e), 233(a)(2), 235, 236, 237, and 243.

SPECIAL USE ZONING (*See* CONDITIONAL USE ZONING.)

SPECIFICATION CODE A building code establishing construction requirements by reference to particular construction methods and materials, as distinguished from a performance code.

SPECIFICATIONS (specs) The written description that accompanies a set of working drawings and describes the work to be performed and the materials to be used in conjunction with a construction project.

SPECS (*See* SPECIFICATIONS.)

SPECULATOR A person, group, or other entity that attempts to make a profit by buying property, holding it for either long or short periods, and selling it at a higher price.

SPLIT-LEVEL HOUSE A house designed with living areas on two or more levels constructed less than a full story apart.

SPONSOR An entity that assumes liability for a particular type of effort or enterprise.

SPOT CLEARANCE The removal of certain, usually slum properties on a selective basis in an area dotted by such properties, as under a rehabilitation program.

SPOTTED SURVEY A survey of land showing the dimensions of improvement(s) located thereon and their relative position on the site—prepared by a registered surveyor. (*See also* LOAN SURVEY, PLAT OF SURVEY.)

SPOT ZONING The zoning of a parcel, tract, or other area incongruous with surrounding uses and in variance with established zoning regulations.

SPRAWL (*See* URBAN SPRAWL.)

SPREAD The difference between the cost of money to a lender and the "cost" for which (or interest rate at which) it is loaned to a borrower.

SQUARE-FOOT COST The cost per square foot of a building or of a land tract established by dividing its total cost by the total number of square feet—for buildings, on each floor measured to the surface of the outer wall. (*See also* CONSTRUCTION COST PER SQUARE FOOT.)

SQUATTER Someone who occupies another's property illegally.

STABILIZED INCOME The probable income from rents and other normal and necessary sources over a specific period.

STABILIZER VALUE The value based on normal market conditions, which excludes such factors as abnormal inflation or depression periods, short supply of materials, work slowdowns, etc.

STACK   A pipe extending upward through a building and through the roof to ventilate the plumbing system.

STAIRWAY [HUD]   One or more flights of stairs and any landings or platforms connected therewith to form a continuous passage from one floor to another.

STAMP, STAMP TAXES   (*See* TRANSFER AND STAMP TAXES.)

STANDARD DWELLING   (*See* STANDARD HOUSING UNIT.)

STANDARD HOUSING UNIT   A dwelling unit that meets minimum standards of occupancy. (*See also* SOUND HOUSING.)

STANDARD METROPOLITAN STATISTICAL AREA (SMSA)   Area defined by the U.S. Bureau of the Census as an integrated economic and social unit with a recognized large population nucleus. An SMSA generally consists of one or more county areas, primarily nonagricultural and closely related to a central city or cities of 50,000 or more. (In New England, SMSAs consist of groups of cities and townships rather than of entire counties.)

STANDBY COMMITMENT   A loan commitment of the difference between the minimum and maximum amount of a permanent loan, usually by a secondary lender or lending source. Also called "gap commitment."

STANDBY FEE   Fee charged by a lender for a loan commitment; usually it is forfeited if the loan is not made within a specified period.

STATE [FHA]   Includes the several states, Puerto Rico, the District of Columbia, Guam, the Trust Territory of the Pacific Islands, and the Virgin Islands. For properties insured under Title VIII, the term "state" includes the Canal Zone and Midway Island in addition to the above.

STATE AND LOCAL FINANCIAL ASSISTANCE ACT OF 1972   (*See* GENERAL REVENUE SHARING.)

STATE ECONOMIC OPPORTUNITY OFFICE (SEOO)   The SEOO is the prime mechanism by which OEO seeks to aid state governments in their efforts to eradicate poverty within their boundaries; it acts as adviser to the Governor on antipoverty matters, mobilizes and coordinates antipoverty resources at the state level, gives technical assistance to CAAs and other

OEO grantees, and participates in the monitoring and evaluation of OEO-funded programs. (*See also* COMMUNITY ACTION PROGRAM.)

STATE HOUSING DEVELOPMENT AGENCY (*See* STATE HOUSING FINANCE AGENCY.)

STATE HOUSING FINANCE AGENCY According to the Housing and Community Development Act of 1974, any public body or agency, publicly sponsored corporation, or instrumentality of one or more states which is designated by the governor (or governors in the case of an interstate development agency) to finance, assist in carrying out, or to carry out housing development or certain housing development-related activities.

STATE LAND DEVELOPMENT AGENCY Any state or local public body or agency with authority to act as a developer in carrying out one or more new community development programs, or any agency or instrumentality of these entities.

STATUTORY REGULATION Regulation established by law.

STATUTORY ROOM COST [public housing] Maximum amount that can be spent by a local housing authority for dwelling construction and equipment per room as established by statutory regulations. (*See also* PROTOTYPE COST LIMITS.)

STATUTORY TENANT A tenant whose lease is protected by provisions of law or other regulations.

STOOP A porch, platform, or entrance stairway in front of a house door.

STORM SEWER Sewer designed to carry surface water only, as distinguished from a sanitary sewer.

STORY That part of a building included between the surface of any floor and the surface of the floor next above or of the ceiling. (*See also* HALF STORY.)

STRAIGHT-LINE DEPRECIATION Depreciation for tax purposes of the value of a building at a fixed rate throughout the anticipated useful life of the building.

STRAW, STRAW CORPORATION (*See* DUMMY.)

STREET   A public thoroughfare affording the principal means of access to abutting property. (*See also* COLLECTOR STREET.)

STREET FURNITURE   A collective term including the many above-ground items found in the right-of-way of a street: lighting fixtures, traffic signs, signals, signal control boxes, fire hydrants, benches, mailboxes, plant boxes, trash receptacles, etc.

STREET LINE   The dividing line between a street and a lot.

STRIP DEVELOPMENT   Developed area along a main thoroughfare characterized by rows of retail stores and similar commercial buildings.

STRUCTURAL ALTERATIONS   Any change in the supporting members of a building, such as bearing walls or partitions; columns, beams, or girders; or any structural change in the roof, but not normally including extension or enlargement of the building.

STRUCTURAL LUMBER   Lumber measuring 2 inches or more in thickness and width, with designated working stresses assigned. (*See also* FACTORY AND SHOP LUMBER, YARD LUMBER.)

STRUCTURE   Any facility constructed or erected on the ground or attached to a facility located on the ground, including all types of buildings, billboards, signboards, etc. (Fences and boundary or retaining walls are not considered structures.)

STRUCTURE COSTS   Costs of foundations, frame, shells, interior finish and of mechanical, plumbing, and electrical systems.

SUBCHAPTER S CORPORATION   Corporation formed under the provisions of Sections 1371 to 1379 of the Internal Revenue Code to realize certain tax and nontax benefits. It is similar to a partnership under certain conditions stipulated in the Code, such as that the corporation cannot have more than ten shareholders, have any shareholder which is not an individual (except an estate), have more than one class of stock, or derive more than 20 percent of its gross receipts from passive investment sources—e.g., rents. The corporation is exempted from paying corporation income taxes, and the owner/taxpayer is personally taxable on all net income of the corporation.

SUBDIVISION   Land which is divided or proposed to be divided into lots (usually fifty or more), whether contiguous or not, for the purpose of sale or lease as part of a common promotional plan; where subdivided land is offered for sale or lease by a single developer or a group of developers acting in concert; and where such land is contiguous or is known, designated, or advertised as a common unit or by a common name. Also called "addition."

SUBDIVISION REGULATIONS Local ordinances, similar to zoning ordinances, governing the process by which building lots are created out of large land tracts—including site design and relationships and allocation of costs of public facilities between the subdivider, local taxpayers, and the governing body.

SUBGRADE The elevation established to receive top surfacing or finishing materials.

SUBLEASE A lease between a lessor and a third party.

SUBMARGINAL LAND Land whose value is negative by virtue of its location, topography, soil conditions, or another reason. The term is used to imply that, were the land available for free, it would not be developable or productive.

SUBORDINATION AGREEMENT Provision in a contract through which an owner of real estate grants a prior claim on his assets to a mortgagee.

SUBSCRIPTION AND PURCHASE AGREEMENT Document which serves as a contract of sale and a prospectus in the selling of a condominium unit.

SUBSIDENCE The sinking or settlement of ground, usually caused by a mining activity below the surface.

SUBSIDIZE To provide a subsidy.

SUBSIDY [housing] Grants of money by a governmental or other entity to reduce the cost of one or more of the housing components (i.e., land, labor, management, money, materials, taxes) to lower the cost of housing to the occupant.

SUBSTANDARD HOUSING A dwelling unit which is either dilapidated or unsafe, thus endangering the health of the occupant, or which does not have adequate plumbing or heating facilities.

SUBSTANDARD NEIGHBORHOOD A neighborhood characterized by an inordinately high number of substandard houses and/or other conditions that render the neighborhood inferior to others.

SUBSTANTIAL REHABILITATION [HUD] Improvement of the condition of property from deteriorating and substandard to good condition.

SUBSTITUTION PRINCIPLE Commonly held principle that the value of property is established by the sales price of a similar and substitutable property, all other things being equal.

SUBSURFACE RIGHT [real estate] The right to ownership of everything beneath the surface of the property.

SUBURB The area surrounding a central city; suburban areas may or may not be independently incorporated and they may be within the municipal limits of a central city or not.

SUM OF THE DIGITS DEPRECIATION (SUM-OF-THE-YEARS DIGITS DEPRECIATION) Method of depreciation of residential rental property only—since the 1969 Tax Reform Act—for tax purposes, in which the total number of useful life years of the property are added together (e.g., for a structure with twenty useful years, $1 + 2 + 3 + 4 + 5 + 6 + 7 + 8 + 9 + 10 + 11 + 12 + 13 + 14 + 15 + 16 + 17 + 18 + 19 + 20 = 210$ years) to become the denominator in the calculation of the depreciable value in a given year; the numerator is the remaining useful life of the property (e.g., in the first year it is twenty, in the second it is nineteen, etc.). Thus the formula for establishing the depreciable value in the first year for real estate with a twenty-year life would be $20/210$ times the depreciable base.

SUNDRY EXPENSES [HUD] Forms, stationery, office supplies, messenger and armored car service, office rent, advertising for bids, fiscal agent fees, collection agent fees, court costs (if not chargeable to tenants), fees for accounting and audit services, and certain express, freight, and drayage charges.

SUPERBLOCK A very large block within a city; frequently formed by combining or consolidating several smaller blocks through an urban renewal program.

SUPERSESSION The transition of a tract or of an area from a less to a more profitable use, as when rural land is superseded by urbanized uses.

SUPERSTRUCTURE   The portion of a building above ground level or above its foundation.

SUPERVISED LENDING INSTITUTION [FHA]   A mortgagee subject to the inspection and supervision of a governmental agency, which is required by law to make periodic examinations of the mortgagee's books and accounts, and which has a certain net worth as stipulated by federal statutes and/or regulations.

SUPERVISING ARCHITECT   The architect in charge of supervising construction activities to assure that they comply with design plans and specifications; distinguished from the design architect, although they are often one and the same.

SUPPLEMENTAL GRANT [urban renewal]   A grant from HUD to a local public agency to cover an amount necessary to enable the local agency to borrow funds from private sources for carrying out urban renewal activities.

SUPPLEMENTARY LOAN [FHA]   A loan, advance of credit, or purchase of an obligation representing a loan or advance of credit made for the purpose of financing improvements or additions to a project or facility.

SURCHARGE   Additional rent charged to tenants who consume utility services in excess of the amounts allowed in the rent.

SURETY BOND   A bond issued by an insurance company guaranteeing the performance of a contract or agreement of a person, group of persons, company, or corporation.

SURFACE PARKING   An open parking area, as distinguished from a parking garage.

SURPLUS LAND PROGRAM   Authorized by the Housing Act of 1949 and later amendments; provides HUD advisory services and counseling involving the sale, exchange, or donation of government land, property, and goods, to provide a national demonstration designed to create complete new communities and neighborhoods on surplus federal land in urban areas as well as on surplus land available under state and local jurisdictions, and to demonstrate a joint public-private capability to create total new communities rather than simply more housing projects or residential subdivisions.

Federal property sold or leased under this program may be used for the provision of rental, cooperative, and homeownership housing for persons with low and moderate incomes and related public, commercial, and industrial facilities. Land sold or leased to nonpublic developers for these purposes must remain in these uses for a period of not less than forty years unless the Secretary of HUD and the administrator of the General Services Administration jointly approve a change of use after twenty years.

City, county, and state governments and nonpublic developers may apply.

SURVEY [real estate]   The process by which a parcel of land is measured and its area is ascertained.

A document indicating the legal description, boundary lines, and dimensions of real estate and the location of buildings or other improvements. (*See also* LOAN SURVEY, PLAT OF SURVEY, SPOTTED SURVEY.)

SURVEY AND PLANNING APPLICATION (S&P) [urban renewal]   Technical document prepared by a local public agency on which preliminary evaluation of a proposed project is made by HUD. The application shows project boundaries, properties tentatively designated to be cleared or rehabilitated, plans for complying with minority group housing and low- and moderate-income relocation housing requirements, the preliminary financing plan for the project, and the amount of the request for federal funds required to plan the project and to implement it.

Before submittal of an S&P to HUD, approvals must be obtained from the commissioners of the local renewal agency, from the local planning body, and from the local governing body.

SUSPENSION [HUD]   A disqualification from participation in HUD programs for a temporary period of time because a contractor or grantee is suspected, upon adequate evidence, of engaging in criminal, fraudulent, or seriously improper conduct.

SUSTAINING OCCUPANCY   The point at which a new project can support its own expenses with income received from rentals.

SWAG   (*See* SCIENTIFIC WILD-ASS GUESS.)

SWALE   A flattish depression of the ground surface which conveys drainage water but offers no impediment to traffic, as do ditches or gutters.

SWEAT EQUITY   The equity one develops by contributing his labor or services instead of capital. (*See also* SELF-HELP AND MUTUAL SELF-HELP PROGRAM.)

SYNDICATE   A group of investors or the formation of a group of investors organized to undertake a particular venture or type of ventures.

SYNDICATION   The selling of equity in a project to one or more investors not including the actual developer.

SYSTEMS CONSTRUCTION   Construction of a building or buildings using building systems such as industrial housing components.

T

TAKE-BACK MORTGAGE   Mortgage held by the seller of a property.

TAKE DOWN   (*See* PROGRESS PAYMENTS.)

TAKE OUT   Permanent financing which replaces an interim or construction loan.

TANDEM PLAN   The purchase by the Government National Mortgage Association of certain mortgages at par for subsequent resale at market prices to the Federal National Mortgage Association, with the difference funded from the U.S. Treasury.

TANGIBLE ASSET   Asset for which a value can be established—e.g., real estate, equipment, furniture, inventories.

TAX ABATEMENT   Concession by a taxing authority under which, for a specified period of time, a property is exempt from local taxes or pays a reduced rate of taxes for that period of time.

TAXABLE INCOME   In simplest terms, the sum of cash flow, plus amortization, minus depreciation.

TAX-ANTICIPATION BOND   A bond issued by a taxing authority in anticipation that it will be repaid from tax receipts.

TAX BASE [real estate]   The assessed valuation of all real estate located within the jurisdiction of a taxing authority.

TAX DEED   A deed transferred by a taxing authority to a purchaser of a tax lien placed on a property on which the taxes have not been paid.

TAXES DURING CONSTRUCTION [FHA]   Taxes accrued during the construction period for which interest is computed, provided the amount has been paid in cash to the taxing authority or is deposited in escrow with the mortgagee.

TAX EXEMPTION   Privilege accorded to certain types of corporations or other organizations freeing them from the payment of taxes.

TAX FLOW   Income from an investment that is either taxable or lost (and therefore deductible).

TAX-FREE EXCHANGE [IRS]   Provision in Section 1031(a) of the Internal Revenue Code that no gain or loss from or exchange of property is recognized if property held as an investment or for use in a business is exchanged solely for real estate of like kind, to be held for a similar use.

TAX INCENTIVE   Beneficial status accorded to certain types of organizations, investments, or other activities intended to stimulate, in the public interest, a payer of income or real estate taxes to do or refrain from doing something.

TAX ISLANDS   Small governmental principalities that contain several large business establishments paying large amounts of taxes but few residents who benefit from such revenues to the governmental entities.

TAX LIEN   A lien against a deed as a result of nonpayment of taxes.

TAX PARTICIPATION   Provision in a lease stipulating that the lessee will pay all or part of the real estate tax on the property leased.

TAX SHELTER   An investment which, because of provisions of the Internal Revenue Code, results in a savings in income tax payments.
    An income tax deduction without a cash outlay.

TECHNICAL ASSISTANCE PROGRAM (TAP) [FHA]   A technical assistance project developed under the provisions of Section 106(a).

TECHRETE SYSTEM [construction]   An American building system consisting of precast bearing walls that support pretensioned precast floor planks which are clamped to the walls by post-tensioned steel rods.

TEMPORARY HOUSING   Housing units intended or provided for use for only a short term, as for temporary relocation purposes or to house victims of disaster.

TEMPORARY LOAN [construction]   (*See* CONSTRUCTION LOAN.)

TEMPORARY RELOCATION   A move of a family unit for its safety and welfare or for the convenience of the relocating agency, which does not remove the family unit from the agency's relocation workload.

TENANCY AT WILL   Occupancy arrangement providing that either the landlord or the tenant can cancel the arrangement at will.

TENANCY BY ENTIRETY   Form of ownership in which a husband and wife are viewed as one person.

TENANCY IN COMMON   An estate or interest in land held by two or more persons, each having equal rights of possession and enjoyment, but without any right of survivorship between the owners. Also called "cotenant."

TENANT   Any person in possession of real property with the owner's permission, usually according to the provisions of a lease.

TENANT COMMISSIONER [public housing]   A public housing tenant who serves as a member of the board of commissioners of a local housing authority.

TENANT HANDBOOK   Booklet or pamphlet prepared by a landlord and/or tenants explaining tenant rights and responsibilities, procedures and policies not set forth or not understandable in a lease, information about services available to tenants, etc.

TENANT MAINTENANCE   Usually includes but not necessarily limited to the maintenance by tenants of lawns adjacent to units, interior painting, and care of common halls and stairways.

TENANT ORGANIZATION   Formal or informal organization of a group of tenants through which tenants communicate with the landlord and vice versa and through which various tenant services and activities can be organized and conducted.

TENANT PROFILE   A statistical composite of the characteristics of an existing or a projected group of tenants occupying an existing or a proposed housing project or area; the profile normally includes the ages of the family heads, sizes of the families, ages of the dependents, source and amount of income to the tenants and the degree of income performance, racial and ethnic characteristics, ratio of ownership to rental units, and attitudes toward the community.

TENANT PROGRAMS AND SERVICES [public housing]   The development and maintenance of tenant organizations which participate in the management of projects; training tenants to manage and operate such projects and the utilization of their services in project management and operation; counseling on household management, housekeeping, budgeting, money management, day care, and similar matters; advise on resources for job training and placement, education, welfare, health, and other community services; services which are directly related to meeting tenant needs and providing a wholesome living environment; and referral to appropriate agencies when necessary for the provision of such services.

TENANT SELECTION CRITERIA [public housing]   Criteria established by local housing authorities, pursuant to provisions of HUD administrative requirements until 1974 and, as of 1974, pursuant to a requirement in the Housing and Community Development Act of 1974 under Title II—Assisted Housing, Section 6(c)(4), to assure that public housing projects include families with a broad range of incomes and assuring that assignment of tenants to dwelling units in such projects will avoid concentrations of low-income and deprived families with serious social problems.

TENANT SERVICES   (*See* TENANT PROGRAMS AND SERVICES.)

TENDER   An offer of an amount of money.

TENEMENT   An apartment or flat built for rental purposes.
A building containing tenements.

TENNESSEE VALLEY AUTHORITY (TVA)   The Tennessee Valley Authority is a corporation created by act of Congress May 18, 1933, to conduct a unified program of resource conservation, development of the Tennessee Valley region, and to advance the region's national defense capabilities. All functions of the Authority are vested in its three-member board of directors, appointed by the President with the consent of the Senate. The board reports directly to the President. Offices of the board and general manager are in Knoxville, Tennessee.

TENURE   The possession or the right to possess and use property; the term or duration of possession.

TERM   Duration—as the term of a mortgage or of a lease. (*See also* TERMS.)

TERMINAL INTERVIEW   Interview with tenant vacating a housing unit who has developed a delinquent rent account.

TERMINATION CHARGE   The charge paid by a mortgagee to the FHA in consideration of terminating a contract of insurance pursuant to the joint request for such action made by the mortgagor and mortgagee.

TERMS   The provisions or arrangements embodied in a business deal or contract; terms include financial arrangements, term, and date of possession. (*See also* TERM.)

TERRACE   A raised level or platform of earth, which may or may not be surfaced, usually adjoining a building.

TERRAZZO   Floor construction using a mixture of marble chips and cement ground to a smooth finish. Thin metal strips are used to outline a design and prevent cracking.

TESTATE   The estate or condition of leaving a will at death. (*See also* INTESTATE.)

TESTATOR or TESTATRIX   A person who makes or has made a testament or will.

TEST BORINGS   Borings into the ground to test subsurface conditions of a building site.

THROUGH LOT   An interior lot having frontages on two streets and distinguished from a corner lot. (*See also* CORNER LOT, INTERIOR LOT.)

TIME OF THE ESSENCE   Clause which, when used in contracts, relieves the offended party when the offender refuses to deliver possession at the time agreed.

TIME-SERIES CHART   A chart indicating statistical variations over a period of time.

TIME SHARE OWNERSHIP PLAN (TSO)   A property ownership agreement in conjunction with vacation housing usually, under which a number of individuals or families can totally own a vacation condominium unit, each owner holding title to the unit for a specified time each year.

TIPPING POINT   The percentage of occupancy by minorities reached in a housing project, neighborhood, or community at which members of majority groups can be expected to move out in large numbers, leaving the project or area for occupancy entirely or virtually entirely by minorities.

TITLE [real estate]   The legal sum of all evidence which constitutes a proof of ownership.

TITLE I [FHA]   (*See* TITLE I PROPERTY IMPROVEMENT LOAN INSURANCE.)

TITLE I—COMMUNITY DEVELOPMENT   Major provision of the Housing and Community Development Act of 1974, the purposes of which are essentially the same as those encompassed by Title I—Urban Renewal of the Housing Act of 1949 and its numerous subsequent amendments, with some expansion of scope of activities. The 1974 act, through this title, provides for the following:

1. The phasing out of all Title I—Urban Renewal activities (including the Community Renewal Program, General Neighborhood Renewal Program, Neighborhood Development Program, Section 115 housing rehabilitation grants, the Section 116 demolition grant and the Section 117 federally assisted code enforcement programs, and most other related and ancillary programs), the Demonstration Cities Program ("Model Cities Program"), Section 702 basic water and sewer facilities grants, and Section 703 neighborhood facilities grants—as well as other programs and grants embodied in the 1949 housing act

2. The consolidation of forms of federal financial assistance (previously, largely all categorical grants) into a system of block grants available to units of general local government

3. The elimination of the feature of a "local share" required of participants and its supplanting by a 100 percent federal share

4. The required preparation of a "housing assistance plan" by participants, according to specific criteria established in the act

Block grants received under this title may be used to conduct all activities permitted under supplanted and consolidated programs, as well as for certain other additional activities approved by HUD.

(*See also* BASIC GRANT AMOUNT, COMMUNITY DEVELOPMENT PROGRAM, DISCRETIONARY GRANT, ENTITLEMENT AMOUNT, HOLD-HARMLESS AMOUNT, HOLD-HARMLESS GRANT, HOUSING ASSISTANCE PLAN.)

TITLE I LAND   Land in an urban renewal project area.

TITLE I MOBILE HOME LOAN INSURANCE   Authorized by Title I of the National Housing Act as amended by the Housing and Urban Development Act of 1969; provides mortgage insurance through FHA to make possible reasonable financing of mobile home purchases; FHA insures lenders against losses on loans. Insured loans may be used to purchase mobile home units by buyers intending to use them as their principal place of residence. The maximum amount of the loan is established by statute. The borrower must give assurance that his unit will be placed on a site which complies with FHA standards and with local zoning requirements.

The loan term may extend for up to twelve years and thirty-two days (fifteen years and thirty-two days in the case of two or more modules).

TITLE I PROPERTY IMPROVEMENT LOAN INSURANCE   Authorized by the National Housing Act as amended; provides FHA mortgage insurance to facilitate the financing of improvements to homes, including multifamily structures and other existing structures, including nonresidential or non-farm structures; uses and use restrictions vary with the type of structure. Eligible borrowers include the owner of the property to be improved or a lessee having a lease extending at least six months beyond loan maturation.

TITLE I—URBAN RENEWAL   That portion of the Housing Act of 1949 as amended which contains most of the basic legislative provisions pertaining to the urban renewal program. Title I authorizes most of the federal financial assistance and technical aids for communities participating in the program.

The Housing and Community Development Act of 1974 provides for the phasing out of Title I—Urban Renewal activities and for their supplanting by Title I—Community Development.

(*See also* TITLE I URBAN RENEWAL PROJECTS.)

TITLE I URBAN RENEWAL PROJECTS   Authorized by the Housing Act of 1949 and later amendments; provides HUD project grants, direct loans, and mortgage insurance to provide financial assistance for the rehabilitation or redevelopment of slums or blighted areas. This program provides grants, planning advances, and temporary loans to eliminate blight in urban areas through surveys and planning, land acquisition and clearing, rehabilitation of existing structures, new building construction, and the installation of public improvements including streets and sidewalks, utilities, incidental recreational areas, flood protection, and the preservation of historic structures. A federal grant may cover two-thirds (population over 50,000) or three-fourths (population 50,000 or under) of the cost of renewal activities. Funds may not be used for the construction of buildings.

Local public agencies, which can be a local or county renewal agency or housing authority or a local or county department of government, depending upon state enabling legislation, are eligible.

Project area residents may benefit.

The local governing body must enact a resolution approving the urban renewal project. The locality must adopt a Workable Program for Community Improvement certified by the Secretary of HUD, and the area to be assisted must be a slum, blighted, deteriorated, or deteriorating area or a vacant, unused, underused, or inappropriately used area and otherwise acceptable to the Secretary.

Application procedure: Three separate applications must be submitted: (1) Survey and Planning Application which defines the area and proposed general treatment. Approval of this application provides funds for planning the project and a reservation of money for the projects to enter execution after planning; (2) Part I Loan and Grant Application contains the Urban Renewal Plan for the area and costs for the project in execution; (3) Part II Loan and Grant application, contains the local approvals of the Urban Renewal Plan and other aspects of the renewal project. After approval of the Part II application and execution of the loan and grant contract, the project can enter execution.

Formula and matching requirements: the applicant must provide at least one-third or one-fourth of the loan and grant funds needed to carry out project, depending upon the community's population. The average length of the assistance period is ten years; the LPA receives planning funds in the form of repayable direct advances during the planning stage. During the execution stage, it receives temporary loans and capital grants.

The Housing and Community Development Act of 1974 provides for the phasing out of such projects and for the supplanting of the urban renewal program through Title I—Community Development.

(*See also* NEIGHBORHOOD DEVELOPMENT PROGRAM.)

TITLE IV NEW COMMUNITIES ASSISTANCE Guarantee of new community financing by HUD, authorized by the Housing and Urban Development Act of 1968. (*See also* NEW COMMUNITY DEVELOPMENT PROGRAM, TITLE VIII NEW COMMUNITIES LOAN GUARANTEES, TITLE X MORTGAGE INSURANCE FOR LAND DEVELOPMENT AND NEW COMMUNITIES.)

TITLE IV OPEN SPACE LAND PROGRAM Authorized by the Housing and Urban Development Act of 1970; provides HUD grants to help communities meet the rapidly growing recreation needs of urban areas by assisting these communities acquire and develop park land.

Eligible acquisition costs include those for acquiring title to, or other interests in, open space in urban areas, demolition of inappropriate structures where developed land is being acquired, and real estate services. Acquisition costs may also include underdeveloped land in a planned development sector, such as urban shaping areas to guide urban development and the acquisition of historically significant structures listed on the National Register of Historic Places. Eligible development costs include roadways, landscaping, basic utilities, recreational facilities, swimming pools, improvements of acquired structures, preservation of historic and architecturally significant structures listed on the National Register of Historic Places, etc.

Acquisition and development of the open-space land must be in accord with a unified and officially coordinated program for development of open-space land as part of local and areawide comprehensive planning. Major construction, such as marinas, is not eligible under this program.

State and local public bodies, including Indian tribes, bands, groups, and nations legally authorized to undertake an open-space project may participate.

No more than 50 percent of total cost of acquisition and development of open space land in urban areas and historic preservation will be provided by HUD. Not more than 75 percent of the total cost of acquisition of underdeveloped or predominantly undeveloped land for urban shaping purposes will be provided by HUD.

The length of the assistance period for approved project is twelve months from date of contract execution to complete activity. Payments are made on a reimbursable basis only. Partial payments may be made when project activities are 25, 50, and 75 percent completed.

TITLE V RURAL HOUSING LOANS   (*See* RURAL HOUSING LOAN).

TITLE VI [civil rights]   Section of the Civil Rights Act of 1964 and later amendments applying to HUD programs.

TITLE VII COMMUNITY DEVELOPMENT TRAINING GRANTS   Authorized by the Housing Act of 1964; provides project grants through HUD to help states develop or expand programs that provide skills needed for community development to technical, professional, or subprofessional personnel. This program assists in developing training programs for employees of state and local governments, public agencies, or private nonprofit organizations with a community development responsibility, and for persons soon to be employees of such governmental or nonprofit agencies.

States, U.S. territories, and the District of Columbia are eligible. Trainees must be employed or must be training to be employed by a governmental or public body responsible for community development or by a nonprofit organization conducting housing and community development programs. At least 50 percent of the total cost of the state program must be borne by the state. The nonfederal share of costs may be provided either in cash or in noncash contributions of goods or services. Matching formula applies to the total state program; individual projects within the program need not be funded on a 50-50 basis.

Grants are made on an annual basis, with the period of performance running from July 1 through the following June 30.

TITLE VII NEW COMMUNITIES LOAN GUARANTEES Authorized by the Urban Growth and New Community Development Act of 1970 (Housing Act of 1970); provides FHA mortgage insurance to encourage the developmenth of well-planned, diversified, and economically sound new communities, including major additions to existing communities.

Eligible costs which may be financed with the proceeds of a guaranteed loan for real property acquisition and land development include those incurred as part of a community development project. Eligible costs for land development include clearing and grading land and installing and constructing water lines and water supply systems, sewerage, roads, streets, drainage facilities. Also included are other preparation of land for residential, commercial, industrial and other uses, including construction of public facilities. Other buildings are not eligible costs unless needed in connection with water supply or sewage disposal installation or a utility line, or unless the building is to be owned and maintained by residents of the new community under joint or cooperative arrangements. Development must be in accord with comprehensive areawide planning and must preserve and enhance the environment, contribute to the welfare of the area of which it is part, provide substantial amounts of low- and moderate-income housing, and encourage social innovation and the use of new technology.

Private new community developers and public land development agencies (including regional or metropolitan public bodies) are authorized to act as developers for new community development programs under state or local law. However, obligations of public land development agencies may not be guaranteed if the income from such obligations is exempt from federal taxation.

The amount of guarantee cannot exceed $50 million for any single project. In the case of public land development agencies, guarantees for the principal obligation cannot exceed 100 percent of the Secretary's estimate of the value of real property before development and the estimate of the cost of land development. For private developers, guarantees may not exceed the sum of 80 percent of the estimated value of real property before development. Length and time phasing of assistance is not limited by law.

(*See also* NEW COMMUNITY DEVELOPMENT PROGRAM, TITLE IV NEW COMMUNITIES ASSISTANCE, TITLE X MORTGAGE INSURANCE FOR LAND DEVELOPMENT AND NEW COMMUNITIES.)

TITLE VIII HOUSING   (*See* CAPEHART-WHERRY HOUSING.)

TITLE X MORTGAGE INSURANCE FOR LAND DEVELOPMENT AND NEW COMMUNITIES   Authorized by the Housing and Urban Development Act of 1965 and later amendments; provides FHA mortgage insurance to assist the development of large subdivisions or new communities on a sound basis; FHA insures lenders against loss on mortgage loans. These loans may be used to finance the purchase of land and the development of building sites for subdivisions or new communities, including water and sewer systems, streets, lighting, and other installations needed for residential communities. Nonresidential buildings, such as schools or commercial buildings, are not included except for water supply and sewage disposal installations, clubhouses, and parking garages owned and maintained jointly by property owners. The maximum amount insurable is $25 million.

Prospective developers, subject to the approval of FHA, are eligible. Public bodies are not eligible.

Land development must meet statutory and FHA requirements and receive all governmental approvals required by state or local law or by the Department of Housing and Urban Development. Eligibility as a "new community" requires specific findings of substantial contribution to the sound economic growth of the area and may require the approval of the local governing bodies and the governor of the state.

The maximum amount of the loan guarantee may not exceed 50 percent of estimated value of the land before development plus 90 percent of estimated cost of development or 75 percent of the estimated value upon completion, whichever is less. The current maximum interest rate is established by the Secretary of HUD; the mortgage insurance premium varies, depending upon the term and purpose of the loan. The FHA application and commitment fee is $4.50 per $1,000. The service charge by the mortgagee is 2 percent of the total mortgage amount.

The mortgage term may extend for ten years, but it may be longer for separate mortgages for water and for sewerage systems or for development of a new community.

TITLE XI MORTGAGE INSURANCE FOR GROUP PRACTICE MEDICAL FACILI-TIES   Authorized by the Demonstration Cities and Metropolitan Development Act of 1966; provides mortgage insurance through FHA to help finance the development of group practice medical facilities. FHA insures lenders against loss on mortgage loans. These loans may be used to finance the construction or rehabilitation of facilities, including major movable equipment, for the provision of preventive, diagnostic, and treatment services by a medical, dental, osteopathic, podiatric, or optometric group.

Eligible for this insurance are private nonprofit sponsors (1) undertaking to provide comprehensive health care to members or subscribers on a group practice prepayment basis or (2) established for the purpose of improving the availability of health care in the community, which will make the group practice facility available to a medical, osteopathic, podiatric, optometric, or dental group for use. The owner (mortgagor) of the facility must be organized on a nonprofit basis but may make it available to a practicing group through a lease.

The maximum insurable mortgage in most cases would be equal to 90 percent of the estimated replacement cost of the facility, including major movable equipment. The maximum interest rate is established by the HUD Secretary, to which is added ½ percent for mortgage insurance premium. The mortgage term may extend for twenty-five years.

TITLE ABSTRACT   (*See* ABSTRACT OF TITLE.)

TITLE DEFECT [real estate]   Any legal right held by others to claim property or to make demands upon the owner. (*See also* ENCUMBRANCE, LIEN.)

TITLE EXAMINATION   The search and review of public records relating to a title.

TITLE INSURANCE   (*See* INSURANCE OF TITLE.)

TITLE PLANT   The total facilities—records, equipment, fixtures, and personnel—required to function as a title insurance operation. Technically, the organization of official records affecting real property into a system which allows quick and efficient recovery of title information.

TITLE SEARCH   An examination of public records, laws, and court decisions to disclose the current facts regarding ownership of real estate.

TOILET ROOM [HUD]   (*See* HALF-BATH.)

TOPOGRAPHIC MAP (topo)   Map showing the surface features of an area of ground.

TORRENIZED LAND   Land subject to a Torrens system.

TORRENS SYSTEM   A system of recording the ownership of title to land in which the governing body issues the certificates of title which serve as title insurance.

TOTAL ANNUAL RETURN TO INVESTOR   Net cash income plus tax savings derived from ownership of a project.

TOTAL DEVELOPMENT COST (TDC)   The total cost of development of a given project, including the costs of land, planning, all fees, construction financing, construction, landscaping, and off-site improvements. (*See also* ESTABLISHED INVESTMENT.)

TOTAL DOLLAR RETURN   The total number of dollars earned from an investment.

TOT LOT   Special play area for children who are too small to use ordinary playground equipment or too young to play with groups of older children.

TOWN HOUSE   (*See* ROW HOUSE.)

TOWNSHIP   A division of territory 6 miles square, containing thirty-six sections or 36 square miles.

TRACING   Duplication of a drawing by copying the lines and lettering as seen through a transparent sheet of paper, vellum, or tracing cloth.

TRACOBA SYSTEM [construction]   A French concrete panel system of building consisting of load-bearing cross walls and on-site factory-cast parts (Tracoba "1") and a separate Tracoba "4" of on-site casting using steel tunnel forms.

TRACT   An area of land. Generally refers to a large area of land.

TRACT BUILDER   A builder who buys tracts of land for subdivision into lots, on which he builds houses for sale.

TRACT HOUSE   A house located in a subdivision—generally characterized by repetition of design, architectural features, and price—distinguished from a house that is custom designed and custom built for a particular owner.

TRAFFIC MODEL [transportation]   Mathematical equations that express the relationship between an area's traffic pattern and its land-use and socio-economic characteristics. Traffic models simulate actual traffic conditions and help provide an understanding of existing and probable future problems.

TRAILER   A mobile home (which is what owners prefer to call them). Campers or camper trailers are sometimes called "trailers." (*See also* MOBILE HOME.)

TRAINING GRANTS   (*See* TITLE VII COMMUNITY DEVELOPMENT TRAINING GRANTS.)

TRANSFER AND STAMP TAXES   Taxes paid to local or state governments in connection with the execution or recording of mortgages or other instruments.

TRANSFER FEE [FHA]   Charge by FHA for the substitution of mortgagors. The charge is 50 cents per $1,000 on the mortgage amount.

TRANSFER TAXES   (*See* TRANSFER AND STAMP TAXES.)

TRANSIENT HOUSING [HUD]   Housing units intended for occupancy for periods of less than thirty days or housing in which the occupants are provided customary hotel services such as room service for food and beverages, maid service, furnishing and laundering of linen, and bellboy service.

TRANSITIONAL AREA   Usually, a part of a city undergoing racial transition in the occupancy of dwellings.

TRANSOM   A small window installed over a door, intended to admit light or to provide ventilation.

TREAD   Horizontal face of a step.

TRIBUTARY LENDING   The lending of money, usually by a savings and loan association, for special-purpose properties such as certain commercial buildings and housing units for the elderly.

TRIP [transportation]   One-way movement of one person between an origin and a destination. Includes walking to or from the means of transportation.

TRIP ATTRACTION [transportation]   That which gives motivation, specific direction, and destination of a trip—e.g., going downtown.

TRIPLEX   A building comprised of three dwelling units, each with a front and rear or side door and yard. (*See also* ROW HOUSE.)

TRIP PRODUCTION [transportation]   The motivation to make a trip—e.g., going to work.

TRUSS [HUD]   A structural framework composed of a series of members so arranged and fastened together that external loads applied at the joints will cause only direct stress in the members.

TRUST [real estate]   A right of property held by one for the benefit of another.

TRUST DEED   A mortgage or deed of trust.

TRUSTEE [real estate]   A person holding property in trust.

TUCK-UNDER PARKING   Parking space(s) provided under a residential unit (usually a townhouse), generally characterized by the absence of a garage door. (Some think of tuck-under parking as a carport under the unit.) Such parking-space design minimizes the need for surface parking.

TURNKEY I [public housing]   (*See* TURNKEY PUBLIC HOUSING.)

TURNKEY II [public housing]   A program for private management of public housing or the training for homeownership given public housing tenant residents participating in the Turnkey III or Turnkey IV program.

TURNKEY III AND IV HOMEOWNERSHIP FOR LOW-INCOME FAMILIES AND MUTUAL HELP FOR INDIANS [public housing]   Authorized by the U.S. Housing Act of 1937 and later amendments; provides direct loans and formula grants through HUD to provide, through local housing authorities, low-income families with the opportunity of owning their own homes. The purpose is to assist local public agencies in providing housing purchase opportunities for low-income families by crediting the amount budgeted for routine maintenance, which is performed by the tenants, to family equity accounts. When family income increases to the point where it can obtain permanent financing for the unit or when the equity account equals the unamortized debt and closing costs, ownership passes to the family. Originally the units are owned (Turnkey III) or leased (Turnkey IV) by the local public agency. The unit must be legally discrete and can be part of a planned unit development, condominium, or cooperative. During the period of tenancy, the family makes payments representing between 20 and 25 percent of its income. The Turnkey III homes are amortized over a period of thirty years and the Turnkey IV assistance is for twenty years. The mutual-help program for Indians allows families to contribute their labor in the construction of the housing. They may also contribute the building site and, where feasible, indigenous building materials.

Local housing authorities established by a local government in accordance with state law, authorized public agencies, or Indian tribal organizations are eligible. The proposed program must be approved by the local governing body.

Low-income families interested and demonstrating potential for homeownership may benefit.

Annual contributions are made by HUD to local public agencies for use as subsidies to homebuyers and to cover debt service. There are no matching requirements. Length of the annual contributions commitment is approximately twenty-five years.

TURNKEY LEASING [public housing]   Housing constructed by private sponsors for lease to a local housing authority for use of its low-income tenants.

TURNKEY-MUTUAL HELP—NEW CONSTRUCTION [public housing]   New Turnkey public housing units, including site, which are constructed by a developer (seller) in whole or in part with labor of prospective occupants to be credited to them as equity toward ultimate home ownership and are purchased by a local housing authority upon completion pursuant to an agreement entered into prior to start of construction.

TURNKEY—NEW CONSTRUCTION [public housing]   New Turnkey public housing, including site, which is purchased by a local housing authority from a developer (seller) upon completion of construction pursuant to an agreement entered into prior to start of construction.

TURNKEY PROJECT   Project in which all components are organized and developed by one entity and sold to another for a lump-sum price, at which point the developer "turns the keys" over to the purchaser in exchange for payment.

TURNKEY PUBLIC HOUSING   An approach to public housing development through which a local housing authority invites competitive proposals from private developers for the design and construction of a stipulated number, and frequently a stipulated type, of housing units on land provided by the developer. The successful offerer-developer provides his own construction financing. Upon completion of the development of the project, the authority purchases the housing for a lump-sum price and the developer "turns the keys" to the housing over to the authority. Turnkey public housing projects are distinguished from conventional projects.

TURNKEY REHABILITATION [public housing]   Existing housing units, including site, which require substantial alteration, repair, or improvement at a cost ratio of 20 percent or more of total development cost for multifamily housing or 25 percent or more of total development cost for single-family housing (detached, duplex, or row house); such housing is (to be) purchased from the owner upon completion of the work pursuant to an agreement entered into prior to start of the work.

TWENTY PERCENT GAP [public housing]   The financial "gap" which must exist, by law, between the highest rent charged for public housing units and the rents charged in a given community for private rental housing unassisted by public subsidy which is deemed to be decent, safe, and sanitary housing. The requirement was established in the Housing Act of 1949. The Housing Act of 1961 eliminated the requirement in the case of elderly families.

Title II—Assisted Housing (Section 201) of the Housing and Community Development Act of 1974 eliminated the 20 percent gap requirement.

TWILIGHT ZONE   Area of a city officially or unofficially earmarked for slum clearance over an extended period, during which blight can be expected to increase in severity.

TWO-TIER PARTNERSHIP   A partnership having an interest in a second partnership.

U

UNDERWRITING   Analysis of the extent of risk assumed in connection with a loan; the process of preparing or arranging the conditions of a mortgage and the subsequent decision to approve or disapprove a loan application.

UNIFORM BUILDING CODE   National code published by the International Conference of Building Officials; prominently used especially in the Western states.

UNIFORM RELOCATION AND REAL PROPERTY ACQUISITION POLICIES ACT OF 1970   An act to provide for uniform and equitable treatment of persons displaced from their homes, businesses, or farms by federal and federally assisted programs and to establish uniform and equitable land acquisition policies for federal and federally assisted programs. Approved January 2, 1971, and subsequently amended.

UNITED STATES   (*See* entries beginning U.S.)

UNIT OF GENERAL LOCAL GOVERNMENT   As defined in the Housing and Community Development Act of 1974, any city, county, town, township, parish, village, or other general-purpose political subdivision of a state or United States territory.

Depending on the context of the reference, a unit of general local government also includes states, Indian tribes, bands, groups, and nations, including Aleuts and Indians and Eskimos of Alaska; a local public body or agency, community association, or other entity may sometimes also be referred to as a unit of general local government.

UNIT YEARS   The age of a project multiplied by the number of housing units.

UNTENANTED HAZARD   A derelict building that constitutes a hazard because it is easily entered by vandals or others who might suffer injury or endanger their health and safety or that of the surrounding neighborhood.

UPSET PRICE   The maximum or minimum price above or below which no sale or purchase can transpire according to the terms of a contract.

URBAN AREA [census]   Places with populations of 2,500 or more, whether incorporated or not.

URBAN BEAUTIFICATION AND IMPROVEMENT PROGRAM   Established under the provisions of Section 706 of the Housing Act of 1961, the program was intended to help communities carry out programs for the beautification and improvement of publicly owned and controlled land in urban areas.

URBAN COMMUNITY DEVELOPMENT SPECIAL REVENUE SHARING   A Nixon administration proposal that would consolidate several existing categorical grant programs available to states and local communities for certain community development programs. (*See also* GENERAL REVENUE SHARING, HELLER-PECHMAN PLAN, SPECIAL REVENUE SHARING.)

URBAN COUNTY   As defined in the Housing and Community Development Act of 1974, any county within a metropolitan area which (1) is authorized under state law to undertake essential community development and housing assistance activities in its unincorporated areas, if any, which are not units of general local government and (2) has a combined population of 200,000 or more (excluding the population of metropolitan cities within the metropolitan area) in such unincorporated areas and in its units of general local government (*i*) in which it has authority to undertake essential community development and housing assistance activities and which do not elect to have their population excluded or (*ii*) with which it has entered into cooperation agreements to undertake or to assist in the undertaking of such activities.

URBAN MASS TRANSPORTATION ADMINISTRATION (UMTA)   This operates under the authority of the Urban Mass Transportation Act of 1964 as amended. UMTA was established as a component of the Department of Transportation by Section 3 of the President's Reorganization Plan 2 of 1968, effective July 1, 1968.

The missions of the UMTA are to assist in the development of improved mass transportation facilities, equipment, techniques, and methods; to encourage the planning and establishment of areawide urban mass transportation systems; and to provide assistance to state and local governments in financing such systems.

URBAN OBSERVATORY PROGRAM   A HUD-sponsored research program conducted by the National League of Cities/U.S. Conference of Mayors under arrangements with a selected group of cities and local universities.

URBAN PLANNING GRANTS *(See* SECTION 701 COMPREHENSIVE PLANNING ASSISTANCE.)

URBAN PROPERTY PROTECTION AND REINSURANCE Authorized by the Urban Property Protection and Reinsurance Act of 1968 and later amendments; provides insurance through the Federal Housing Administration to assure availability of essential insurance coverage for urban property, particularly that located in areas possibly subject to riots or civil disturbance.

Federal reinsurance against excess losses resulting from riots and civil disorders is available only to property insurance companies that cooperate as risk-bearing members of a state FAIR Plan. The state FAIR (Fair Access to Insurance Requirements) Plan is designed to assure reasonable access to basic property insurance (fire, extended coverage, and vandalism and malicious mischief) to any property owner in a designated urban area. FAIR Plans operate in 26 states, District of Columbia, and Puerto Rico (December 31, 1970).

URBAN REDEVELOPMENT *(See* URBAN RENEWAL.)

URBAN RENEWAL Process through which deteriorated neighborhoods are upgraded through clearance and redevelopment or through rehabilitation and through the installation of new, or modernization of existing, public improvements. Urban renewal activities may be financed with a combination of federal and local funds or strictly with private funds. *(See also* NEIGHBORHOOD DEVELOPMENT PROGRAM, TITLE I URBAN RENEWAL PROJECTS.)

URBAN RENEWAL ADMINISTRATION (URA) Until HUD received Cabinet status in 1965, the URA was the constituent agency of the Housing and Home Finance Agency that administered the federally assisted urban renewal program. *(See also* TITLE I—URBAN RENEWAL.)

URBAN RENEWAL AGENCY (URA) *(See* LOCAL PUBLIC AGENCY.)

URBAN RENEWAL AREA A slum area; a blighted, deteriorated, or deteriorating area; or an open-land area which is approved by a local governing body and HUD as appropriate for an urban renewal project. *(See also* TITLE I URBAN RENEWAL PROJECTS.)

URBAN RENEWAL HANDBOOK The official HUD statement establishing the federal policies and requirements for the administration of federally assisted urban renewal programs—the basic issuance used to promulgate permanent policy and requirements for local administrative officials and to establish broad national objectives and detailed requirements; oriented to the local public agency that administers an urban renewal program at the local level.

URBAN RENEWAL HOUSING (*See* SECTION 220 MORTGAGE INSURANCE FOR HOMES IN URBAN RENEWAL AREAS.)

URBAN RENEWAL PLAN Detailed proposal prepared by a local public agency indicating specific plans for property acquisition or rehabilitation, demolition, clearance, installation of public utilities and facilities, eventual marketing of cleared land, land use, design controls, property management, relocation, and most other aspects of project activities. (*See also* TITLE I URBAN RENEWAL PROJECTS.)

URBAN RENEWAL PLANNING The stage of an urban renewal project during which the Urban Renewal Plan is prepared. (*See also* TITLE I URBAN RENEWAL PROJECTS.)

URBAN RENEWAL PROJECT Specific and official program undertaken by a local public agency in an urban renewal area to prevent and eliminate slums and blight. May involve slum clearance and redevelopment, rehabilitation, conservation, or a combination thereof; acquisition of open spaces or of land for open space dedication; building and/or housing code enforcement. Depending on the type of project involved, it may include acquisition of land; demolition of structures; installation of streets, parks, and other improvements; disposition of acquired land for uses specified in the Urban Renewal Plan; and the carrying out of plans for voluntary rehabilitation of nonacquired structures in the areas. (*See also* NEIGHBORHOOD DEVELOPMENT PROGRAM, TITLE I URBAN RENEWAL PROJECTS.)

URBAN SPRAWL Formless dispersal of a congested urban area with little or no regard for the interrelationships of such factors as logical transportation, employment, health, and recreational needs; the growth of a metropolitan area through the process of scattered development of miscellaneous types of land use in isolated locations on the urban fringe, followed by the gradual filling in of the intervening spaces with similar uses.

URBAN SYSTEMS ENGINEERING DEMONSTRATION Established under the provisions of Section 701(b) of the Housing Act of 1954 and later amendments to encourage public bodies to employ systems of engineering and systems analysis techniques through the use of computer technology in developing areawide public service systems.

U.S. DEPARTMENT OF HOUSING AND URBAN DEVELOPMENT (*See* DEPART-
MENT OF HOUSING AND URBAN DEVELOPMENT.)

USE DENSITY The percentage of land that can be covered in relation to
a particular use as established by zoning ordinances or city planning
criteria.

USEFUL LIFE For tax depreciation purposes, the period over which a
property may be expected to be useful to the taxpayer in the production
of his income.

USE VALUE A property's value when it is specifically designed only for a
certain purpose and therefore would be of marginal value to another
owner.

U.S. HOUSING ACT (USHA) Law passed by Congress in 1937 which established the U.S. Housing Authority and its programs. Many of the
provisions of this act were rewritten and/or changed in Title II—Assisted
Housing of the Housing and Community Development Act of 1974.

U.S. HOUSING AND HOME FINANCE AGENCY (HHFA) (*See* HOUSING AND
HOME FINANCE AGENCY.)

U.S. HOUSING AUTHORITY (USHA) Federal authority established by
Section 3 of the U.S. Housing Act of 1937. First established as a federal
agency in the U.S. Department of the Interior. In 1939, USHA was transferred to the Federal Works Agency; in 1942, to the National Housing
Agency, when it was renamed the Federal Public Housing Authority; in
1947, renamed the Public Housing Administration, it became a constituent
agency of the Housing and Home Finance Agency. In 1965, the Public
Housing Administration and the Housing and Home Finance Agency
were absorbed by HUD.

U.S. PUBLIC HOUSING ADMINISTRATION (PHA) (*See* PUBLIC HOUSING
ADMINISTRATION.)

U.S. URBAN RENEWAL ADMINISTRATION (URA) (*See* URBAN RENEWAL
ADMINISTRATION.)

USURY The loaning of money at an unlawfully high rate of interest.

UTILITY (*See* PUBLIC UTILITY.)

UTILITY ANALYSIS Report projecting the estimated monthly cost of furnishing lighting, refrigeration, cooking, hot water, space heating, or other utility services under each of the feasible methods of utility supply; the study takes into account the costs of fuel and energy, the costs of maintaining the various utility systems and equipment, and the capital costs of the utility systems and equipment.

UTILITY COSTS [HUD] Amounts not included in rent paid by a tenant for water, electricity, gas, heating and cooking fuels, refrigeration, trash and garbage collection, and sewage disposal. Utility costs do not include the cost of telephone service.

VACANCY LOSSES Income not received by management because of units being unrented.

VACANCY RATE The percentage of a locality's available housing stock that is vacant.

VALUATION The estimated value of a property.

VALUE-IN-USE (*See* USE-VALUE.)

VANDYKE A reproduction of a tracing resulting in a copy producing white lines on a brown background or brown lines on a white background.

VARIABLE RATE MORTGAGE Mortgage permitting that the contract interest rate be adjusted upward or downward as interest rates change with economic conditions.

VARIANCE A modification or variation of the provisions of established governing regulations. Usually refers to a variance of the zoning regulations.

VAULT An arched ceiling.

VENDEE [real estate]   A purchaser of real property.

VENDOR [real estate]   A seller of real property.

VENEERED WALL [HUD]   A wall with a masonry face which is attached but not so bonded to the body of the wall as to exert a common reaction under load.

VERY LOW INCOME FAMILIES   As defined in the Housing and Community Development Act of 1974, families whose incomes do not exceed 50 percent of the median family income for a given area, as determined by the Secretary of HUD, with adjustments for smaller and larger families. (*See also* LOWER-INCOME FAMILIES, LOW-INCOME FAMILIES.)

VERY LOW INCOME HOUSING REPAIR LOANS [rural]   (*See* SECTION 504 HOUSING LOANS.)

VEST [real estate]   To pass to a person an immediate right.

VESTEE [real estate]   A nonlegal term coined by title insurance companies and used by them to indicate the owner of real property.

VESTIBULE   A small area or passageway located between outer and inner doors of a building.

VEST-POCKET HOUSING   (*See* IN-FILL HOUSING.)

VEST-POCKET PARKS   Parks built on vacant parcels in built-up areas of cities. Frequently serve only as playgrounds or tot lots.

VETERAN   A person who served in the active military service of the United States during certain established periods and who has been discharged or released under conditions other than dishonorable.

VETERANS ADMINISTRATION (VA)   The VA was established as an independent agency under the President by Executive Order No. 5398 of July 21, 1930, in accordance with an act of July 3, 1930. This act authorized the President to consolidate and coordinate federal agencies especially created for or concerned in the administration of laws providing benefits for veterans.

VA administers laws covering a wide range of benefits for former members and dependents and beneficiaries of deceased former members of the Armed Forces. VA also administers laws which provide certain benefits to current members of the Armed Forces and to dependent children of seriously disabled veterans.

The Loan Guaranty Service works to facilitate the extension of credit for the purchase or construction of homes, including mobile homes, and the acquisition and operation of business and farming enterprises by veterans.

VETERANS CERTIFICATE OF ELIGIBILITY   The official certificate issued by the Secretary of Defense to FHA which establishes that the person designated on the certificate as a serviceman has met the eligibility requirements set forth in Section 222 of the National Housing Act as amended.

VETERANS HOUSING PROGRAM [direct loans]   The Veterans Administration may make loans generally up to a maximum amount established by statute to eligible applicants for any of the following purposes: (1) purchase or construction of a dwelling to be owned and occupied by the veteran as his home; (2) construction on land owned by the veteran of a farm residence to be occupied as his home; (3) repair, alteration, or improvement of a farm residence or other dwelling owned by the veteran and occupied as his home. Restrictions are that (1) the home must be located in a housing credit shortage area designated by the Administrator of Veterans Affairs; (2) loans for construction or purchase of a home completed less than one year must meet VA minimum construction standards for housing credit shortage areas; (3) the nature and condition of other housing must be suitable for dwelling; (4) the loan may not exceed the VA determined reasonable value of the property; (5) the veteran must be unable to obtain financing from private lenders or the Secretary of Agriculture under the Bankhead-Jones Farm Tenant Act or the Housing Act of 1949 for the particular loan purposes.

VISUAL RIGHTS   Property owner's right to view or to be viewed, free of such encumbrances as vegetation, structures, billboards, etc.

VITAL STATISTICS   Statistics related to births, deaths, ages, race, marriages, health, and similar characteristics of a population group.

VOLUNTARY REHABILITATION [urban renewal] [HUD]   Structural or other substantial repairs to or alterations of any building or other improvement on land within an urban renewal area undertaken by an owner of any interest in such real property for the sake of conforming to the property rehabilitation standards set forth in the Urban Renewal Plan.

VOLUNTARY TERMINATION [FHA]   The termination of the mortgage insurance contract between FHA, the mortgagor, and the mortgagee upon request by the mortgagor and the mortgagee (for which no cancellation fee is charged by FHA).

VOLUNTEERS IN SERVICE TO AMERICA (VISTA)   Authorized by the Economic Opportunity Act of 1964 and later amendments to supplement efforts to eliminate poverty by enabling persons from all walks of life and all age groups to perform meaningful and constructive service as volunteers in situations where the application of human talent and dedication may help the poor to overcome the handicaps of poverty and to secure opportunities for self-advancement.

Provides volunteers who are willing to live and work with the poor. The volunteers live on subsistence allowances in urban slums, in rural poverty areas, on Indian reservations, and in migrant camps. Many volunteers contribute specific skills as lawyers, health technicians, and architects. Volunteer activities focus on six program emphasis areas: health, education and manpower, economic development, social services, housing, and community planning.

Volunteers are not to displace employed workers nor shall an agency supervising any volunteer program receive compensation for services of volunteers. Volunteers are not to be involved in labor or antilabor organizations, nor shall volunteers engage in partisan political activity.

Sponsors applying for VISTA Volunteers must be nonprofit; they may be public or private. The project in which they propose to use the volunteers must be poverty connected. Volunteers must be eighteen years of age or older.

Persons who are assisted by VISTA Volunteer activities must be poor, and VISTA work must directly benefit the poor. There is usually not a direct beneficiary eligibility test, since in most cases volunteers are working with community groups which are basically poor but which may include individuals not poor by government definition.

WAGE AND HOUR LAW (*See* FAIR LABOR STANDARDS ACT OF 1938.)

WAINSCOT An interior wall lined with wood, wood panels, or other surface material, and usually only along the lower part of the wall.

WAIVER OF LEGAL NOTICE [lease] Agreement by tenant that the landlord may institute suit without any notice to the tenant that the suit has been filed, thus preventing the tenant from defending against the lawsuit.

WALK-UP APARTMENT A nonelevator, multilevel structure containing two or more dwelling units, in which the units are separated horizontally by floor and/or ceiling structural elements.

Also an apartment in a walk-up apartment building.

WALLBOARD Panels fabricated from an artificial substance to substitute for plastered walls or ceiling.

WARRANTED PRICE A price established for a property which is deemed fair and just by both a seller and a buyer.

WARRANTY [real estate] An agreement and assurance by the grantor of real property for himself and his heirs to the effect that he is the owner and will be responsible.

WARRANTY DEED A deed containing a warranty.

WATER AND SEWER GRANTS (*See* SECTION 702 BASIC WATER AND SEWER FACILITIES GRANTS.)

WATERSHED Usually, a mountain range or other elevated area that separates the drainage areas of rivers.

Also, the area so drained.

WATER TABLE The point in the depth of the soil below which it is saturated with water.

WAY   A street, alley, or other thoroughfare or easement permanently established for passage of persons or vehicles.

WEEP HOLE   One of several small holes left in a wall, such as a retaining wall or foundation, to permit surplus water to drain.

WELFARE RENT [public housing]   The rental charge to a welfare recipient based on the average rent included in a locality's welfare budgets for families in private housing, or the average project operating cost on a per-unit per-month basis, or the highest rent to which a welfare agency will agree.

WET MODULE   Modular construction component comprising all or part of a kitchen and/or bathroom and/or a utility service module.

WHOLESALE PURCHASE [utilities]   Purchase by management of water, fuel, or energy for an entire project; consumption is recorded and billed to the project on the basis of master meter readings. Distinguished from retail purchase.

WINDFALL PROFITS   Profits paid to developers or others as a result of their obtaining loans or contracts significantly above the actual development cost of a project.

WORKABLE PROGRAM   (*See* WORKABLE PROGRAM FOR COMMUNITY IMPROVEMENT.)

WORKABLE PROGRAM CERTIFICATION   Official HUD approval of a locality's Workable Program for Community Improvement and adherence to its features.

WORKABLE PROGRAM FOR COMMUNITY IMPROVEMENT (PFCI)   A locality's official document asserting active progress in seven areas of community improvement: (1) codes and ordinances to establish adequate standards of health and safety under which dwellings may be built and occupied; (2) comprehensive community plan to provide a framework for improvement, renewal, and blight prevention and for sound community development in the future; (3) neighborhood analyses to develop a comprehensive review of blight—where it is located, its extent, and actions needed to eliminate it; (4) administrative organization to establish clear-cut authority and responsibility to coordinate the overall Workable Program and the capacity to administer it and related activities; (5) financing to provide funds for staff and technical assistance, for public improvements, and for renewal activities; (6) relocation resources available to persons displaced by public action; (7) citizen participation in the planning and implementation of the Workable Program.

Without this document and evidence of a locality's adherence to it, HUD can disqualify the locality from participating in certain federal programs (as a result of the Housing Act of 1954).

WORK INCENTIVE PROGRAM (WIN)　Authorized by Title IV-A of the Social Security Act and later amendments; provides formula grants through the Social and Rehabilitation Service of HEW to state welfare agencies to help persons receiving Aid to Families with Dependent Children become self-supporting. State welfare agencies provide necessary child care to persons referred by them to state public employment offices for training and employment under the Work Incentive (WIN) program. Under this program, day care services in or out of the home are provided for WIN enrollees and those obtaining jobs afterward. Persons employed as a result of the WIN programs continue to receive financial help with the child care until other satisfactory child care arrangements can be made.

WORKING CAPITAL [FHA]　Money available for the cost of renting and equipping a project once it is ready for occupancy.

WORKING DRAWINGS　Plans and drawings showing dimensions and other information required to guide workmen in the construction of a building. Working drawings are supplemented by specifications.

WORK ORDER　A form, prepared with a specified number of copies, used following a tenant complaint or request for maintenance work or following the discovery of the need for any repair work.

WRAPAROUND LOAN　Transaction in which a borrower, owing on a first loan and wishing to obtain a second loan against whatever is the security, obtains the second loan in the desired amount plus the amount of the first loan. The borrower then makes debt payments only on the wraparound loan, which payments, in turn, pay the debt service on the first loan as well.

WRITE-DOWN [urban renewal]　The difference between the cost of purchasing and clearing built-up areas in urban renewal projects and the